KOREAN
COOKING

WALTHAM FOREST LIBRARIES

904 000 00418400

KOREAN COOKING

DISCOVER ONE OF THE WORLD'S GREAT CUISINES
WITH 150 RECIPES SHOWN IN 800 PHOTOGRAPHS

YOUNG JIN SONG

WITH PHOTOGRAPHY BY MARTIN BRIGDALE

southwater

This edition is published by Southwater,
an imprint of Anness Publishing Ltd,
108 Great Russell Street,
London WC1B 3NA;
info@anness.com

www.southwaterbooks.com;
www.annesspublishing.com

If you like the images in this book and would
like to investigate using them for publishing,
promotions or advertising, please visit our website
www.practicalpictures.com for more information.

© Anness Publishing Ltd 2014

All rights reserved. No part of this publication
may be reproduced, stored in a retrieval system,
or transmitted in any way or by any means,
electronic, mechanical, photocopying, recording
or otherwise, without the prior written permission
of the copyright holder.

A CIP catalogue record for this book
is available from the British Library.

Publisher: Joanna Lorenz
Project Editor: Emma Clegg
Home Economist: Lucy McKelvie
Photographer: Martin Brigdale
Stylist: Helen Trent
Illustrator: Rob Highton
Introduction Text: Young Jin Song
    and Catherine Best

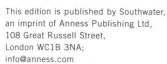

**Waltham Forest
Libraries**

904 000 00418400	
Askews & Holts	27-Jan-2015
641.5951 SON	£7.99
4554131	S

PUBLISHER'S NOTE
Although the advice and information in this book are
believed to be accurate and true at the time of going to
press, neither the authors nor the publisher can accept
any legal responsibility or liability for any errors or omissions
that may have been made nor for any inaccuracies nor
for any loss, harm or injury that comes about from following
instructions or advice in this book.

NOTES
Bracketed terms are intended for American readers.
    For all recipes, quantities are given in both metric and
imperial measures and, where appropriate, in standard cups
and spoons. Follow one set of measures, but not a mixture,
because they are not interchangeable.
    Standard spoon and cup measures are level.
1 tsp = 5ml, 1 tbsp = 15ml, 1 cup = 250ml/8fl oz.
    Australian standard tablespoons are 20ml. Australian
readers should use 3 tsp in place of 1 tbsp for measuring
small quantities.
    American pints are 16fl oz/2 cups. American readers
should use 20fl oz/2.5 cups in place of 1 pint when
measuring liquids.
    Electric oven temperatures in this book are for conventional
ovens. When using a fan oven, the temperature will probably
need to be reduced by about 10–20°C/20–40°F. Since ovens
vary, you should check with your manufacturer's instruction
book for guidance.
    The nutritional analysis given for each recipe is calculated
per portion (i.e. serving or item), unless otherwise stated.
If the recipe gives a range, such as Serves 4–6, then the
nutritional analysis will be for the smaller portion size,
i.e. 6 servings. The analysis does not include optional
ingredients, such as salt added to taste.
    Medium (US large) eggs are used unless otherwise stated.
    Main front cover image shows Spicy Stir-fry Squid –
for recipe, see page 155.

Contents

AN INTRODUCTION TO KOREA

The countries of North and South Korea form an area of vibrant contrasts. They embrace light-filled bustling modern cities, natural landscapes seemingly unchanged over centuries, and traditional cultures developed over time. The geography and seasonal changes dictate how to work the land, and farmers grow a mixture of arable crops, rice and cattle wherever the mountainous terrain flattens out enough to be tilled. The diversity of Korea also unfolds within the country's eating traditions, showing the influence of Buddhism and Confucianism, the use of seasonal local ingredients and the culture of sharing multiple dishes.

NORTH AND SOUTH

The two countries are deeply divided between the Communist North and the democratic South. It is difficult for outsiders to obtain much information about everyday life in North Korea; but from what we understand about the country, the people live in a relatively restricted fashion, a real contrast to life in bustling, prosperous South Korea. However, longstanding Korean food and farming traditions persist throughout the country, with fresh and natural ingredients grown or fished locally in what is a productive, industrious land.

THE LANDSCAPE OF KOREA

The small Korean peninsula, a spit of land pushing into the sea, is joined to the mainland only on its northern edge, where it touches the giant land masses of China and Russia. A tiny stretch of the border, only 19km (12 miles) long, skims the southern edges of Siberia just south of Vladivostok. The remainder of the border follows the winding courses of two rivers for 1,400km (880 miles) to

Above: A young farmer surveying the landscape near Kyongju, South Korea. Cultivating the land provides many of the major ingredients essential to Korean cooking.

separate Korea from the ancient land of Manchuria, now known as China. The eastern side of the country is protected from the Pacific Ocean by the curving islands of Japan. The enmity between these two countries over many centuries is underlined by the fact that the Koreans now prefer to call the stretch of water which divides them the East Sea, rather than the older name, the Sea of Japan.

Korea has a rich variety of natural fauna and flora, from the native broad-leaved trees of the south of the country, which flourish in the humid climate, to spikier pine trees, larch and juniper in the colder north. Luckily, there are no active volcanoes in Korea, but a number of hot springs mean that the earth is quietly rumbling not far below the surface, and small earthquakes are common.

Left: Farmworkers picking tea leaves in Boseong, South Korea, famous for its green tea leaves. If leaves are picked before 20 April, they are thought to be of the very best quality.

Above: A farmer in traditional costume; indigenous farming and self-sufficiency is of high importance to the Koreans.

Above: Traditional Korean houses with tiled roofs, and the commercial centre of Seoul seen in the distance.

Above: A paddy field in Magoksa, South Korea – half of Korea's arable land is given over to the cultivation of rice.

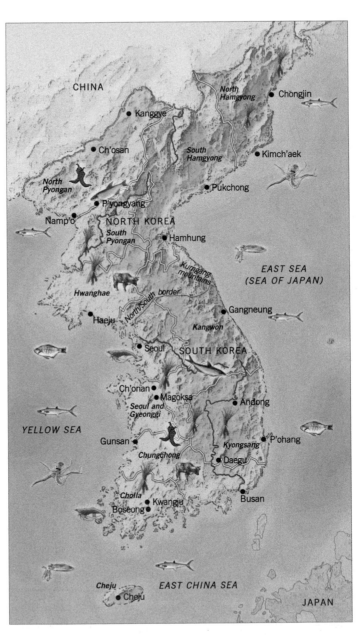

Above: The presence of warm and cold currents around the coastline of North and South Korea attracts a variety of fish and shellfish. The land is 30 per cent arable, half of which is rice cultivation; other key crops include herbs, spices and chillies.

THE KOREAN CLIMATE

The terrain is both rugged and beautiful, and the climate comprises similar harsh extremes: blazing heat in the humid summer and snow in the icy winter. The southern regions have a similar climate to that of Japan, with warm, wet summers and a regular monsoon season which brings half the year's rainfall in a few weeks. Farther north, it is much drier and colder, with snow on the mountains and freezing temperatures in winter.

COUNTRY LIFE

Korea is described as the Land of Morning Calm, and outside the cities, this is clearly borne out by cloud-enshrouded mountains dominating the landscape, blanketed by lush meadows and dotted with picturesque villages. Working monasteries open their doors, and the friendly locals welcome travellers enthusiastically, happy to share their meals with interested tourists.

The farmers of Korea do, however, have a challenging brief against the twin limitations of mountainous terrain and encroaching cities. On every square metre of level ground you will find either buildings or agriculture. Where there is room for farming, they raise animals for meat – beef and pork being the most popular meat in Korea – or grow rice, which fills over half the fields of Korea and forms the delicious, glutinous base of every Korean meal. Where other crops are grown, they are usually barley, wheat and corn to mill into flour for pancakes and fritters, or a great variety of delicious vegetables and fruit.

Above: The dramatic Kumgang mountains in North Korea are located on the east coast, just above the north/south country border.

CITY LIFE

Korea is a fascinating blend of the fiercely traditional and the breathtakingly modern. The great cities are like neon tigers, with skyscrapers soaring into the air. Seoul's lights shimmer and sparkle, reflected in the waters of the Han River, and everywhere there is a vibrant sense of a thriving, prosperous, 21st-century society. There has been a general drift of the country's population to the big cities of South Korea, several of which have more than a million inhabitants packed tightly into a small area. Most of these people live in 20-storey high-rise blocks of apartments, which resemble each other so closely that they often have ornate murals painted on the side to differentiate one block from the next.

Some Koreans still live in a traditional way even in the big cities, though many younger people now embrace a Western way of life and most learn English with an eye to their future prosperity. However, the family remains an important part of life, and Koreans generally show great respect for older people in society.

Harvests from the sea

The peninsula is set in some of the world's best fishing waters, so seafood is a major source of protein in the diet. The intricate coastline and numerous islands, inlets and reefs, and the presence of a warm and a cold current, attracts a great variety of species. There is a huge tidal flow on the western side of the country – the tides rise and fall 5 to 8 metres (17 to 27 feet) every day – keeping a wonderful variety of fish moving in shoals all around the coastline. The street markets overflow with fish, prawns (shrimp), crabs, oysters and octopus, and this harvest is served in every form – raw, stir-fried, grilled (broiled), stewed, pickled and dried.

Left: A typical Korean village surrounded by rice fields. Rural life centred on the village, and was based on the mutual solidarity of the inhabitants.

Above: The harbour city of Busan, South Korea, is home to one of the largest and busiest ports in the world.

Above: A traditional bell pavilion in Daegu, South Korea, stands in the shadow of modern high-rise apartments.

Above: The city of Pyongyang at sunrise. Pyongyang is the only large city in North Korea.

Above: The deceptive veneer of Seoul's towering skyline disguises a city of great contrasts, where ancient temples jostle for position with modern skyscrapers.

Korea's main cities

Seoul (South Korea) – population 10.3 million	A pulsating 21st-century city, full of busy people and with a thriving night life. Tall new buildings dominate the business districts, and the living areas are densely packed with apartment blocks. There are many vehicles on the roads, leading to appalling traffic jams and pollution.
Busan (South Korea) – population 3.7 million	The largest port in Korea, built on the south-eastern coast facing Japan. Busan attracts many tourists to its beautiful beaches and shopping streets. It is proud of its heritage as an ancient city and the summer capital of Korea.
Pyongyang (North Korea) – population 3 million	Generally rebuilt since the Korean War, with many monuments and huge buildings, some of the grandest remaining empty. There is a shining new metro system; yet most people in the city walk or cycle, and there are very few cars.
Daegu (South Korea) – population 2.5 million	Inland city and centre of a web of transport networks, built at the junction of two rivers centuries ago. It is now a thriving business hub with a lively sporting life, the home of Korean baseball.

THE REGIONS OF KOREA

The remarkably varied terrain of Korea, with its craggy mountains in the east and tidal mud flats in the west, its cold, dry northern hills and humid, fruitful zone in the south, divides itself naturally into provinces along the natural boundaries of mountains and rivers. Until recently, cultural differences between these provinces were very marked and there was little interaction between the people from one side of the mountain peak and those on the other side. Regional variations in language and customs arose and were perpetuated through the ages, giving a subtle difference to the cuisine and food customs of these different parts of the country.

THE PROVINCES OF NORTH KOREA

North Korea is to some extent hidden from the West by the secretive Communist regime which has been in power since Korea was divided after the Second World War, and there have been rumours of great poverty and even food shortages despite its natural resources.

Pyongan region

In the north-west of North Korea lies the province of Pyongan, which contains the capital city, Pyongyang. Much emphasis has been placed on new building in the capital and the government takes great pride in such massive developments as the gleaming

metro system, wide new roads that remain largely empty, and the "Grand People's Study House", a monumental educational establishment that dominates the city from a hilltop.

The Pyongan region is a land of flattish fields and river valleys in the west, with the River Chonchon, a major waterway, flowing right across the centre of the region. Farther east the remote, jagged mountain peaks rise above the plains and the climate is much cooler, with freezing winter temperatures during several weeks of the year.

Above: Oyster mushrooms, a key ingredient in Korean cooking, being harvested in Janggang, North Korea.

The western side of the province is the agricultural centre of North Korea, where most of the food is grown in a traditional way handed down from centuries past. Rice is the main crop, of course, but there is a variety of vegetables too, including cabbages, pumpkins, bell peppers and onions. All around the west coast the fishing fleets venture out into the teeming waters to catch carp, mullet and sardines, as well as shellfish such as clams, oysters and crabs.

Farther east the local industries are based on forestry and mining, and food has to be transported to these areas for the workforce. There is also great poverty here, and catastrophes such as flooding in the coastal plains can cause terrible hardship and a shortage of food.

Hamgyong region

The Hamgyong province touches the border with Siberia and China at its northern end and descends down the east coast of Korea past the industrial

Left: Pyongyang Grand People's Study House is of monolithic proportions, with 600 rooms housing 30 million books.

city of Hamhung. This is mountainous country, with the peaks rising to over 2,500m (8,200ft) to the west and forming a natural boundary which would have been very difficult to pass through before modern technologies. Hot springs gush forth from this rocky country, and spas have formed around them to make use of the medicinal qualities of the water.

It is a province of heavy industry based on mining and construction, as well as making plastics and machinery in the many factories on the east coast. Naturally, as the province snakes down the coastline, fishing is the other main occupation, but here the fish are different from those caught in Pyongan province to the west – cod, mackerel and turbot abound in the colder, fresher eastern waters, as well as seafood such as octopus and a regional delicacy, *wakame* seaweed, which is also popular in Japan just across the sea.

The province also has its own very popular speciality fish, known as *myongtae*, which is dried and then used in many favourite Korean recipes throughout the country.

Hwanghae region

The Hwanghae province forms the southernmost part of North Korea, located just below Pyongan province, on the western side of the country. This area is one of lush plains with fertile fields growing rice and cereals, as well as vegetables, apples and other fruits; the Hwanghae region is blessed with mild temperatures that are ideal for agriculture.

Once again fishing forms a major part of the region's industry and therefore its cuisine. Clams and oysters, eel and salmon, laver and kelp form part of the sea's rich harvest, all of which are key ingredients in favourite Korean dishes.

Above: Vegetables are prepared to make kimchi, a traditional dish of fermented vegetables, which is served at every meal.

Below: A carpet of red chilli peppers is laid out to dry outside the Ulmil Pavilion in Pyongyang, North Korea.

THE PROVINCES OF SOUTH KOREA

South Korea is of a similar size geographically to the North, but the similarities end there. The country has embraced Western capitalism with fervour, which means that many of its people now work in manufacturing and service industries rather than as agricultural labourers or fishermen.

Seoul and Gyeonggi region

The capital region of South Korea contains the thriving, ever-growing city of Seoul, where over 10 million people are packed into a small area of flat land encircled by mountains. Smaller cities have sprung up around the capital, making this region the most economically vibrant area of Korea.

Seoul is a city near the west coast, relying for its prosperity on administration and the head-office functions of Korean firms such as Samsung and LG. This means that over 6 million people commute to work in the city daily, causing a problem of traffic congestion and air pollution which the government is working to relieve.

Kangwon region

To the east of Seoul lies the province of Kangwon, which borders the East Sea and faces Japan over the water.

Above: A woman sells laver bread at a market at Yeosu, on the south-western tip of Korea.

Once again, mountains run from north to south through the province, dividing it into eastern and western Kangwon. This is an area that used to rely mainly on mining for its prosperity, but competition from abroad has led to a decline in this industry and the area now suffers from a significant depopulation – the whole province contains less than 2 million people, or under a fifth of the population of Seoul.

Agriculture in this region is mostly concerned with cattle rearing on ranches, and deforestation has been a problem as the land is cleared for this purpose. Beer barley is a favourite crop, and brewing is becoming one of the area's major industries.

A serious food culture

The people of the Seoul and Gyeonggi region are very hardworking and industrious, and this includes their attitude to food – it's a major interest and passion for many people. Not only do they take great care in preparing traditional dishes for the evening meal; the nightlife in Seoul also encourages the consumption of tasty snacks bought from street vendors while strolling through the shopping and entertainment areas after work.

Above: Seoul's street vendors sell a tantalizing array of delicious foods. These tend to be eaten as snacks, rather than full meals.

Chungchong region

This province is located just south of the city of Seoul and benefits hugely, economically speaking, from its proximity to the buzzing, lively capital of Korea. The land is reasonably flat, especially in the south of the region, and as a result farmers are able to grow crops such as rice and corn, as well as raise cattle for both milk and meat. Ginseng, garlic and tobacco are grown too, farther inland on the hilly slopes. Unusually for Korea, a dramatic 75 per cent of the population of this region are involved in farming and food production.

Transportation links are good from the countryside to the city, building an effective infrastructure that means the huge and growing urban population can buy fresh food, which they are unable to grow themselves in densely populated Seoul and other cities. New industries have grown up along the coast, reflecting the rising prosperity of the region, but there is still room for traditional fishing in the warm seas, and the locals are particularly fond of oysters, clams and other seafood.

Cholla region

A long and intricate coastline dominates this province in the south-west of Korea. It includes the far western and southern coasts of Korea, where many tiny inlets and small islands divide the low-lying land from the sea. It is a fertile land, like the Chungchong region, and similar crops are grown here, including rice, sweet potatoes and tobacco, and is now also being reclaimed from the sea for agricultural and industrial use.

Tourism is another major industry in Cholla province, growing fast in recent years. Tourists are attracted to the area to take part in water sports such as diving and fishing, and for the constantly warm temperatures, both on the coast and in inland areas where there are several beautiful lakes and rivers full of fish.

Kyongsang region

Farther round the southern tip of Korea to the east lies Kyongsang province, which is another area of rocky coastline with inland rivers and mountains rising above the coastal plains. Unlike Cholla province, the Kyongsang region contains several bustling major cities which have grown up along the eastern seaboard, including Busan and Daegu, the second and third cities of South Korea. Regional dialects and customs

Above: Persimmons are hung up to dry in South Kyongsang province. Once dried the persimmons, or kkotgam, are a traditional winter delicacy.

have persisted here despite the pace of 21st-century life, as the mountains to the north and west prevented fast, reliable communications until comparatively recently. The Racktong river flows majestically through the centre of the region, leaving flat fertile land in the gentle valleys, with fields of rice as far as the eye can see. Many other crops are grown, including the ubiquitous garlic, tobacco and red chilli peppers. On the southern edge of the Kyongsang province the climate is warm and humid for most of the year, and this provides ideal conditions for growing oranges, watermelons and ginseng.

KOREAN ISLANDS

The seas around the southern and western edges of South Korea are liberally sprinkled with small islands, some of which are inhabited, while others are excellent wild habitats for all kinds of animals and birds. The fishing waters around and between the islands are well stocked with a huge variety of seafood.

Left: Shellfish is prepared at Yongduam (dragon head) rock on Cheju, South Korea's largest island.

Cheju region

Located off the southern coast of Korea, Cheju is the biggest of the thousands of islands in this region. This volcanic rock rises from the sea around South Korea's biggest mountain, Halla-san, some 1,950m (6,400ft) high. The isolation of Cheju island from the mainland has led to many fascinating customs, including the carving of a very impressive "stone grandfather" (*dol hareubang*) out of lava. The tradition survives that the women of Cheju are the head of the family, and earn a living as free divers for abalone and conch shells.

The generally mild temperatures (a mixture of continental and oceanic climates) and beautiful and dramatic landscape have established Cheju as a popular tourist destination these days, and it offers a variety of sporting activities, ranging from hiking in the mountains to horse riding and swimming. The climate is warm nearly all the year round, an ideal temperature for growing fruit, and oranges, tangerines and pineapples flourish in groves among the volcanic rocks. Fresh fish and shellfish abound in the region and lucky visitors may find them for sale on the beach just minutes after they have been caught.

HISTORICAL INFLUENCES

Korea has always been a crossroads of cultures, absorbing the influences of the surrounding countries while developing a distinct national identity.

From the middle of the 1st century BC Korea began to develop as a recognizable country. This was the beginning of the era of the Three Kingdoms: Koguryo, Paekje and Silla. The kingdoms fought among themselves for dominance until the end of the 7th century, when Silla defeated the other two, with Chinese aid, and unified the peninsula under central rule.

MONGOLIAN AND CHINESE INFLUENCE

The southern migration of Mongolian tribes to Korea in the 1st century BC from Manchuria (now China) brought great changes, in cultural and agricultural terms. The shamanistic beliefs of the Mongols were adopted by the Koreans, as were their cultivation techniques. The Mongols taught the Korean people how to farm the plains, raise cattle and grow crops, and this influenced the country's cuisine, which then started to move away from a predominantly seafood-based diet.

The origins of the Korean tofu and vegetable casserole *chungol* can be traced back to Mongolia. The Koreans adapted the recipes of migrating Mongol tribes from the north, using local

ingredients to produce regional variations in which the flavours were carefully matched to accompanying dishes.

THE INFLUENCE OF BUDDHISM

At the end of the 7th century Korea entered a long stable period based on Buddhist culture. This had a great effect on the nation's gastronomy, as the slaughtering of animals was prohibited under Buddhist principles.

Diets changed with this dramatic reduction in the consumption of meat, and vegetables took on a much more

Above: The influence of Buddhism in Korea led to the elevated importance of vegetables, over meat, in Korean food.

significant role. Temple meals consisted of soup, rice and vegetable dishes, and omitted strong-smelling ingredients, such as garlic or spring onions (scallions). This influence is still apparent in the *namul* vegetable dishes of modern Korea, and the technique of marinating in soy sauce, rice vinegar and sesame seeds has barely changed. Interestingly, the simple porridge and vegetable dishes of the Buddhist monks have found a new popularity with today's health-conscious citizens.

CONFUCIANISM

The Buddhist culture flourished into the Koryo dynasty (935–1392). However, although the monks still wielded some influence, the kings of the Koryo dynasty adopted a Chinese governmental approach, which brought the influence of Confucianism to the country and incidentally led to more meat eating.

Towards the end of the Koryo dynasty the Mongols took control of Korea and ruled for around 100 years, before being ousted by General Yi Seong-Gye, who seized political and military power and, in 1392, established the amazingly long-lived Chosun (Yi) dynasty, which ruled for over 500 years until 1910. Confucianism became the

Above: A group of novice Buddhist monks in Seoul, aged between 5 and 7, sheltering from the rain after a head shaving ceremony to celebrate Buddha's birthday.

Above: A Confucian temple in South Korea. Based on the teachings of a Chinese sage, Confucianism is based around the importance of morality, and the cultivation of the civilized individual. The philosophy has had a significant influence on Korea.

The Korean barbecue

The Chinese had developed sophisticated techniques for seasoning and cooking meat, mostly derived from the Mongolian use of the barbecue. This was hugely influential in Korean cooking and they adopted the principles while retaining their own traditions. Meat was seasoned and cooked on the barbecue, and then wrapped in vegetable leaves to provide complex flavours and help to create meals that were nutritionally balanced. Documents from this era refer to this style of meal: "In the springtime the wind carries the irresistible scent of wild vegetables over the mountain and the Koryo people enjoy meat with fresh green leaves." This concept of wrapping meat in green leaves influenced the Chinese in their turn, and seafood wrapped in lettuce leaves remains a popular dish in both China and Korea today.

state creed, and the Chinese influence steadily took hold, heralding a new era in the national cuisine.

CHINESE INGREDIENTS

Closer ties with China meant that a wide range of spices and seasonings became available, an important driving influence in determining flavour trends. Black pepper and vinegar, molasses and rice wine were now enjoyed by many Koreans.

Tofu was another Chinese ingredient that had a tremendous impact when introduced to Korea. Its ubiquity in Korean cooking, and versatility in different dishes, has meant it is now more popular in Korea than in its native China. Many other dishes from China were introduced after the Korean War, with Chinese restaurants becoming very popular. However, over the past five decades their recipes have been adapted to create popular dishes that are distinctly Korean in their use of local ingredients and spices.

JAPANESE RULE

The Japanese asserted their authority over their neighbours in the 19th and 20th centuries, attempting to impose by the use of force their own religion and education system, and even the adoption of Japanese names by the Koreans. The Koreans fought back with their own independence movement, and after the Second World War, gained freedom from the Japanese.

However, the period of Japanese colonial rule brought many different ingredients to Korea, including the *maki* roll, *sashimi* and *udon* noodles. While the preparation and cooking methods have remained the same as in Japan, the choice of sauces and spices gives a uniquely Korean taste to these dishes, and these adaptations have travelled back to Japan where they are becoming increasingly popular.

THE SEPARATION OF NORTH AND SOUTH

Since the division of Korea into North and South in 1953, after the Korean War, the country has been physically divided by a DMZ (De-Militarized Zone) roughly along the 38th parallel, and the North has withdrawn into isolation from the rest of the world, while the South has enthusiastically embraced the technology and industry of the 21st-century world.

Above: The traditional ceremonial dress of the Confucianist village of Chunghak-dong, in South Korea.

FESTIVALS AND CELEBRATIONS

As in many other Asian countries, delicious seasonal dishes and beverages are enjoyed during festivals throughout the year. Exciting and elaborate recipes are an integral part of Korean celebrations, from the spicy drinks associated with New Year to the hot chicken stew made to fortify the body against the great heat of the summer.

Religious festivals are now less widely observed in this predominantly secular society, but there are many occasions such as weddings and birthdays when family and friends celebrate together.

SEASONAL FESTIVALS

Korea's agricultural society has always been well aware of the importance of the changing seasons, and this is reflected in time-honoured festivals that celebrate these transitions in nature with food and drink and much merrymaking.

New Year

February is the time the lunar New Year is celebrated, and during this period Koreans enjoy *sujunggwa*, a spiced punch made with dried persimmons and cinnamon. During this celebration they remember their departed ancestors, and revere their elders with a formal bow.

The traditional meal for this day is a soup called *tteokguk*, where long strips of rice cake (flavoured with the aromatic herb, wormwood) float in a clear beef broth. It is said that you cannot become another year older without eating a bowl of *tteokguk*. Another New Year's feast-day dish is the fragrant beef stew, *galbi tang*.

Above: South Korean Buddhists in traditional costume with lanterns at a parade to celebrate the birthday of Buddha on 15 May.

First Full Moon Day

In springtime Koreans celebrate the First Full Moon Day, which is known as *Jeongwol Daeboreum*. On this day they perform a series of rituals to help prevent bad luck throughout the forthcoming 12 months, waking at dawn to drink rice wine and crack walnuts while praying for good health over the coming year. The two favourite dishes for *Jeongwol Daeboreum* are *ogokbap*, a recipe of steamed rice mixed with five other grains, and *mugeun namul*, which is a medley of vegetable dishes such as mushrooms, radish leaves and steamed shoots of young ferns.

Buddha's birthday

The birthday of Buddha on 15 May is a day of celebration and a national holiday. Every temple is decorated with colourful lanterns and holds a special ceremony. In Seoul there is a weeklong festival, the first day with a lantern parade stretching for several kilometers through the heart of Seoul, leading up to the day itself, where religious ceremonies in the morning are followed by a street fair.

Above: The traditional Korean New Year's Day celebration is a formal occasion, which includes ceremonial prayers and food.

Right: October's Silla festival hosts an array of traditional dancing, music, and religious ceremonies as a celebration of Korean history and culture.

The festival of *Sambok*

At the height of summer the three hottest days are celebrated at the Festival of *Sambok*. Called *Chobok*, *Jungbok* and *Malbok*, these days are held in honour of the beginning, middle and end of the lunar calendar's hottest period. The classic dish that is eaten at *Sambok* is *samgyetang*, which is a soup containing a whole chicken stuffed with rice, ginseng and red dates. These strong-tasting ingredients are believed to boost stamina, and also to give the population the energy to withstand the blazing heat of this time of year.

The festival of *Chuseok*

In the autumn Koreans hold a day of harvest thanksgiving called *Chuseok*. On this day they visit their ancestors' graves to give thanks for a plentiful harvest, and to pray for the well-being of their loved ones. Crescent-shaped rice cakes (*songpyeon*) are eaten with a taro soup (*torantang*). The *songpyeon* are stuffed with beans, nuts and seeds, and then presented at the ancestral memorial service, along with fruit from the harvest.

The festival of *Donji*

The winter solstice of *Donji* towards the end of December is the final festival of the year in Korea. This is the shortest day of the year, and a herald of the bitterly cold weather that will follow for several months. On this day *patjuk* is eaten, a red bean porridge that contains balls of rice. For Koreans the colour of this dish is of particular significance, as it is an ancient belief that red will drive away evil spirits and ward off bad luck. By eating this porridge on *Donji* a long-held tradition claims that the whole family will then be kept safe from harm throughout the bleak and frosty winter months that follow.

Right: South Korean dancers performing the "O-go Mu" dance at a festival to celebrate the New Year.

Left: The bride pours wine for the groom, a traditional part of the North Korean wedding banquet.

Wedding sweets

The bride will offer date sweets, made of whole red dates dipped in sugar syrup and rolled in sesame seeds, to her new husband and his family. These are linked in chains and presented on a lacquer platter to her guests, who return the compliment by throwing some of the dates over the couple, just as people in the West throw confetti or rice.

WEDDINGS AND BIRTHDAYS

As well as festivals to mark the passing year, Koreans enjoy many other celebrations that involve some fragrant and unusual dishes. Weddings and birthdays are particular favourites and are a great chance for families and friends to get together and socialize over a celebratory meal.

The wedding feast

On the day of a traditional wedding in Korea, a grand banquet is held to commemorate the event. Ceremonial tables are filled with drinks and laid items that have great significance for the bride and groom. The importance of these two people on this day is reflected in pairs of utensils and foods: for example, two vases filled with bamboo accompany two lit candles, and a brace of chicken is included to symbolize integrity. There are also two bowls filled with rice to ensure wealth, along with red dates, chestnuts and gingko nuts to guarantee their descendants' prosperity. None of these is intended to be eaten by the guests or wedding party; they are part of the complex ritual that surrounds wedding celebrations in Korea.

The wedding banquet itself is usually a plentiful and extravagant affair, with a great number of different small dishes served to the family and guests. Among these the most traditional and popular is a bowl of noodles served in broth, which is imbued with particular significance. In Korea the eating of noodles is associated with a long life, and during the centuries of the Koryo and Chosun eras these dishes were reserved for the upper classes. The inclusion of noodles on the tables of festivals and celebrations reflects both the promise of a long and happy life

Above: The bridegroom and his retinue as he travels to the ceremony.

Above: A wedding in Seoul. A traditional marriage used elaborate rituals, including ceremonial bowing and gifts, but most modern-day ceremonies are much simpler.

Right: A festival to celebrate the birthday of North Korea's leader, Kim Jong Il.

and the status of enjoying a dish traditionally reserved for the elite. For a wedding this is seen as a signifier of the good health and long lives of the bride and groom, and also of the eternal bond of their marriage.

The thin noodle *somyun* is also particularly associated with the wedding table, to the extent that the question "Where can I have *somyun* noodles?" is often used to imply that the person enquiring is getting married.

The influence of the elaborate style of cuisine favoured by the imperial court can also be seen in *gujeolpan*, a dish often made for weddings which consists of many different kinds of meat and vegetables with tiny thin pancakes, carefully arranged and served on a special divided plate.

Birthday celebrations: the first year of life

Another occasion surrounded with traditional rituals, a birthday often involves a symbolic celebratory meal. Before a child even reaches their first birthday, a small festival is celebrated on the 100th day after their birth and a simple meal consisting of rice cakes is prepared. This is a tradition that has survived from a much older era when disease took the lives of many children before this date, making it an important milestone for those that survived.

1st birthday rice cakes

A favourite Korean custom involves sharing rice cakes made for a child's first birthday party with 100 people to ensure that the child will live to a venerable age. Rice cakes are even mailed to friends and distant relations who are unable to attend the celebrations in person. The recipients then mail back lengths of thread to the baby, expressing the hope of longevity, and grains of rice, symbolizing future wealth.

While this celebration remains popular, it is now less important than the child's first birthday, called *Dol* in Korea. On this day a ritual meal is prepared, with offerings of rice and soup made to the spirits in gratitude for having kept the mother and child safe from harm. The family and friends then enjoy a glass of rice wine, accompanied by rice cakes and red bean cakes sweetened with honey, to celebrate the child's first birthday. To ensure the continued well-being of the child, and to bring them good luck and joy, red bean cakes are also placed as offerings at the four compass points within the house.

Birthday celebrations: the 60th year

The 60th birthday, which is known as *Hwangop*, is another important festival in Korean culture, as it marks the day when a person has completed the zodiacal cycle. Observed with an extravagant feast, this is a time of great celebration, and reflects the fact that in times gone by comparatively few individuals lived to be 60. This made it all the more important to mark the occasion.

On *Hwangop* the grown-up children traditionally honour their parents with a grand banquet and then propose a toast to their longevity. There is much eating and drinking and merrymaking, although in recent times this has begun to resemble a more Western celebration, with the addition of a birthday cake. However, one dish is still eaten in accordance with the old traditions: a bowl of seaweed soup. This is the same kind of soup that is traditionally given to women just after childbirth, as it is believed that the minerals in the soup help to improve circulation and restore the stamina of new mothers. Eating this dish on one's birthday celebrates birth and also honours the role of the mother.

The few Koreans who made it to their 70th birthday in centuries gone by would have been honoured with another feast on this special day which was known as *Koh-cui*, meaning old and rare. A very similar pattern of celebration with a banquet took place as for *Hwangop*, the 60th birthday. Nowadays many more Koreans reach the milestone of 70 and so enjoy another grand-scale party.

KOREAN CUISINE

The cuisine of Korea is truly the undiscovered gem of Asian cooking: a treasure trove of exotic scents and flavours. Despite the cross-cultural exchanges with China and Japan, and the significant influence they have both had on the evolution of Korean cuisine, it remains quite distinct from either. The cuisines of all the countries share the balance of salty, bitter, hot, sweet and sour – the "five flavours" – but cooking techniques and ingredients create a marked culinary difference between the three.

THE SPECIALITIES OF KOREA

In Korea, certain key flavours such as garlic, ginger and soy sauce lend themselves to common preparation techniques such as pickling or grilling (broiling). Then there are the signature dishes, such as *kimchi* (pickled vegetables, often cabbage), *bulgogi* (barbecued meat or fish) and *namul* (vegetable side dishes).

One might expect the Koreans to stir-fry in a wok like the Chinese, or eat ingredients raw like the Japanese, as these characteristics would be consistent with their geographical proximity. However, the Koreans have developed their own methods of

cooking, including preservation techniques that give their cuisine a unique array of flavours.

From mild rice dishes and delicate soups, through to pickled vegetables and fiery seafood stews, there is something wonderfully mysterious about the taste of Korean food. Whereas the flavours in Chinese and Thai dishes are easily identifiable, Korean cooking blends fresh and preserved ingredients to create complex tastes. In Korea there is also a

Above: The method of making kimchi *varies greatly from region to region, but it always contains fermented vegetables.*

generosity of spirit and a desire to share and please, which characterize the experience of eating.

CHARACTERISTIC FLAVOURS

As in Japan, rice, pickles and meat or fish form the basis of the diet. However, the spices and marinades are distinctive

Above: A fish stall in Gonju, in the Gyeonggi region of South Korea.

Above: Korean soups vary from light, highly flavoured broths in summer to substantial stews laden with fish or meat, rice and vegetables in winter months.

Homemade seasonings

Traditionally every family would make their own soy sauce, *doenjang* (soya bean paste) and *gochujang* (chilli paste), storing them in earthenware jars in the back yard. Preparing these seasonings was a significant event in the culinary calendar, as without them cooking became all but impossible.

Above: After rice, garlic is the second-largest cash crop in Korea, most of which is grown in the south-west.

to Korea. Food is predominantly seasoned with the traditional key flavours of garlic, ginger, soy sauce, spring onions (scallions) and sesame oil, plus the careful use of sugar and rice vinegar. The Koreans are the greatest consumers of garlic in the whole of Asia. Delicious spice pastes are used in many dishes with either the fermented soya bean paste, *doenjang*, or the ubiquitous *gochujang*, red chilli paste, providing the foundation of a multitude of recipes.

Koreans tend to make a combination of freshly prepared and preserved foods for each meal, rather than preparing just one main dish. The strong taste of Korean food originates both from their love of pungent flavours, and from the preservation techniques that allow those flavours to develop and intensify.

In addition Koreans make use of ingredients in different ways to their neighbours; for example, sesame seeds are always toasted before being added to cooking, to emphasize their nutty flavour. By enhancing certain flavours, and mixing fresh and pickled tastes, Korea has found a culinary identity unlike any other in Asia.

With globalization and the influence of the Western food industry, Korean cuisine is evolving at a dramatic rate. However, despite these multicultural influences, the basic diet remains the same as it has for centuries.

SEASONAL CONTRASTS

Like other countries in the temperate zone, such as Japan, Korea has four distinct seasons. Spring brings countless hours of sunshine, gentle breezes and azure skies. In summer the weather becomes hot and humid, with heavy monsoon rains from late June. Autumn is dry and cloudless, with plenty of sunlight, followed by the arctic air of winter, bringing bitterly cold, dry weather and some snow to the region.

Each of these four seasons provides a variety of ingredients for the Korean kitchen, and certain dishes are traditional at particular times of year. On the hottest days of summer, for example, Koreans eat *samgyetang*, a soup made with chicken, red dates and ginseng, as it is said to provide vitality and stamina to survive the heat. Similarly, *kimchi*, the pickled vegetable dish, is a staple food through the long, harsh winters when fresh vegetables are scarce. Korean cuisine embraces the seasonal variety of its ingredients, and blends the food of the sea, the field and the mountain, reflecting a diverse and bountiful terrain.

THE INTRODUCTION OF RICE

Rice proved itself early in the country's history as a staple ingredient for the Korean diet. It grows well in the varying climate, and its inviting taste and the ease with which it could be cooked also had a great effect on the cuisine. Rice became an essential feature of most meals, adopting the same role as bread in the West, and played a major part in establishing the Korean style of eating. It was served as the foundation of the meal, and around this began to grow the idea of cooking a number of small accompanying dishes of soup, meat, vegetables and seafood. Having rice at every meal, and in many dishes, also helped to form the Koreans' sociable way of eating, with each diner partaking freely of any dish on the table.

THE CHILLI PEPPER

Another revolutionary event in Korean culinary history was the introduction of the chilli pepper in the 16th century. In 1592 and 1597 the Japanese invaded Korea, but they were eventually beaten off in 1598 with help from the Chinese.

Below: The heat of chillies is intrinsic to Korean cooking, but their fire is just one element of this multi-layered cuisine.

Catholic priests from Portugal travelled with the Japanese troops and brought with them the chilli plants and seeds from the New World – a long round trip from South America to Asia, via Europe. Prior to this, spiciness had been imparted with the Chinese Sichuan peppercorn, but Korean cooks were wholeheartedly seduced by the flavour and heat of the chilli pepper.

The Koreans adored spicy food, and created *gochujang*, a red chilli paste that has become a basic ingredient in every Korean kitchen. Countless dishes were built upon its fiery kick, and traditional techniques for preserving

Above: North Korean women harvesting rice at a farm in Uiji county, North Pyongan province.

vegetables were brought to life with its strong, pungent flavour. Koreans believe that red is a colour which offers protection from the devil, and this may also have had a bearing on the all-pervading use of *gochujang* in their cooking.

HEALTHY EATING

Since the 17th century the Koreans have been increasingly preoccupied with food and health. Various documents were written at that time on

Royal court cuisine

Imperial cuisine is a tradition kept alive by a few restaurants in Korea, mainly in Seoul, where the super-wealthy go to enjoy an expensive meal of meticulously prepared dishes, balancing warm and cold, spicy and mild, soft and crisp, solid and liquid, and a range of colours, all of which may take hours or days to prepare. Even the serving dishes are carefully chosen to reflect the colours or shapes of the food. Although this is not a daily experience for most Koreans, the aim of a careful balance in their food is kept alive through a simpler mixture of the staple dish, rice, and a selection of side dishes (*banchan*).

Right: Dried roots, seeds, flowers, fruit, herbs and fungi on display at the Herbal Medicine Market, in Yangnyeong, Seoul.

the subject of farming and horticulture, and new ingredients were introduced in an effort to promote a balanced diet.

Sweet potatoes, for example, were brought from Japan in the 18th century to help stave off famine, and quickly became a common ingredient. These potatoes were not only eaten as a vegetable, they were also made into noodles, known as *dangmyun*, which are still found uniquely in Korea.

Modern Korean cuisine is rich in seafood, vegetables and grains, and always provides generous amounts of protein and fibre. Most dishes have a moderate number of calories and are low in fat, making for a healthy and well-balanced diet.

FOOD AS MEDICINE

The Koreans recognize medicinal qualities in a wide variety of their foods and beverages, and also use seasonings and spices as an effective treatment for certain ailments. A daily dose of either sea kelp or carrot juice, for example, is recommended for those suffering from high blood pressure, whereas an increased intake of seaweed or vinegar is considered as an excellent measure to help prevent a heart attack. Asthmatics are

recommended Asian pears, apricot kernels and extracts from the leaves of gingko trees.

The heavily mountainous region in the east encourages the growth of culinary and medicinal herbs and plants. The country is the world's largest producer of ginseng, a sweet, liquorice-flavoured root that has been credited with being everything from an aphrodisiac to a restorative. Ginseng is used to make a renowned Korean tea thought to provide enhanced stamina, and to help high blood pressure. Angelica, a peppery herb with edible leaves and roots, and wormwood, a bitter, aromatic herb, also grow abundantly on the high-altitude slopes, and are used in Korean temple cooking and for the treatment of certain illnesses.

THE HARMONY OF OPPOSITES

One of the fundamental principles of Eastern philosophy is that of the two universal opposing forces of yin and yang. This concept has a strong influence on Koreans' thinking and

Left: Fermented soya bean cake for sale at the Herbal Medicine Market in Yangnyeong, Seoul.

their approach to cooking, and is reflected in the ingredients selected by chefs when preparing dishes with the intention of achieving harmony in flavour, colour and presentation. Traditional Korean cooking – from the dishes of the royal court to simple family meals – uses green, red, yellow, white and black ingredients in equal amounts, to ensure evenness in the diet and to reflect the theory of the five elements from traditional Chinese philosophy: wood, fire, earth, metal and water. The dishes will also have harmonizing yin and yang values: hot and spicy yang foods stimulate the body, whereas cool yin foods calm and nourish the system. Neutral foods are a balance of yin and yang. The perfect meal will contain yang dishes to heat up the body and yin dishes to cool down the brain.

So Korean cooking is an enticing fusion of flavours and textures, mixing dishes from the simple vegetarian fare of Buddhist monks with those from the banqueting tables of kings. Various cultural influences combine ingredients and techniques in fascinating ways, creating perhaps unfamiliar, but delectable meals.

EATING TRADITIONS AND ETIQUETTE

Left: Villagers enjoy a traditional Korean meal which is accompanied by soju, *a distilled grain liquor.*

(broiled) meat or fish dish is traditionally accompanied by rice, soup and salad, along with a selection of pickled vegetables, or *kimchi*. The dishes will reflect a range of preparation techniques as well as different ingredients – maybe steamed rice, a simmered casserole of vegetables or fish, and a piece of meat quickly grilled. Sometimes the Koreans eat raw fish dishes, rather like Japanese sushi.

The main dishes are shared between all the diners. Because of this style of eating there is a real spirit of fellowship when dining Korean-style, and this is accentuated by the common practice of cooking food on a gas or charcoal grill at the table, giving mealtimes an inviting, domestic feel.

While the idea of sharing an abundance of small dishes is the same as the Spanish *tapas* style of dining, the Korean approach requires all the dishes to complement each other. To this end, the recipes of certain dishes will be altered depending on the other dishes being served so that all the elements work in harmony with each other.

All Korean meals are designed to include a harmonious assortment of dishes, and to enjoy the experience of Korean dining fully this is the perfect approach. When you are preparing any of the recipes in this book you should choose a number of dishes – maybe three or four – of contrasting texture and colour, and varying in taste, and serve them together with a dish of rice and a bowl of soup for each person. You will then be sampling a Korean evening meal as it would be eaten in many family homes throughout the peninsula, from a farmhouse in the chilly northern mountains to a high-rise apartment in the bustling cities of the south.

A VARIETY OF TASTES

A typical Korean meal will have a selection of small dishes, rather than a single main dish for each person, and all the food is served together rather than as different courses. A grilled

Traditional Korean dining

Although there is no prescribed order for eating the many dishes served at a traditional meal, many Koreans like to start with a small taste of soup before then sharing the other dishes among themselves. The formation of menus will vary depending on the number of dishes and the occasion, from a mere three or four for an informal family supper to many exotic and glamorous dishes at major celebrations for weddings, special birthdays and festivals.

Right: Koreans taking tea in a tea house. A low table and floor seating is the traditional practice.

Left: Restaurant diners in Seoul. The barbecue hot plate is a standard feature, along with a range of side dishes.

time these traditions have relaxed, although there are some basic rules by which Koreans still abide. One of these is to allow an older person to sit at the most respected seat at the table, which is the one that is closest to the fireplace or with the best view of the entrance.

Koreans will never pour their own drinks; they believe it is courteous for their companion to pour for them. Both hands are used to receive a drink, and it is more important to accept the drink than actually to drink it; declining the first glass is considered terribly impolite, and it is better to accept the glass and simply touch it against the lips than to refuse it entirely.

The correct amount to drink is a matter of some debate in Korea, and tastes have become more bacchanalian in recent years. However, the traditional wisdom is summed up by an old saying, which translates as "Don't stop after one glass; three glasses is lacking, five glasses is proper and seven glasses is excessive."

Below: A traditional Korean tea ceremony in Seoul, South Korea, forming part of a wedding celebration.

DRINKING

Korean cuisine includes both alcoholic and non-alcoholic drinks, and there are many traditional varieties of both available to drink with meals or snacks or simply as a thirst-quenching brew.

Non-alcoholic drinks

Koreans tend to drink mainly water or *boricha*, a tea brewed from roasted barley, with their meals. Green tea is also very popular; this is a drink that was introduced with the rise of Buddhism in the 7th century as an indispensable part of temple ceremonies. During the Koryo dynasty (918–1392) tea became popular among the upper classes and nobility, too, even finding a place in the rituals of the royal court.

Alcoholic drinks

Koreans also drink a wide range of alcoholic beverages including the local wine, *chungju*, a variety of domestically brewed beers, and *makgoli*, a potent milky-white rice drink. However, the most famous drink in Korea is *soju*, a rough rice wine with a fearsome kick, which was traditionally distilled in

Buddhist monasteries. The popularity of *soju* cannot be overestimated, and no Korean meal is really complete without a glass of this potent liquor.

Drinking etiquette

In the past, Korean drinking was steeped in convention and ceremony, to show respect to drinking companions. Over

TABLE SETTINGS

The classic Korean table setting is one of the most impressive aspects of Korean cuisine and is quite unique, both in its selection of dishes and in its form of presentation. As in other Asian countries, an individual bowl of soup and a dish of rice are provided for every person dining. However, what sets the Korean table distinctively apart from its Asian neighbours is the fact that all the dishes are served simultaneously rather than as one course after another.

The table setting is seen as an important element to enjoying Korean cuisine, and allows dishes to complement one another in terms of flavour while maintaining a nutritional balance. Table settings are normally defined by the main dish, except in the case of ceremonial meals.

THE *BANSANG* TABLE

The most common table setting is based around the serving of a bowl of rice as the main dish, known in Korean as

Right: The Korean Bansang *setting consists of a main dish, a rice bowl and sauces with a number of side dishes, or* chups, *ranging from three to twelve. This one shows a three-*chup *setting.*

Above: A table setting for a wedding celebration, with cutlery and glasses provided for each stage of the meal.

bansang or *bapsang*. Directly translated, *ban* or *bap* means cooked rice and *sang* means table, and this form holds true for other table settings. If the main dish served were based on noodles, *myun* in Korean, then the table setting would be *myunsang*, or "noodle table". There are also more elaborate table settings that are defined by an occasion, for instance weddings, birthdays or anniversaries, but these are lavish and have much more sophisticated rules.

Above: Traditionally Korean diners ate their meals at floor height, sitting on cushions. This is still relatively common.

On a traditional *bansang* table setting the main rice dish would be served with soup, a plate of *kimchi* and a selection of side dishes referred to as *chups*. The number of side dishes included on the table is reflected in the name given to the setting, with three-, five-, seven-, nine- and twelve-*chup* settings the most traditional.

Historically this figure was a reflection of social status, with both three- and five-*chup* meals the staple among the lower classes, and seven- and nine-*chup*

Above: This traditional Korean table arrangement incorporates many small, tasty side dishes to augment the obligatory rice dish.

Eating from the same bowl
Koreans believe that eating food from the same bowl as their fellow diners makes for closer relationships. It is not considered impolite to ask the host for an individual bowl or plate, but it is a rarity among a people whose Confucian ideals value fellowship and mutual respect.

---

meals reserved for the upper classes and nobility. Twelve-*chup* meals, or *surasang*, were only allowed to be served to the king, with the expanse of dishes spread across three separate tables. These more ostentatious royal menus often took days to prepare and offered a complex blend of warm and cold dishes, with mild and spicy ingredients and a harmony of textures and colours, all of them served according to a specific ritual.

Regardless of whether the table has a three- or a twelve-*chup* setting, the notion of harmony is still important, and culinary contrasts are reflected in the choice of dishes. Hot dishes are served alongside cold ones, with mild and spicy ingredients designed to complement one another while exhibiting an interesting diversity. Crunchy vegetables are offset by velvety stews and porridges, while meat, seafood, vegetables and rice are balanced in equal measure.

The Korean dining table
Any formal table setting is based around a complex historical design, rich with significance. The classic Korean table is round, symbolizing the sun and the yang virtue, whereas its four legs point to the ground, signifying the yin properties of the earth. Korean dining tables used to be low, and the diners would sit around them on floor cushions; these days tables have become more Westernized, with chairs rather than cushions.

LAYING THE TABLE

For each person who is dining, a covered bowl of rice is set on the left and a bowl of soup on the right. A second row of bowls is formed behind these containing the dipping sauces and *kimchi*, while the side dishes are placed to flank this arrangement. Hot or cooked dishes always go on the right, while cold dishes or fresh vegetables sit on the left. Large communal dishes, such as stews and noodle bowls, are always placed in the very centre of the table to allow them to be easily shared between all the diners.

A long-handled, shallow spoon (*sutgarak*) and a pair of silver or stainless-steel chopsticks (*jeotgarak*) are placed next to each soup bowl to complete the table setting. Unlike most other Asians, the Koreans prefer to use a spoon rather than chopsticks as the main table utensil. Rice, soups and stews are eaten with the spoon, whereas chopsticks are used for the drier side dishes, although the two are never used simultaneously (see also p37). This spoon culture indicates a marked difference in eating habits to those of both China and Japan, where bowls are designed to be small enough to lift them in order to hold them close to the mouth when eating with chopsticks. Korean food is served in larger, heavier bowls and it is considered bad manners to pick up tableware while eating.

The preference for spoons over chopsticks is due to the softer, more liquid nature of the dishes that make up Korean cuisine. The substantial *chige* casseroles that are so popular would be very difficult to eat with chopsticks, as would the various mixed rice and porridge dishes.

In the big cities of South Korea, a meal, especially with traditional dishes, is still considered to be the highlight of an evening's entertainment. Even emigrating families living in Europe or the USA preserve their traditional ways of cooking and eating.

FOOD THROUGH THE KOREAN DAY

One of the most intriguing things about the Korean way of life is the different way they organize their mealtimes during the day compared to the way that is usual in the Western world. There is no rigid structure of breakfast, lunch and dinner, with different foods for each one, particularly breakfast. Koreans would consider it strange to eat breakfast cereals or toast, fried eggs and bacon or even muffins only at breakfast time, and at no other time during the day.

BREAKFAST

The Korean family will start the day, as long as there is time before dashing off to work, with a good serving of rice and accompanying dishes, quite similar in character to those eaten during the evening, although the preparation and variety may not be so elaborate. These days many townspeople are too busy to prepare a huge breakfast of the kind needed by farmers working in the fields in past times, so they will eat just soup and rice, or a few side dishes, or rice and *kimchi* for breakfast.

If there is no time to prepare anything at home for breakfast, busy people still manage to eat before starting work by fitting in a quick visit to a café or street stall serving a traditional Korean breakfast of rice, soup and meat or fish.

Some of the big cities have rows of "breakfast cafés", with their fronts open to the street, and a row of earthenware pots (*tukbaege*) on the stoves inside containing a simmering porridge-type mixture made of beans, rice or other grains, which are cooked with a lot of water until they are really soft. When you order your breakfast, a raw egg will be broken into the pot and you mix it in yourself when it arrives at the table. There is also a special porridge made of pine nuts, but this would only be eaten on feast days and birthdays, as pine nuts are so expensive.

A Korean breakfast feast

If you are feeling particularly hungry, you might be tempted to try eating all this for breakfast before a hard day's work.

- A *tukbaege* containing rice and beansprout porridge, with a raw egg broken on top and mixed in at the table
- Tofu and vegetable soup
- Cabbage *kimchi*
- Grilled (broiled) fish
- Aubergine (eggplant) salad
- Steamed shrimps
- Stir-fried beef strips
- And finally, a cup of barley tea to aid the digestion

LUNCH

The midday meal is a similar feast, but on a smaller scale than breakfast. This is when most working Koreans will throng the cafes and restaurants for a quick snack, or pick up a pancake or two from a street stall. Children and agricultural workers tend to take their lunch to school or work with them – this will often include easily transported favourites such as *kimbap*, the Korean rice and seaweed roll.

DINNER

The evening meal is the big event of the Korean day for all families. Most dinners are still cooked by the women in the family, whether or not they work outside the home, and they do not seem to consider it too much of a hardship to spend most of their free time preparing food. Of course, the range of dishes and length of time needed to make them will be defined by the amount of time available. Nevertheless, the evening meal is extremely important in most Korean families, and great care is usually taken to balance the dishes almost without anyone being aware of the time and effort this takes.

Not only will the cook of the family be thinking about the evening meal during the day, she (or sometimes he) will be planning ahead to make sure

Above: Early-rising Korean families enjoy a full and varied breakfast which, though less elaborately prepared than dinner, consists of many of the same staple ingredients such as rice, soup and kimchi.

Right: Hard-working Korean cooks can save time by using dried goods, but these are generally used to prepare the traditional components of a meal, not as ready-made meals.

that there are fresh vegetables in the house, a good stock of rice, and, of course, a pot of *kimchi* to go with every meal.

READY-MADE FOOD

Nowadays Korean food stores sell all sorts of convenience foods such as ready-made soy sauce, *doenjang* (fermented soya bean paste) or *gochujang* (chilli) paste, these all being ingredients that would have been made at home in the days when most women's main job was looking after the house and the family. But now, with more Korean women working outside the home, convenience food starts to establish its place. It is now also possible to buy ready-made *kimchi*, instant soup and stock mixes, dried fish and herbs, along with a great many other ingredients.

Despite this, the culture of fast food has made very little impact on the big cities of South Korea. The idea of a ready meal would be impossible to contemplate, simply because one dish popped into the microwave and eaten in front of the TV would not constitute a proper dinner to a Korean who had been brought up on a beautifully arranged selection of *banchan*, rice, soup and stew, with a piece of fish or meat grilled at the table. The point of Korean food stores is for convenience, to save the cook a little time by doing some of the pre-cooking preparation. But it is still the case that spending many hours planning meals, buying and combining ingredients, cooking, serving and eating as a social activity are still deeply ingrained within the Korean culture.

Right: Lunch is often eaten on the go. Children tend to take nutritious prepared lunches to schools, and busy workers stop briefly for lunch at local restaurants.

STREET FOOD AND SNACKS

Koreans take their food very seriously, and spend a lot of time preparing it and eating it according to traditional rituals. However, a more relaxed cuisine is available on the street, in the form of tasty little snacks, freshly cooked by street vendors and either munched straight away or, if you can wait, wrapped up to be taken home.

EATING ON THE STREET

The Koreans are sociable people, and love to stroll around their city shopping centres or town markets, or perch on chairs at the roadside, eating mouthfuls of spicy hot dishes in the winter or cold refreshing ones in the summer, and chatting to friends and acquaintances on the street.

Rice rolls (kimbap)

One of the most popular savoury snacks is kimbap, which is a tasty roll rather like Japanese sushi. Kimbap consists of seasoned rice and a medley of little morsels of fried egg, vegetables, meat or fish, all spread on a piece of dried laver, the flat dark-green seaweed, and rolled up. Each bite reveals a whole series of flavours, which are expertly bound together by the spicy rice.

Savoury pancakes (pajeon)

At the next stall you might find a cook expertly frying small pancakes called pajeon. These will always be based on a batter of eggs and flour, and include the ubiquitous spring onions (scallions), green chillies and a selection of other ingredients. It's yet another opportunity to eat kimchi (kimchijeon), this time incorporated into the pancake batter and eaten with a spicy soy sauce dip; or seafood such as oysters (gool pajeon), just a few chopped pieces added to the pancake while the underneath is cooking.

These pancakes are always fried gently so that there is plenty of time for the filling to cook with the batter and for the flavours to mingle. They are served pale beige and soft, not brown and crispy. The simplest version and the cheapest consists of just the batter and spring onions (scallions), and these are very popular all over the country.

More elaborate pancakes are usually the province of restaurants, but you may find some street vendors making them with buckwheat flour or rice flour, or even with cooked rice or ground cooked mung beans mixed into the batter, and a wider range of other ingredients on top including strips of beef or pork, radish, carrot, mussels, clams and anything

Above: Delicious savoury pancakes are served stuffed with spring onions, chillies and meat, seafood or vegetables.

else that comes to hand. A dipping sauce will be a necessary accompaniment to serve alongside these more intricate dishes.

Other savoury snacks

What else can be found to eat in the open air? Other savoury dishes include dumplings (mandu) with a filling of meat, fish or vegetables, or savoury sausages of pork, noodles, vegetables and seasonings packed inside a pig's intestine. To accompany these strong meaty flavours, you may find little slices of liver or lung as well as your small container of spicy dipping sauce. Absolutely nothing is wasted in Korean cooking.

Sweet pancakes (hotteok)

A plain pancake batter is the base of hotteok, but the sweet sauce is folded inside so that all the ingredients, honey, cinnamon, chopped nuts or brown

Left: Shoppers enjoy street food as a delicious and fortifying snack; not a full meal, which is normally eaten at home.

Left: Fishcakes on skewers steaming over potatoes and spring onion broth.

BAR SNACKS

Koreans enjoy a special range of snacks (*anju*) made to accompany alcoholic drinks, and these are often found in places such as karaoke bars. They tend to be finger foods, such as nuts, small portions of the rice/seaweed roll *kimbap*, pieces of steamed squid or octopus, and chopped fruit. In fact they are a bitesize version of the side dishes, *banchan*, which accompany every main meal in Korea.

Street food etiquette

Koreans will often eat snacks while strolling through the streets, window-shopping or chatting to friends. If they are particularly hungry and have bought something quite substantial, such as a seafood pancake with some rice, a sauce and a drink, there may be some chairs and tables provided by the stall so that they can sit down and appreciate the food in comfort.

sugar, are incorporated with the batter mixture into a soft cake. These are winter favourites, ideal to warm you up on a freezing day.

Cakes and pastries

Sweet things often come in unusual shapes – for instance:
• *bungeoppang* (goldfish bread), a small pastry in the shape of fish with a sweetened red bean puree inside
• *gukwappang*, a similar sweet mixture shaped like a flower
• *gyeranppang*, shaped like a shell.
Rice cakes are popular at every festival throughout the year, with both sweet and savoury mixtures inside, sometimes both, according to the season.

DRINKS

Korean street stalls sell a wide variety of drinks, both hot and cold, alcoholic and non-alcoholic. A favourite is the grain spirit, *soju*, a small shot glass of which can be swallowed quickly for winter warmth. Cold punches are favourites during the summer, especially the classic persimmon

punch, containing spices, fruit and honey to counteract the tart flavour of the persimmon. This punch is considered the most refreshing drink in Korea, and it is one that balances the strong tastes of most Korean food better than a more subtle wine or fruit juice.

Right: Koreans enjoying a picnic, which would typically include pajon (griddle cakes), kimchi *and* hwajon (rice cakes).

EQUIPMENT,
INGREDIENTS &
BASIC RECIPES

This chapter looks at key equipment, ingredients — ranging from

vegetables and fish to spices, garnishes and fruit — and a selection

of basic recipes for preparing the stocks and sauces that characterize

Korean food. This is the first step towards enjoying a Korean meal

with a steaming pot of rice, fragrant side dishes, marinated meat on

the grill, a bowl of soup and a dish of spicy kimchi.

PREPARING AND SERVING FOOD

Korean cooks know the importance of fresh ingredients, but have also developed ways of storing food for the lean months of the year. When food is fresh and of top quality, it will be cooked quickly in a wok or on a grill; less prime cuts of meat and fish are more likely to be simmered slowly on the stove. A pan of rice steams gently in every Korean kitchen until the grains become really soft and glutinous. Out-of-season food is preserved in pickled or dried forms to be eaten during the freezing winter months. The notable exception is that hardly any dishes are baked; this is because the traditional Korean kitchen had a wood-fired stove, but no oven. The combination of

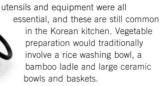

Right: Cast iron griddles have a variety of uses. A flat griddle is perfect for pancakes.

Above: A shallow, heavy-bottomed, casserole dish is ideally suited for long, slow cooking.

cooking techniques leads to the typical adventurous Korean meal, with a variety of tasty dishes to eat with the rice.

COOKING EQUIPMENT

Traditionally, food preparation and preservation was time consuming. Wooden, bamboo, ceramic, stone and metal cooking

utensils and equipment were all essential, and these are still common in the Korean kitchen. Vegetable preparation would traditionally involve a rice washing bowl, a bamboo ladle and large ceramic bowls and baskets.

For the preparation of preserved foods, such as *kimchi*, condiment mortars, grinding stones and pestles, sieve knives, chopping boards, dough boards and rice cake pattern makers would all have been necessary, as well as oil presses to extract oil from plant seeds such as sesame seeds, beans, rape, red (bell) pepper and castor beans, which are roasted, steamed and then squeezed in an oil press.

For the cooking and heating of food there would have been iron pots, frying pans, steamers and grills. Other implements in the traditional Korean kitchen would be a rice scoop, ladles and a funnel. And for serving dishes on the table, there would have been a

Below: A wok is found in most Asian kitchens, perfect for preparing quick, delicious food.

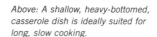

Below: Traditional cooking utensils and serving implements give a dinner party an authentic Korean edge.

Below: A traditional rice sieve. Washing rice until the water runs clear removes excess starch.

charcoal brazier to warm ceramic bowls or casserole pans. This method of warming food on the table remains strong in Korean families today.

While modern appliances such as rice and gas cookers and noodle makers have now taken over the Korean kitchen, cutting down the preparation time and making the cook's life much easier, many of these traditional implements and methods are still integral to food preparation as well as presentation.

COOKING TECHNIQUES

Fresh food is usually cooked quickly in the Korean kitchen, but cooks also use many different techniques, which have evolved over the centuries to extract every last drop of flavour and goodness from other ingredients.

Above: Rice is typically served from a large dish into individual covered bowls.

Barbecuing and grilling

Bulgogi is one of the signature dishes of Korean cuisine. For this, high-quality meat – usually beef – is sliced paper-thin and marinated in a blend of soy sauce, sesame seeds, spring onions (scallions) and ginger. After the flavours have permeated the meat, the beef slices are cooked in a dome-shaped pan placed over a charcoal brazier. The pan has a channel that catches the delicious juices produced during cooking, and they are eaten with rice and vegetables. As the marinade cooks it forms an appetizing glaze over the meat, which is then eaten either with spicy dipping sauce or

wrapped in green leaves with slices of fresh garlic and green bell pepper. Grilling over charcoal is a hugely popular method of cooking, and echoes barbecue techniques introduced by the Mongols. Traditionally a metal brazier, also called a Korean barbecue, is used for making *bulgogi* on the table. It can also be prepared on a griddle plate and then served at the table. It is often done at the table in restaurants, usually on a gas grill.

Slow cooking

Rice is served with every meal, and is always steamed gently, either in an iron pot or a bamboo steamer, and nowadays often in a rice cooker. Soups and stews are an important part of the Korean diet, and these vary from the simplest mixture of seasonal vegetables and stock to a hearty blend of meat or fish and vegetables. Slow cooking on the stove in an earthenware pot called a *tukbaege* allows the flavours to mingle, and produces fabulous casseroles that are brought to the table still bubbling hot. A flameproof casserole can also be used for such dishes.

Above: Beef being cooked on a table barbecue, from which diners would then help themselves.

Stir-frying

Finally, the Korean cook will make great use of the wok to stir-fry a mixture of ingredients – fish, seafood, vegetables – with a strong-tasting sauce. This healthy cooking process preserves vitamins and minerals, and keeps the delightfully crunchy texture of the food.

Above: A modern rice cooker will cook rice perfectly and free up space on a stove top.

PRESERVATION OF FOOD – *KIMCHI*

Ask any Korean which dish he or she cannot live without, and they will answer "*kimchi*". This tasty preparation makes full use of cabbage and other seasonal vegetables, which are preserved by blending them with seasonings and sauces and storing them in large earthenware jars to keep cool and ferment over the long winter months. *Kimchi* jars were generally stored outside in the courtyard, or buried in the ground; these days refrigerators are a better option, but you will still see rows of *kimchi* jars on top of the flat roofs of apartment buildings in the big cities.

Kimchi pots vary in size and shape, and contain anything from one to 40 gallons of this delicious preserve. An earthenware lid sits on top and the sealed pots preserve the strong flavours for months. When the jars are opened, the contents will have absorbed all the delicious fiery flavours – a perfect contrast to the chill of the wintry weather.

Koreans will literally eat *kimchi* on every day of the year and traditionally prepare a large amount during *kimjang* season, which occurs around the time of the autumn harvest. This is an important social event, when *kimchi* ingredients are blended together in copious quantities. Help is often drafted

Above left and right: Traditional woven dishes and platters are a practical and attractive method for serving up dry and fried foods.

in, and neighbours and friends who have worked hard on *kimchi* preparation all day are usually rewarded with a meal prepared by the family.

SERVING FOOD

Because the presentation of Korean food still has a strong formal element, considerable emphasis is placed on the nature and presentation of the implements that are used at the table (see also pages 24–27).

Above: Large earthenware jars used for fermenting kimchi. *These jars are often placed outside during the colder months so that the* kimchi *is refrigerated while it matures, a process that can take months.*

Above: The unusual combination of using both chopsticks and a spoon to dine with is unique to Korea.

Above: Large ceramic bowls are typically used for holding dishes such as soups and stews, from which all diners serve themselves.

Above: Heavy bowls with thick wooden bases retain heat and protect the often highly laquered table tops.

Above: Korean chopsticks are usually made of silver or brass and can be very highly ornamented at the untapered end.

Serving dishes tend to be of ceramic or stone, and incorporate large bowls for casseroles and soups as well as a selection of smaller dishes for side dishes and *kimchi*. Wooden, bamboo and metal dishes also feature, bamboo as platters for rice rolls or pancakes. Bamboo containers are also used for preparing vegetables.

Koreans always use a spoon in combination with chopsticks (generally a flat circular spoon with a straight handle), with the spoons being used for rice and soup and chopsticks for everything else. Chopsticks are held between the thumb and fingers of the right hand and are levered to pick up food portions. Traditionally made of brass or silver in Korea, they are now more commonly made of

stainless-steel, in the Korean style of medium length rods that taper to a square blunted end.

When eating with Koreans, avoid picking up the served-up bowls to eat from them, which is considered impolite, and serve the food to your own plate before eating. For anyone who is unused to eating with chopsticks, a knife and fork along with a spoon is quite acceptable. Spoon and chopstick holders can be made of porcelain, wood or silver and are an important feature of the formal table setting.

Porcelain is the preferred material for water glasses. For alcohol, glassware or crystal glassware is preferred, although porcelain can be used for serving rice wine or other alcoholic beverages.

Organizing a Korean meal

It is customary at any Korean meal for several small dishes of different food to be served at the same time. This is organized in the kitchen by having a rice dish in a bamboo steamer over a wok on the stove, while a dish or two of *kimchi* is ladled out from the pot. An additional recipe involving pancakes or vegetable fritters, for example, can be stir-fried while the rice is cooking, and a pot of soup or a casserole of meat and vegetables can be kept warm in another clay pot until the rest of the meal is ready.

Now the rice is strained through a bamboo or metal strainer and served in individual bowls, with the side dishes (*banchan*) set out in ceramic dishes. The casserole pot (*tukbaege*) is brought to the table straight from the stove. Sometimes a barbecue plate may be used, consisting of an ironware hot plate set into a wooden surround so that the food stays hot and the fingers stay cool.

Left: A ceramic platter with three "chup" or side dishes for serving at the Korean table.

TRADITIONAL FLAVOURINGS

Seasoning food carefully and plentifully is a must in Korea. Not only was this habitual because spices would preserve food for the months of scarcity during the cold winters, but Korean cooks make sure that the tastes of individual spices blend with each other and the base of vegetables, meat or fish. Furthermore, the influence of Buddhism can be felt in the belief that balanced seasoning leads to good health – the yin and yang of salty and sweet, spicy and mild makes for a general equilibrium in the body.

The traditional technique of seasoning, known in Korea as *yangnyum*, requires a mixture of spices to be blended with almost medicinal precision. Koreans believe there are five elements – fire, earth, water, wood and metal – that govern everyone's life, and these have their direct counterparts in cooking flavours. The five flavours, salty, sweet, sour, spicy and bitter, balance each other and so should be combined as far as possible at each meal.

The basic seasonings used to create the five different flavours include salt, soy sauce, *gochujang* chilli paste, *doenjang* soya bean paste, vinegar and sugar. Aromatic seasonings include ginger, mustard, pepper, sesame oil, sesame seeds, spring onions (scallions), garlic and

Above: Soy sauce is a regular component of Korean meals.

chrysanthemum leaves. Most Korean dishes are cooked with at least half a dozen different ingredients and seasonings, producing a complex and distinctive taste.

THE THREE MAJOR FLAVOURINGS

While any self-respecting Korean cook would insist on using many different ingredients, there are three flavourings that dominate Korean cuisine and without which almost no Korean recipe is complete. These are:
• soy sauce
• soya bean paste, *doenjang*
• red chilli paste, *gochujang*
The actual process of making *doenjang, gochujang* and soy sauce from scratch is a lengthy and complex one. Nowadays few households still make these condiments, relying instead on store-bought alternatives as basic ingredients, which they then combine in traditional and time-honoured recipes for strong marinades, sauces and dips.

Soy sauce

There are a number of types of soy sauce, the by-product of *doenjang* paste. Light soy sauce is used in soups and to season vegetables, while dark soy sauce is used for roasted, steamed and more hearty dishes.

Soy dip
This dip is widely served with Korean fritters and dumplings, as well as tofu and tempura dishes.

SERVES 4

INGREDIENTS
45ml/3 tbsp dark soy sauce
1 garlic clove, chopped
15ml/1 tbsp cider vinegar
7.5ml/1½ tsp sesame oil
5ml/1 tsp ground sesame seeds

Mix all the ingredients together thoroughly and transfer to a small sauce bowl for dipping.

Doenjang

This paste is made of fermented soya beans. The beans are cooked and dried into blocks, then once the fermentation process has begun with a fine mould appearing on the surface of the blocks, they are added to water and kept in a

Above: Chrysanthemum leaves are used in food, to make tea and as an ingredient in Korean rice wine.

Above: Doenjang *paste, made from fermented soya beans, is commonly used to augment soups and stews.*

Above: Gochujang *is a distinctive dark red chilli paste, its extensive use demonstrates the Korean love of chillies!*

Traditional Flavourings 39

warm place to continue fermenting. Once the process is complete, the liquid is drained off to make soy sauce, and the solids are made into *doenjang*, a salty, tasty paste similar to Japanese miso, ideal for adding a sparkle to stews and soups or for spreading on vegetables such as sticks of celery.

Gochujang

The classic Korean paste called *gochujang* also uses soya beans as a base, but this time red chillies are added for spice, as well as powdered rice, salt and a little honey or sugar, before the mixture is left to ferment in a warm place. This produces a dark red, rich, concentrated paste which is used to marinate meat and is added to many cooked dishes to give them a spicy tang.

Above: Used in Pork Belly with Sesame Dip (see page 178) this sauce combines gochujang *and* doenjang.

Chilli paste and vinegar sauce

This uncooked sauce, called *cho gochujang*, can be used as either a dip or a dressing with any salad dishes or noodles. Its tart pungency is particularly suited to seafood dishes.

SERVES 4

INGREDIENTS
60ml/4 tbsp *gochujang* chilli paste
75ml/5 tbsp water
60ml/4 tbsp cider vinegar
15ml/1 tbsp lemon juice
30ml/2 tbsp sugar
2 garlic cloves, crushed
30ml/2 tbsp spring onions (scallions), finely chopped
5ml/1 tsp sesame seeds
15ml/1 tbsp sesame oil

1 Combine all the ingredients in a bowl and mix them together.

2 Transfer the final chilli and vinegar paste to a small sauce bowl before serving it to accompany any Korean salad dish, or with Chinese leaves.

Stir-fried *gochujang* chilli paste

This sauce, called *yangnyum gochujang*, is often used for the traditional rice dish *bibimbap*. It is also suited to meat and rice dishes.

SERVES 4

INGREDIENTS
15ml/1 tbsp sesame oil
65g/2¹/₂oz beef, finely chopped
2 garlic cloves, crushed
250ml/8fl oz/1 cup *gochujang* chilli paste
30ml/2 tbsp maple syrup
15ml/1 tbsp sugar

1 Coat a wok or pan with sesame oil and heat over medium heat. Add the beef and garlic, and stir-fry until lightly golden brown.

2 Add the chilli paste and 45ml/ 3 tbsp of water, and stir until it has formed a sticky paste.

3 Add the maple syrup and the sugar, and simmer the mixture in the pan for a further 30 seconds before then transferring to a sauce bowl to serve.

FERMENTING AND PRESERVING

Koreans have developed various ways of preserving food. In the days before refrigeration this enabled them to eat well during the winter when fresh vegetables and salads, fresh meat or seafood were unavailable. The tangy, spicy taste of these foods is now associated with Korean cuisine.

Kimchi

Consisting of pickled vegetables and other foodstuffs preserved in earthenware pots, *kimchi* is Korea's most famous culinary export. Made for over 2,000 years, it is believed to be a life-giving dish which encourages good health and stamina. Although any pickled and fermented vegetable mixture can be called *kimchi*, the best-known variety is made with napa cabbage. The vegetables are coated with a mixture that typically includes chilli, ginger, garlic, soy sauce and fish paste, and then sealed in a jar and left to ferment until the flavours have blended. Koreans pickle most vegetables like this, including radishes, cucumber, turnip and aubergine (eggplant), as well as fish, shellfish and fruit. During the fermentation process the vegetables lose much of their flavour, adopting the tastes of the seasonings, but with a greatly enhanced texture.

Kimchi is most often eaten as a side dish at any meal, breakfast, lunch or dinner. However, it also makes a tasty accompaniment to little fried street snacks made of rice and sesame seeds, or may be covered with a thin batter and fried as *kimchi* fritters (*buchimgae*).

Kimchi can also be used in a spicy stew with vegetables such as mushrooms and onions, and tofu or seafood for protein. This is simmered on the stove until everything is really hot and all the textures are soft. Koreans would eat the stew with a crunchy vegetable and some glutinous rice for balance.

There are many *kimchi* variations from the different provinces according to what vegetables or fish are available. For instance, from the province of *Gyeonggi* comes a recipe for turnip

kimchi made with fish sauce, chilli and garlic, onions and salt. A frugal recipe for the winter uses small amounts of cod, which migrates south from the waters around China towards the western coast of the Korean peninsula. The recipe is similar to the one shown here, with the addition of chopped pieces of cod to the soaking brine for a salty, fishy taste. Radish *kimchi* is another favourite, with a recipe known as "Young bachelor *kimchi*" which uses the immature white radish with its fresh green leaves still attached.

Other fermented foods

Jeotgal is a mixture of any seafood, such as fish, shellfish, squid or oysters, including the intestines of the fish so that nothing is wasted, mixed with a salt brine. A colourful dish, it is often bright red with chilli flavouring, and is most often eaten layered with dark green seaweed and pale rice.

Doenjang (soya bean paste) is also fermented and can be preserved for months, taken from the store cupboard whenever needed to brighten a winter stew or vegetable soup.

Below: Traditional cabbage kimchi. *The most famous of Korean dishes, and an essential at every meal, the making of* kimchi *is an ancient and revered art.*

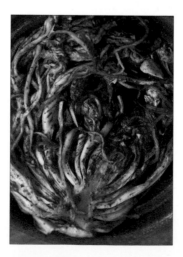

A basic *kimchi* recipe

INGREDIENTS
1 *napa* cabbage (Chinese leaf)
15ml/1 tsp salt, plus salt for brine
15ml/1 tsp sugar
15ml/1 tsp chilli pepper flakes
15ml/1 tsp pine nuts
15ml/1 tsp fresh ginger
15ml/1 tsp fresh garlic
15ml/1 tsp anchovy sauce
a handful of watercress
a handful of green onions
a handful of sliced radish

1 Cut the *napa* cabbage into two.

2 Submerge the cabbage in a couple of handfuls of sea salt and water to cover. Soak for 6 hours, then rinse.

3 Combine the remaining ingredients to form the seasoning.

4 Cut out and discard the hard core of the cabbage halves, and pack the seasoning between each leaf. Wrap one outer leaf tightly around the remaining leaves, and put it all into a sealed ceramic container. Leave for 40 hours and then refrigerate.

SPICES AND OTHER FLAVOURINGS

SPICES

The aromas of *doenjang* (soya bean paste), *gochujang* (chilli) paste and soy sauce pervade the Korean kitchen. However, there are many other favourite flavourings. No Korean cook would consider serving a meal that was predominantly flavoured with only one spice; a mixture should be used to make sure that the balance and harmony of the food is just right.

Garlic

This essential aromatic vegetable is used for everything from seasoning soup to creating marinades for meat and fish. It is also used whole as an accompaniment for grilled dishes.

Above: Garlic's pungent flavour makes it a frequent ingredient in Korean cooking.

Chilli

The chilli pepper is the next most important flavouring after garlic. The Korean version varies from mild to fiery, and, combined with garlic, forms the basis of *kimchi* flavouring.

Above: Chillies only came to Korea in the 16th century, but their fiery heat quickly made them a popular ingredient.

Dried chilli

A single sun-dried red chilli can be used to create a sharp, spicy taste, or used flaked or whole for garnishing and presentation. Sun-dried chillies are often ground into chilli powder, milder than the Indian version, which forms the basis of many Korean recipes.

Ginger

The distinctive sweet piquant taste of ginger is popular all over Asia. Korean cooks, as well as using it in *kimchi*, like to combine its taste with that of other ingredients, creating a new subtle flavour.

Above: The warmth of ginger adds depth to any dish.

Ginseng

A root best known for its medicinal properties and widely used in Korea to make tea, ginseng is also used in cooking, particularly in the summer chicken soup *samgyetang*.

Maca

This green herbal root originates in Peru, and is believed to have strong medicinal and energy-giving qualities.

Right: The green powder of the maca root.

Mustard

A favourite accompaniment to fish, the pungency of mustard sauce combines well with the saltiness of the fish. It is made by mixing dried mustard powder with vinegar, water and a little sugar and salt.

Sesame leaves

These leaves are traditionally used as a green vegetable and have a strong nutty aroma. They are also used in salads and as wraps to eat with rice and *miso*.

Above: Sesame leaves, as well as sesame oil and sesame seeds, are used as flavourings.

HERBS

Green herbs are not generally added to Korean food, and are more likely to be made into tea. Various mixtures of herbs and spices to aid digestion and promote good health have traditionally been concocted to drink after a meal, but the commonest are those made with ginseng, roasted barley or ginger.

DRIED FISH AND SEAFOOD

These are often used to make the stock that forms the basis of soups and stews. Dried anchovies, called *myulchi*, are used to flavour dishes and these tiny fish are surprisingly versatile. Dried shrimps, known in Korea as barley shrimps, have a nice crunchy texture when stir-fried and blend well with the taste of green chilli.

Above: Dried anchovies have a strong salty taste.

FISH SAUCE

An essential ingredient for making a classic fermented *kimchi*; any anchovy or fish sauce can be used. It has a multitude of other uses in Korean cooking too.

LIQUID SEASONINGS

Sesame oil

A vital ingredient, sesame oil has a rich nuttiness that imparts a dramatic flavour to grilled and stir-fried dishes.

Bean oil

Widely used in Korean stir-fry dishes, bean oil is colourless and odourless (unlike sesame oil) and using it allows the flavours of the other ingredients in a dish to remain distinct.

Vinegar

Apple and cider vinegar are the most widely used varieties. Persimmon vinegar is a delicious variant, and has an astringent taste that is quite unlike any other seasoning, but this can be difficult to find outside Korea.

Soju

This Korean rice wine is syrupy and sweet when used in cooking. Japanese *mirin*, although slightly sweeter, is perfectly adequate as a substitute.

NUTS AND SEEDS

Sesame seeds

These are toasted to bring out the distinctive taste, and used as both flavouring and garnish in many recipes. They are also toasted and crushed for sweet or savoury snacks.

Gingko nuts

Used in sweet and savoury dishes, gingko nuts are also served as an alternative to lotus seeds. Grilled and salted, they are a popular snack in both Japan and Korea, and once cooked they turn a delicate shade of green.

OTHER FLAVOURINGS

Salt

Koreans use sea salt, plentiful around this small country. A Korean variation called bamboo salt is made by storing sea salt in bamboo stalks plugged with yellow mud and then roasting it to remove any impurities. This treatment gives the salt a distinctive taste.

Above: The versatility of gingko nuts means that they are used in both sweet and savoury dishes.

Honey and sugar

Both these ingredients are used sparingly as sweeteners in Korean cuisine, as desserts are not the main focus of a meal in Korea. In fact, honey and sugar are more often used in savoury dishes, as part of a recipe for flavourings such as *gochujang* paste. They can also be added to marinades in order to create a sweet and sour flavour combination.

Above: Sesame oil is often added at the end of cooking to impart flavour, rather than as a cooking aid.

Above: Sesame seeds have a distinctive nutty flavour and also add an element of texture to dishes.

Above: The inordinately popular soju, Korean rice wine, is very strong and best served in small shot glasses.

GARNISHES

Korean cooks pride themselves on the presentation of their food. Every Korean meal is carefully and artistically arranged, and are then eaten at the table with corresponding consideration and dedication.

This attention to detail includes garnishing the food, an art that used to be almost unknown in the food culture of the West, but has always been natural to the Koreans. Restaurants in Europe and the USA now understand the importance of presentation to the diners' appreciation of a meal, and how the eye informs the taste buds – the little dots of balsamic vinegar or sauce around the plate are testament to this.

Garnishes can consist of artfully arranged fresh vegetables, salad leaves, nuts and fruit, or cooked delicacies such as egg strips or tiny portions of minced meat. Here are just a few ideas for garnishes commonly found in Korean homes and restaurants.

COOKED GARNISHES

Egg strip

Beaten egg is whisked up with a little salt and maybe some sugar, then fried in oil in a small frying pan. A thin omelette will result, which can then be rolled up when cold and cut into shreds to decorate any dish.

Above: This beef noodle dish is garnished with egg strips.

Two-colour egg strip

A favourite variation on egg strip, where the beaten egg white and egg yolk are cooked separately and then, when rolled and shredded, form a yellow and white pattern over the dish or around the rim.

Egg roll

This is another variation on the egg strip. This time the cooked, cooled omelette is rolled around a few lightly cooked green beans and bright orange carrots, then thinly sliced to make little circles of yellow, green and orange.

Minced meat

Small amounts of minced (ground) meat can be quickly stir-fried in sesame oil and mixed with chopped chillies, garlic and onions. This tasty mixture is then sprinkled on top of noodle soup.

VEGETABLES AND SALAD LEAVES

Watercress

Koreans love watercress, or *minari*, for its peppery bite. It can be cooked in stews and stir-fries, or simply arranged a couple of leaves at a time on top of an orange or red dish so as to give an emphatic colour contrast.

Above: Garnishes extend flavour and add visual interest; the finishing touch on this rice dish is fish roe or tobiko.

Shiitake mushrooms

Dried mushrooms are rehydrated or fresh ones gently fried in oil. They can be arranged in overlapping slices on top of a large piece of meat or a bowl of rice, or floated on top of a delicate soup.

Above: This porridge has a garnish of cress, mushrooms and soy sauce.

Below: Chillies cut into flakes inject colour and piquancy.

Chilli peppers

Red or green chilli peppers are ideal for garnishing as they impart a spicy kick and are a beautiful bright colour.

Dried chilli strips or threads

Sun-dried chillies are made into little flakes, strips or even finer threads. They are often sprinkled on top of a bowl of soup or stew.

Sweet potato crisps

The sweet potato is not an indigenous vegetable; it was brought to Korea by the Japanese in the 18th century. It grows well in Korea, however, and when used as a garnish rather than a main ingredient, it is made into thin crisps, cooked quickly in hot oil.

Spring onions (scallions)

These lend themselves particularly well to fancy garnishing – they can be shredded at one end, sliced into thin diagonal rings or made into little brushes with a ring of chilli in the centre.

Other vegetables

Salad vegetables are sliced finely into little strips and either set on top of a dish or served separately. The vegetables may be served plain or dressed with a little vinegar, sugar, salt and citrus juice. Delicate patterns can be made by cutting cucumber sections or carrots into strips almost to the end, and fanning them out like a flower.

SEEDS, NUTS AND DATES

Sesame seeds

These tiny seeds are usually toasted in a dry pan until they jump and turn brown. They can then be sprinkled on top of soups and stews or served with rice to give a nutty flavour to any dish.

Gingko nuts

Prized for the green colour, that appears when a fresh gingko nut is cooked, these make a good contrast to the predominantly red colour of many Korean dishes.

Pine nuts

These are toasted in a dry pan until they begin to jump around the pan and turn brown. Their taste is brought out by toasting and they blend well with blander dishes such as rice or noodles. Pine nuts can also be sprinkled on top of a stew in the pot before it is brought to the table.

Red dates

Known as *jujube* in Oriental cooking, these medicinal fruits are oblong in shape and turn a reddish brown when ripe. They have a sweet flavour and a vibrant colour, and are ideal for garnishing sweet or savoury dishes. They are also a common ingredient in cakes and cookies.

Above: The sweetness of red dates, or jujubes, is said to be an aphrodisiac.

Above: This salad with persimmons is dressed with chilli and egg strips.

Above: The garnish on this pumpkin congée is sliced red dates and pine nuts.

Above: This salmon teriyaki is garnished with sesame seeds and whole chives.

RICE AND NOODLES

The rich spiciness of many Korean meat and fish dishes needs a plain, starchy foil, and this contrast is provided by rice and noodles. These two plain ingredients absorb the flavours of any accompanying sauce, and fill the stomach with nourishing warmth.

Above: Short grain rice, the favourite of Korea, has a distinctive stickiness.

RICE

The foundation of all Korean meals, rice dishes are eaten throughout the day. In combination with soup and vegetables it forms an essential part of a nutritious and satisfying Korean meal. In fact rice, or *bap* as it is known by Koreans, is so essential to every meal that it has become synonymous with the meal itself. "Did you have *bap*?" is the common way to ask if an acquaintance has already dined, regardless of the other dishes they had. Koreans believe that their strength comes from the continuing consumption of rice, and that it greatly enhances their stamina. These very hardworking people may have a point.

Rice is traditionally cooked on its own in the Korean kitchen, although sometimes other grains such as millet and barley are included to enhance the flavour, one example being the five-grain rice recipe shown overleaf. Beans and chestnuts are occasionally included with rice dishes, and cooked vegetables, meat or fish are often mixed into the dish before serving. The Koreans, just like the Japanese, eat only the sticky short and medium grain varieties.

Right: Pudding or sweet rice is short and fat with a white kernel. When cooked, it becomes glutinous. It is useful as a binder for gravies, sauces, and fillings, or in sweet dishes.

Short grain rice

This is the staple food of Korea. Called *ssal* in Korean, this is close in shape and texture to Japanese rice. It becomes soft and sticky when cooked.

Brown rice

This is normally cooked as a mixture with white rice and other grains, and is considered to have better nutritional value than the common short grain variety.

Glutinous or sweet rice

Slightly longer than the common short grain rice, this is only used in rice cakes, cookies and other sweet dishes, where the grains need to bind together.

Mixed grains

Rice grain mixtures are popular in Korea. They vary from region to region, but typically contain combinations of brown rice, sweet rice, wild rice, barley, hulled millet, green peas, yellow peas, black-eyed beans (peas), kidney beans and red

Below: Millet is often used as part of a mixed grain combination.

beans. The Korean dish called Five-grain rice, or *Ogokbap* combines four other grains (including millet, black beans and sweet beans) with regular rice. Other ingredients can be added, such as soya beansprouts and chestnuts.

Storing rice

Any leftover cooked rice can be stored in the refrigerator, wrapped with clear film (plastic wrap) in order to help preserve the moisture. Don't keep cooked rice for more than a couple of days.

Left: Brown rice is usually combined with other rice types.

RICE RECIPES

Recipes for two widely eaten Korean rice dishes are given here. The flavours in these rice dishes are understated, and are designed to balance and complement highly spiced meat or fish. Knowing how to cook the basic rice recipes that are shown here is an essential requirement for creating the heart of any Korean meal.

Steamed rice

Koreans cook rice in a steamer, but the same flavour and texture can be created with pan-cooked rice. Short grain Asian rice is the best, although pudding rice can be used. Good quality rice will have a sheen, and the grains should also be free from scratches.

Cooking rice

SERVES 4

INGREDIENTS
400g/14oz/2 cups short grain
  white rice or pudding rice
a drop of sunflower oil

1 Rinse and drain the rice in cold water four or five times. Place in a heavy pan and add water to about 5mm/¼in above the rice. Add a drop of sunflower oil to give the rice a shine, cover with a lid and boil.

2 Lower the heat and leave to steam. Do not remove the lid during cooking.

3 After 12–15 minutes turn off the heat and leave the rice, still covered, to steam for a further 5 minutes.

Mixed grains

Plain steamed rice often has grains, beans and lentils added to create the Korean favourite *ogokbap*. These extra ingredients give more of a crunch to the dish, and give exotic combinations of flavours. It is believed that sharing *ogokbap* at the first full moon of the year will bring good luck for the year.

Preparing mixed grains

SERVES 4

INGREDIENTS
40g/1½oz/generous ¼ cup dried
  black beans or sweet beans
50g/2oz/¼ cup barley
50g/2oz/¼ cup millet
50g/2oz/¼ cup brown rice
50g/2oz/¼ cup sorghum or lentils
200g/7oz/1 cup short grain
  white rice
salt

1 Soak the beans, barley, millet, brown rice and sorghum or lentils in cold water for 24 hours. Add the white rice to the soaked grains and beans. Drain and rinse well.

2 Place the rice in a heavy pan and add water (preferably filtered) to about 5mm/¼in above the rice level.

3 Add a pinch of salt, then cover with a lid and bring to the boil.

4 Lower the heat and steam for 12–15 minutes keeping the lid on. Turn off the heat and leave the grains to steam for 5 more minutes.

NOODLES

Korean noodles can be made of different grains and vegetables, the most common being wheat, buckwheat and sweet potato. They are almost as common as rice in Korean cuisine. Noodles should be boiled for a few minutes in lots of water but should never be over-cooked, especially for a stir-fried dish.

Glass noodles

Known as *dangmyun*, these delicate strands of sweet potato starch are also known as cellophane noodles, Chinese vermicelli, bean threads and bean thread noodles. They are often used as the base for noodle soups or stir-fried dishes, and can also be added to casseroles to provide volume and richness of flavour and texture.

Buckwheat and wheat noodles

Thin and brown in colour, buckwheat noodles are known in Korea as *memil*. They have a distinctive crunchy texture and are similar in

Above: Originally from Japan, udon noodles are thicker and softer than other types of noodle.

appearance to a softer variety called *momil*, which are made from wheat flour. These are much better known as the Japanese *soba* noodle.

Udon noodles

Handmade flat noodles, also called udon noodles or *kalguksu*, are made from plain wheat flour and are popular for dishes where a more tender texture is suitable.

Somyun

A thin plain flour white noodle, which is often used for noodles served in broth.

Soba noodles

These noodles, which are of Japanese origin, are made of buckwheat flour (*soba-ko*) and wheat flour (*komugi-ko*). They are of approximately the same thickness as spaghetti, and are prepared in various hot and cold dishes in Korea. They can be bought dried, but they taste best when handmade.

Below: Soba noodles are made from buckwheat and are similar in length and thickness to Italian spaghetti.

Below: Thick udon noodles in a delicate broth make a quick and tasty lunch.

Above: Thin buckwheat noodles are often bound with wheat flour to prevent them disintegrating while cooking.

Above: Glass, or cellophane, noodles are made of mung bean or sweet potato starch and are almost clear when cooked.

Chilled *naengmyun* noodles
Noodles are often chilled after cooking for use in salads and other side dishes.

INGREDIENTS
90g/3½oz *naengmyun* buckwheat noodles

1 Cook the noodles in a large pan of boiling water for 5 minutes. Add a few drops of oil while cooking to help prevent the water from frothing up and boiling over; this also helps to keep the noodles separate when they are drained.

2 Drain the noodles, and then rinse two or three times in cold water until the water runs clear. Chill for 30 minutes.

STOCKS

A good, tasty stock is an essential base for many of the Korean recipes that are introduced here. They will give the depth of flavour that is essential to give an authentic Korean taste to the dish.

STOCK FOR SOUP

A small bowl of soup, steamed rice and some tasty meat, fish and *banchan* (side dishes) is the backbone of a typical Korean meal. Soup is not served as a separate course, but it's often the first thing a Korean diner will taste while the meat is grilling (broiling), keeping hunger pangs at bay with its savoury flavours. At dinner time, soup is usually served in a small dish, one for each person, placed next to the individual rice dish.

One of the most delightful ways to taste this flavoursome brew is while strolling around the town and socializing with friends – it's a common sight to see little cups of piquant soup for sale next to the rice dishes, pancakes and fritters on the stalls of street vendors.

Koreans cook soup, using all sorts of ingredients from meat and vegetables to fish, tofu, seaweed and even tinned food such as hot dogs (the influence of the US troops based here during the Korean War). What they all have in common is a strong, often home-made stock base and

Above: A steaming bowl of hot and spicy beef soup, a delicious and aromatic medley of tastes and textures.

a fiery kick from added chillies, garlic and spices. Korean soup, packed with ingredients, tends to be a heartier dish than many other Asian soups.

HOME-MADE STOCK

There are three basic stock recipes, and these are made whenever they are needed by Korean cooks. These three stocks are based on:
• beef bones, which gives a strong, hearty flavour

Beef bone stock

This is a well-known and versatile stock for Korean dishes. Simply add chopped spring onions and a little seasoning for a wholesome, revitalizing soup. It is also great for fortifying the taste of hearty stews or casserole dishes.

MAKES 1 LITRE/1¾ PINTS/4 CUPS

INGREDIENTS
1–2 beef bones
90g/3½oz spring onions (scallions)
5 garlic cloves
10g/¼oz fresh root ginger
1 leek, halved
90g/3½oz Chinese white radish
5 peppercorns

1 Soak the beef bones in cold water for approximately 2 hours to drain away any excess blood. Add 1 litre/1¾ pints/4 cups water to a large pan, add the bones and bring it to the boil. Immediately drain off the water and rinse the bones.

• beef without the bones for a more subtle meaty dish
• fish or shellfish, for its distinctive salty tang.

Of course, many other variations exist, using any nutritious food available such as pork spine or ox blood; however, these three recipes highlighted above do form the traditional basis of the vast majority of Korean soups and casseroles.

2 Pour 2.5 litres/4⅓ pints/11 cups water into a large pan and add the bones, with the spring onions, garlic cloves, ginger, leek, radish and peppercorns.

3 Bring the stock to the boil, and cook over a high heat until the liquid has reduced by half. Top up the pan with an equivalent amount of water and allow the liquid to reduce again. Repeat one more time until you have just over 1 litre/1¾ pints/4 cups of stock left in the pan.

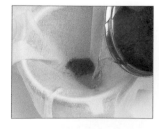

4 Strain the stock into a container and refrigerate for future use in soups and casseroles.

Beef flank stock

Stock made from beef flank, a lean cut, is commonly used for a wide range of Korean soups. It has a much cleaner, lighter taste and consistency than bone broth.

MAKES 1 LITRE/1¾ PINTS/4 CUPS

INGREDIENTS
600g/1lb 6oz beef flank
5 garlic cloves
1 leek, halved

1 Soak the beef in cold water for 2 hours, then drain.

2 Place the beef, garlic and leek in a large pan, and add 2.5 litres/4¾ pints/11 cups water. Bring the pan to the boil, then reduce the heat and simmer for about 2 hours.

3 While the liquid is simmering, skim any fat from the surface of the pan to ensure a more flavourful, leaner stock.

4 Strain the stock into a container for use in soups and casseroles.

Fish stock

A good fish stock is an essential component for fish and shellfish soups or casseroles. Stocks such as this are often boiled for long periods, and the stock can be used several times. This one has a mild seafood flavour and is wonderfully versatile.

MAKES 1 LITRE/1¾ PINTS/4 CUPS

INGREDIENTS
1 square of dried kelp seaweed (about 10 x 10cm/4 x 4in)
5 dried anchovies
¹/₃ Chinese white radish, roughly diced

1 Place all the ingredients in a large pan and add 1.5 litres/2¹/₂ pints/6¹/₄ cups water.

2 Place the pan over a high heat and boil for 15 minutes, after which you should discard the anchovies.

3 Boil the stock for an extra 20 minutes, and then strain thoroughly before use.

Dried anchovy stock

This, a variation of the fish stock, uses dried anchovies, and is commonly used in many traditional soups in Japan and China as well as Korea. The result is a pleasantly mild fishy-tasting stock that will blend well with any fish recipe.

MAKES 1 LITRE/1¾ PINTS/4 CUPS

INGREDIENTS
10g/¼oz dried anchovies
1 litre/1¾ pints/4 cups water

1 Bring the water to the boil in a large pan or wok and then add the 10g/¼oz dried anchovies to the pan.

2 Boil the stock for 2 minutes and then, using a sieve (strainer), remove and discard the anchovies from the pan.

3 Put the anchovy stock in a container before using in a soup or a casserole. Alternatively, cook and refrigerate the stock for future use.

VEGETABLES, SALADS AND TOFU

The Korean diet is a pretty healthy one. The food is mainly low in fat and high in nutrients, with an emphasis on fresh, seasonal food cooked at home and served to be eaten immediately. When fresh ingredients are not available, there is the spicy concoction *kimchi*, which preserves both nutrients and flavour by excluding light and heat in a sealed jar.

Vegetables and salads are a vital part of the Korean diet. They balance the solid base of rice and its accompanying protein, and provide essential vitamins and minerals, and a crucial contrast in flavour, colour and texture.

Vegetables can form the basis of a stew, or be added to a piece of meat or fish as a flavourful and pretty garnish. They make up the majority of the side dishes which are set out for diners to share, featuring any number of vegetables such as aubergine (eggplant), radish, sweet potatoes and mushrooms. There may also be a basket of lettuce or chrysanthemum leaves on the table, ready to wrap a piece of meat. Lastly, of course, there

will be a dish or two of *kimchi*, maybe based on cabbage, radish or turnip.

The high consumption of tofu is linked to Korea's Buddhist roots and to its relatively limited meat resources. Made from sweet soya beans, tofu is still Korea's main source of protein.

KOREAN VEGETABLES

Vegetable and salad dishes vary according to what is in season. The staple vegetables are:

Chinese cabbage

Called *baechu* or *tong baechu* in Korea, this is also commonly known as napa cabbage or Chinese leaves, and nowadays can be found in most supermarkets. It has a long white leaf, and looks quite unlike other round cabbage varieties. It is the key ingredient for traditional *kimchi*.

Chinese white radish

This giant of the radish family can grow to an impressive 30cm/1ft long, and is thick, similar in character to a large parsnip.

Also known by its Japanese name of *daikon* or its Hindi name of *mooli*, this vegetable is simply known in Korea as *moo*. It has an inherent spiciness and sweetness and a pungent flavour.

Leeks

Koreans use *daepa*, a large variety of the spring onion (scallion) that is sweeter and more flavourful than the small green onion. However, leeks have a similar flavour, and the two are interchangeable.

Spring onions (scallions)

These are the most popular garnish for soups and other dishes, sometimes shredded into elaborate shapes like little brushes. Spring onions crop up everywhere, including in *kimchi* recipes, stir-fries, soups, stews and flavoured rice. The Korean variant is virtually identical to the Western equivalent.

Garlic

This staple ingredient is added to many dishes, and features as a pickled vegetable in its own right, ready to use

Above: Cabbage is most commonly found in kimchi, *widely expounded as one of the world's healthiest foods.*

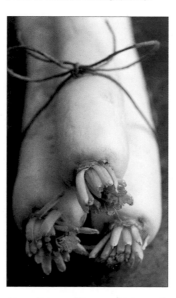

Above: Peppery Chinese radish is usually served cooked, unlike the smaller radishes common to Western kitchens.

Above: Korean food is an amalgamation of carefully constructed flavours; pungent garlic is one of the most popular.

Above: Perilla leaves are reminiscent of mint and delicious in salads.

Right: Soft, sweet mung beans are a Korean staple.

Mung beans

These small round green beans are used in mung bean soufflé and other recipes. The sprouts of the mung bean are also a valuable ingredient, used to make soup or added to stir-fries. Mung beansprouts are favoured over other beansprouts as they have an intense nutty flavour and a pleasing crunchy texture.

Fern fronds

Also known as "fiddlehead ferns", fern fronds are rarely used in the Western kitchen. Wild ferns can be poisonous, so use the dried fern fronds, available at any Asian store. Used as a key ingredient in *yukgejang* soup, these are also seasoned and sautéed for salads.

during the winter when fresh garlic is not available. It comes into its own in the *kimchi* pot, where its full flavour complements the spices, salt and spring onions (scallions).

Perilla

Commonly known as wild sesame leaf, perilla is also called *kenip*. These wonderfully fragrant leaves are used in many ways in the kitchen, and while they look similar to Japanese *shiso*, the flavour is slightly different. The refreshing properties of this herb bring out a naturally fresh taste in many dishes, and it is also used as a wrap for little parcels of grilled meat.

Korean chives

These are similar to Chinese chives in terms of flavour and texture and in Korea are called *buchu*. Korean chives are flat green vegetables and are larger than the herb variety more familiar in Western cooking. This delicate vegetable bruises easily so it should be handled and washed with great care.

Minari

This is a small salad leaf with a wonderful aroma, similar in appearance to watercress, and with a long, crunchy stem. It is used in stews and salads, or can be simply blanched and served with a sweet and sour chilli paste dressing. Watercress can be successfully substituted.

Chrysanthemum leaves

Known as *sukgot* in Korea and cooked in a similar way to spinach, these leaves are strongly aromatic and are often used to suppress the smell of fish or other strong flavours in certain dishes. This herb, with its wonderfully exotic fragrance, can only be found in Korean stores, but the flat-leaf Italian parsley makes a good substitute.

Above: Korean chives are delicately flavoured and make an attractive and tasty garnish.

Above: Beautifully nutty and full of protein, mung beansprouts are a tasty and nutritious ingredient.

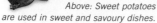

Above: Sweet potatoes are used in sweet and savoury dishes.

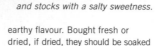

Above: Dried kelp imbues soups and stocks with a salty sweetness.

Above: Rice rolls, wrapped in nori, make a delicious lunchtime treat.

Sweet potatoes

This pink or orange-fleshed root vegetable was brought to Korea by the Japanese and quickly became established as a staple food. Sweet potatoes are eaten in both savoury dishes such as stir-fries, where their subtle flavour blends beautifully with mushrooms and garlic, as well as in sweet dishes such as Sweet Potato Jelly (see page 244), where they are cooked until soft.

Mushrooms

There are several varieties which lend their strong, distinctive flavours to many Korean dishes.

- *Shiitake mushrooms* Called *pyogo* in Korean, these have a flat round cap, and are dark brown with an earthy flavour. Bought fresh or dried, if dried, they should be soaked in warm water to reconstitute.
- *Enoki mushrooms* Also known as *enokitake* in Japanese, enoki mushrooms have a long, thin stem and tiny cap and an extremely delicate, slightly furry texture. They are generally used for garnishing.
- *Oyster mushrooms* A delicate pale grey colour and fan-shaped, oyster mushrooms are often used for casseroles and stir-fried dishes, being mild in taste and silky in texture.

SEAWEED

Used in Korean cooking for centuries, seaweed has a high vitamin and protein content. Three kinds of seaweed are:

Dried kelp

This seaweed is known as *dashikonbu* in Japanese or *dahima* in Korean, and can be found in Asian stores. It has a rich sea flavour, perfectly suited to making soup stock and salads. Kelp should always be soaked before being used.

Nori

This is the Japanese term for the popular edible flat layer of seaweed known as *kim* in Korea. It has a colour somewhere between dark blue and black, and is sold dried in small, very thin sheets. It has a crisp texture and a salty flavour with a distinctly toasty aroma, and is used to make the rice rolls so popular as snacks and lunchbox items in Korea.

Above: Shiitake mushrooms, dried and reconstituted with water, are considered to have superior flavour to fresh.

Above: Fresh enoki mushrooms are mild and fruity, with a delicate crunchy texture that is enjoyed cooked and raw.

Above: Oyster mushrooms are firm and meaty and are an ideal way to add flavour and substance to light meals.

Miyuk

An edible seaweed, known as *wakame* in Japan, *miyuk* is much softer than dried kelp, and contains a range of vitamins that promote good circulation. A popular Korean soup, which is traditionally served at birthday celebrations, is made from *miyuk*. This is also given to new mothers as it is believed to improve the circulation and to help them to regain their strength after childbirth.

Above: Nutritious tofu is the perfect meat substitute.

TOFU

This beancurd cake is made from the milky liquid extracted from soya beans, in a method similar to cheesemaking, with sweet soya beans replacing the milk. Tofu is a good vegetarian option that is commonly used as a meat substitute, and has been a principal source of protein for Koreans since the 15th century, and is combined both with vegetables and with meat. It is both delicious and easy to cook, and you'll rarely find a Korean meal that does not include tofu. Traditional tofu dishes include fried tofu (usually mixed with meat), tofu soup (with vegetables, meat, and noodles), tofu cooked in soy sauce, and *tofu chige* (a spicy soup).

Firm tofu, which is widely available at supermarkets, is pressed from fresh tofu to remove some of the water. It has a much longer product life, but it is not considered as special as fresh tofu.

GRILL ACCOMPANIMENTS – *NAMUL*

Dishes that are grilled are frequently accompanied by side orders of fresh mushrooms, garlic, potatoes and other vegetables in Korea. These side dishes

are known as *namul*. Side dishes can also include meat and fish, and the whole array of zesty, tasty grill accompaniments is known as *banchan*.

Namul recipes vary considerably. Any type of any available vegetable may be used, and any part of the plant. What is more, these little dishes of radish, cucumber, potato, mushroom, and so on can be served separately or mixed in tasteful combinations to make a powerful range of colours, textures and tastes in one dish.

Namul vegetables are often steamed or stir-fried quickly in order to preserve their vitamins. They can also be served raw and crunchy, or preserved as *kimchi*.

Above: This namul *combines soya beansprouts, leeks and sesame oil with a garnish of red chilli.*

Shredded spring onion (scallion)

The ubiquitous spring onion (scallion) often appears as an addition to the lettuce leaf wrap – just a pinch of shredded spring onions will give an enhanced zesty flavour. Here is the recipe for this tasty garnish. Serve with grilled meat and seafood dishes.

SERVES 4

INGREDIENTS
1/2 leek or 4 spring onions (scallions), thinly shredded
30ml/2 tbsp *gochujang* Korean chilli powder
30ml/2 tbsp sugar
30ml/2 tbsp cider vinegar
10ml/2 tsp sesame oil

1 Shred the spring onions and leave to soak in cold water for 5 minutes to make them crunchy.

2 Combine the chilli powder, sugar, vinegar and sesame oil in a small bowl, and mix the ingredients together thoroughly.

3 Add the spring onions to the bowl and coat them with the chilli mixture before serving with dishes such as Braised Mackerel with White Radish (see page 140), King Prawns with Pine Nut Dressing (see page 147) or Grilled Tiger Prawns (see page 152).

BEEF, PORK AND CHICKEN

Korean cooks, as in many Asian countries, turn first to rice and vegetables to form the bulk of their meals. In past years, protein used to come mainly from fish and shellfish, tofu and other soya bean products, and meat was traditionally a luxury ingredient available only to the rich. Now, however, meat is becoming more popular and affordable in Korea and it features in many a favourite recipe.

COOKING TECHNIQUES

Methods of food preparation have changed with the advent of cheaper prime cuts, with the grill or barbecue becoming pretty much indispensable in any Korean household or restaurant. A portable gas or charcoal grill is used to sear the meat for a very short time, sometimes at the table, so that all its flavour and tenderness is preserved. The meat is then cut into pieces and wrapped in lettuce leaves, often sprinkled with spring onions (scallions), garlic and spicy sauces.

Nothing is wasted, however. The prime cuts are usually grilled quickly, but there are many other parts of the animal that are cooked more slowly in stews or soups, including the spine and other bones, the tail and the tongue. Koreans are also fond of using the less attractive cuts of meat in a typical

Above: Beef, marinated in rice wine, here combined with sesame seeds, is an excellent addition to Korean pancakes.

sausage made of chitterlings (the intestines of the pig) stuffed with rice and flavoured with the animal's blood. Finally, the bones are made into stock to extract every last drop of goodness.

BEEF

Nowadays, beef has become the favourite meat in Korea, and there are many inventive ways of cooking the different cuts to tender perfection.

Above: Griddled beef, or bulgogi, *is cooked in a flash and packed with fresh vibrant flavours.*

Bulgogi

This classic dish uses thinly sliced beef marinated in soy sauce and oil with spices and garlic, then cooked quickly on a grill at the table. It results in a juicy slice of beef with added flavour.

Skewered beef

The table grill is also used in a series of skewered beef dishes, where alternate chunks of beef steak and vegetables

Meaty snacks

Not only a major part of each meal, meat also features in snacks to be eaten after work, while stopping off by a stall on the way home or strolling through the markets and shops of a big city. If you can wait, these snacks can also be wrapped up to be enjoyed at home. There's a wide choice for the meat-eater: *kimbap*, with little chunks of meat mixed into the rice filling, or a spicy sausage, or a pancake with tiny strips of pork or beef.

Left: Street food sellers grill or barbecue meat to use in a variety of convenient, tasty and nutritious snacks.

Above: The versatility of beef means that it is enjoyed served in a variety of different ways, cooked and raw.

such as mushrooms and spring onions (scallions) are first marinated in a spicy mix, as for *bulgogi*, and then threaded on to bamboo skewers to be lightly grilled (broiled).

Bulgalbi

This is a chunkier dish, which consists of a hefty piece of beef rib on the bone, cooked at the table after being marinated in a soy sauce mixture. This cut can also be cooked slowly in a *tukbaege* on the stove, simmered with stock and vegetables until meltingly tender.

Below: Slow cooking leaves large cuts of beef perfectly tender.

Above: The finest cuts of raw beef, finely sliced and delicately seasoned, are a Korean delicacy.

Stir-fried dishes

These recipes use beef in finely cut thin strips to add flavour and protein to a predominantly vegetable dish. Cooked in this way, small amounts of best quality beef can be used economically and stretched to feed a whole family – 125g/4¹⁄₄oz of beef is plenty for four people when it is mixed with a large plateful of shiitake mushrooms and spring onions alongside a good mixture of spices, chilli and garlic.

Raw beef

Koreans are very fond of raw beef in a beef tartare dish, where the best cut of meat is very thinly sliced into ribbons, and is then seasoned with sesame oil and displayed in a round flat dish on a base of lettuce leaves. There will be alternating stripes or concentric circles of meat, strips of the hard, grainy Asian pear and garlic, with toasted pine nuts and an egg broken into the centre. When it is time to serve the dish, it is customary for the cook to break the egg yolk, and each diner then dips his portion of meat into the raw egg.

Above: Sirloin steak, cut from the lower portion of the ribs, is the next best cut after the fillet or tenderloin.

Ox meat

In the spirit of good husbandry, making use of everything edible from the countryside, Koreans enjoy pressed ox tongue and oxtail broth, simmered until tender. Oxtails can be bought whole or sliced, and are cooked in stock.

Above: Oxtail has a gelatinous quality that makes it an ideal base for soups and broths.

Then the ox meat can either be extracted and mixed back into the soup, or the oxtail can be left whole for the diners to cut and serve themselves. It has a very strong flavour, so the added seasoning should be gentle – ideally a simple combination of garlic, pepper and onions.

Above: Pork is often treated simply, its blandness used to counter and enhance the vibrant flavours of kimchi.

PORK

Commonly eaten in Korea, pork is probably next in popularity to beef these days. Pigs thrive in the colder climate of the north of the country, where there is less room for grazing because of the mountainous landscape, and raising cattle for meat would not be an economical option. Pork is also a good deal cheaper than beef, and with its blander flavour it absorbs spices and garlic beautifully, making a great base for any number of flavourful recipes.

Grilled steak and ribs

Boneless pork steaks can be treated in the same way as beef, marinated for several hours in a mixture of soy sauce, garlic, chilli and other spices, and then quickly cooked on a grill. Ribs are generally cut longer than Chinese spare ribs, with more meat on the bone. *Kimchi* is the best accompaniment to many a pork dish, as its spicy, tart flavour cuts through the blander, fatty pork.

Samgyupsal

A tasty Korean speciality is known as *samgyupsal*, or "three-layer pork". This is made with a large chunk of pork belly, the "three layers" consisting of the lean meat, a layer of fat, and finally the thick skin. Koreans do not like to eat the fat and skin layers, but keeping them during the cooking process allows the meat to develop a full tender perfection. The whole chunk of meat is first simmered until tender, and then sliced every $^1/_2$cm/$^1/_4$in or so all through the cooked meat part and coated with a seasoning paste made of ginger and toasted pine nuts.

Once the rest of the meal is ready, the piece of meat is steamed gently for a few minutes to heat through, and decorated between the slices with any number of garnishes, ranging from mushrooms, cucumber and chilli threads to sliced egg roll. Each diner pulls off pieces of succulent meat and tasty garnish, leaving the fat and skin below.

CHICKEN

Dishes prepared with chicken are not a favourite of Korean cooks, surprisingly enough. Indeed, despite the fact that chickens are easy to rear and live happily in most climates, they are not a common feature of the Korean countryside and tend to be cooked only on special occasions.

Above: While chicken is not prominent in the Korean diet, it does appear in various recipes.

Samgyetang

Perhaps the best known traditional chicken recipe n Korea is *samgyetang*. This famous Korean stew consists of a small chicken, not more than 450g/1lb in weight, which is simmered slowly over a low heat in a *tukbaege* (or casserole) along with ginseng root, red dates, garlic and rice. *Samgyetang* forms a kind of thick, bright red soup which is believed to be particularly beneficial to the health when eaten during the very hottest days of summer.

Stews, soups and stock

Chicken meat is rarely grilled in the style of the beef and pork recipes that we have already mentioned. It will usually be found in a stew or as the basis of noodle soup. Chicken bones and feet make a good stock, particularly when simmered with ginger and onions.

Deep-fried chicken

Fried chicken is a popular evening snack, especially in Korean bars where they are eaten with beer or *soju*. Korean deep-fried chicken is characterized by a delicate crust, spicy seasoning and deliciously moist meat.

Above: Griddled pork loin should be well done with the exterior seared and slightly blackened.

FISH AND SHELLFISH

The Koreans are fantastically resourceful cooks. They use a multitude of ingredients; they cook their food quickly to preserve its nutritional value; and what they can't eat straight away they preserve for the winter. Above all, they make proper use of the abundant harvest of the sea.

GOOD FOOD FROM THE SEA

This is a country bounded on three sides by water. The land mass of Korea is only about 1,000km (620 miles) long from north to south, but It has a coastline measuring over 8,000km (about 5,000 miles) with over 3,000 islands dotted around the southern and western coasts. So it is no wonder the Korean diet is so rich in fish and shellfish of all kinds.

What is more, the kinds of seafood available vary considerably from one part of the country to another. In the colder waters of the north, cod and other cold-water fish abound, particularly in the winter months when they migrate around the Chinese coast. Farther south in the Yellow Sea, crabs, oysters and other shellfish live in the tidal mudflats; and around the southernmost tip of Korea, into the East Sea facing Japan, there are thousands of squid to be caught and dried in the sun. Busan, South Korea's busy second city and a major port on the south-east coast, has a huge fish market where every kind of seafood is set out for sale every day.

CORNUCOPIA OF SPECIES

There are so many types of fish and shellfish commonly used in Korean cuisine. They are made into stews, soups, stir-fries, grills, street snacks; served with rice, with noodles, with pancakes, as fritters; dried and crushed into paste or sauce or used as a crunchy garnish; even dished up raw, or even live on the plate.

Right: Large prawns are prepared to make the most of their delicious flavour.

Right: Blue crabs live, and are eaten, in abundance around the coasts of South Korea.

Crab

Blue crab is found in the southern part of Korea, in abundance in the muddy tidal estuaries and in the calmer waters between the islands. Crabs are usually cooked live. The cook will plunge them into freezing cold water to stun them before simmering them in boiling stock with lots of vegetables and spices for an excellent casserole. Crab salad is another favourite: the raw crab meat is gently steamed to preserve its flavour, then mixed with crunchy sliced Asian pear and other salad vegetables in a sweet and sour dressing.

Squid

Around the island of Ullung-do, off the east coast of Korea, squid are plentiful. They can be seen drying in the sun all day, draped over washing lines and on roofs. Every bit is eaten, either fresh and cooked or dried as a snack. A local recipe for stuffed squid, fills the seasoned body with a tofu, egg and flour mixture and, after steaming, is then served sliced.

Prawns and shrimps

These are cooked quickly, usually steamed or grilled. Large prawns (shrimp) or tiger prawns are seasoned and marinated before being threaded on to skewers for grilling. They are usually served with a dipping sauce or just lemon juice to bring out the flavour.

Octopus

The Koreans eat octopus both cooked and raw, although the raw version may seem unnecessarily chewy to the Western taste. Once an octopus is tenderized and gently simmered, it retains a chewy texture, but becomes a delicious delicacy that lends itself to dipping in a spicy sauce, or can then be added to a stir-fried mixture of large spring onions (scallions), ginger, *gochujang* paste and sesame oil.

Above: Octopus is a choice Korean ingredient, which becomes delightfully tender with cooking.

Abalone

The beautiful abalone shell with its iridescent inner layer lives on the rocks beneath the warm waters around Cheju island off the south coast of Korea. The cleaned shells are a favourite tourist souvenir, and the flesh is eaten chopped up in stews and soups, often mixed with rice in a thick soup garnished with sesame seeds. Canned abalone is available as an acceptable alternative to the fresh variety, which can be difficult to find. It is a source of selenium, magnesium and vitamins B and E.

Above: Oysters are served cooked in pancakes, soups and stews and are said to have health-giving properties.

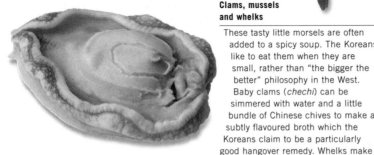

Above: Abalone is a highly prized ingredient in Korea for its unique flavour and health-giving properties.

Clams, mussels and whelks

These tasty little morsels are often added to a spicy soup. The Koreans like to eat them when they are small, rather than "the bigger the better" philosophy in the West. Baby clams (*chechi*) can be simmered with water and a little bundle of Chinese chives to make a subtly flavoured broth which the Koreans claim to be a particularly good hangover remedy. Whelks make popular street snacks, dipped into soy sauce with the usual accompaniments of chilli powder, sesame oil and garlic.

Oysters

In the cold winter months, you can find oysters of the best quality around the Korean coast. They are believed to give strength and good health. One favourite recipe is oyster pancakes, *gool pajeon*, which are little fritters of egg, rice flour, chilli and oysters, gently fried on both sides until tender.

Anchovies

These little fish are eaten fresh (both raw and cooked) or preserved. They can be simply dried and then reconstituted when needed, or they

Above: Anchovies are a staple of Korean cooking and can be served dried, cooked or raw.

Above: Tasty baby clams are cooked in broth and served as a restorative to those nursing a hangover from too much soju. The small size of these clams in no way diminishes their flavour.

Left: Pollack is undervalued in the Western kitchen, but with its flaky white flesh it is a cheap and environmentally friendly alternative to cod.

Hae san mool jungol

Korean cooks are more than happy to mix fish and meat. Major celebrations such as weddings and birthdays may include the famous buffet-style dish, *hae san mool jungol*, a stunning assortment of seafood, vegetables and steak, all carefully arranged in a large pan and then gently cooked together in beef broth. The flavours of the meat and fish will be blended beautifully in the savoury broth with a good few spoonfuls of spicy seasoning paste in the centre.

Right: Delicate skate wings are unique for their soft bones and delicious iridescent flesh. In the Korean kitchen the subtle flavours may be enjoyed by poaching the fish and serving in a salad.

can be made into anchovy paste to be added in small quantities whenever a strong fishy taste is required.

Anchovies are very popular, especially around the southern coast of Korea where an Anchovy Festival is held every year in the late spring, with street processions, feasting and fireworks.

Cod

During the winter months, shoals of cod migrate south past the Korean peninsula in search of warmer currents. On the way they are fished, cooked fresh, or dried and salted for cooking later in the year. The cod is a prized and expensive fish, so small amounts are generally made to stretch a long way in a vegetable stew, or seasoned well so that the flavour carries through a large bowl of rice. Pieces of cod can also be preserved with vegetables in a form of *kimchi* known as *seuck bak ji*, a preparation method where both the cod and the cabbage are soaked separately overnight in brine before adding spices and sealing them into jars. Pollack is used as a good alternative to cod.

Other salt-water fish

As with their meat dishes, the Koreans use everything edible in the sea, and enjoy flounder, mackerel, sea bass, red snapper, monkfish, herring, bream, skate, pollack and many more. These fish are a great source of low-fat protein, particularly for those near the coast who can buy them fresh from the local market. A piece of fish per person can be simply marinated and grilled (broiled) at the table, or a smaller amount can be divided among many diners by adding vegetables and tofu in a stew or fish soup.

Above: Dried pollack is a classic Korean ingredient. It is eaten as a snack, but is most commonly found in soups and broths.

Below: Large, freshly caught fish, such as bream, are a healthy and nutritious addition to the diet; simply marinated and grilled, or added to a fish soup.

FRUIT, SWEETS AND DRINKS

Sweet recipes are generally associated with special celebrations such as weddings and birthdays, or are eaten between meals as snacks. This is because the Korean diet is based on savoury dishes, and once you have filled up with spicy, savoury delicacies with a bowl of rice, there is little need for a sweet course afterwards.

Above: Astringent persimmons, fresh or dried, are a mainstay of Korean cooking.

FRUIT

Orchards abound in the lush green plains and river valleys of central Korea, although the farmers are now finding it difficult to combat the low price of fruit flooding the country from China, just across the border. Apples are still the most common crop grown in Korea,

followed by mandarin oranges, persimmons (often used in savoury recipes for their astringent quality), peaches, grapes and the grainy Asian pears, which are used as a garnish in a variety of savoury dishes.

SWEETMEATS AND CAKES

The festival of *Chuseok*, in the middle of the autumn season, is the best time to find *songpyeon*, sweet rice cakes filled with honey or maple syrup or a sweetened red bean, nut and seed mixture. These are part of the offerings made in thanks for a good harvest, and to pray for a good year to follow.

One dish sometimes eaten as a dessert after a meal is *tteok*, which is a cake-like confection based on rice sweetened with honey and a variety of fillings, such as sesame seeds, sweet pumpkin, dates and pine nuts. The ambivalent attitude of the Koreans to sweet things means that these little cakes are sometimes turned into savouries with beef and vegetables, and served as a light meal at lunchtime.

Other little cakes may be served at any time of day with a cup of barley tea, and are typically made with great care. These delicate confections of

Above: Universally popular, mandarin oranges are one of Korea's most prolific crops and are exported worldwide.

quickly cooked light dough are often coloured with natural ingredients, such as pumpkin (orange) and seaweed (green), and then twisted into attractive shapes.

Above: The Asian pear is grainy in texture and refreshing and light in flavour.

Above: A busy market street in Gonju, South Korea, with fruit and vegetable stalls selling onions, tomatoes, melons, apples and oranges.

DRINKS

Koreans enjoy both alcoholic and non-alcoholic drinks. They are as inventive with both as with their food, using local ingredients and combining them in delicious recipes to get just the right balance of sweet and sour, tart and smooth.

Tea

The best-known non-alcoholic drink is roasted barley tea, *boricha*. Most Korean households will serve this pale

Above: Barley tea is drunk hot or cold and most often consumed between meals to aid digestion.

Left: Two friends share a pot of green tea and a plate of traditional rice cakes in a tea house in Korea.

brew, either at intervals through the day or in little china cups as an aid to digestion after dinner. It is simply made by dry-roasting barley in a large pan until the grains turn brown. The barley is then cooled, added to a pan of boiling water and simmered until ready, which is when the water has taken on the colour of the roasted barley. The tea can be served at any temperature, depending on the occasion, but it is usually drunk hot in winter and cold in summer.

Koreans do also drink all kinds of other flavoured teas. These can be based on rice, corn, ginger, ginseng, fruit or herbs, and tend to be served hot or cold depending on the season, as with *boricha*. Fiery ginger tea is for the winter months, and cooling ginseng or fruit tea goes down better on hot summer days.

Punch

There are many recipes for non-alcoholic mixed fruit punch, but the best-loved mixture is persimmon punch, *sujeonggwa*. The beautiful orange persimmon is quite widely grown in Korea. It is dried and left to soften after harvesting and then steeped in cold water with a large amount of ginger root, cinnamon and sugar. The colour is beautiful – a deep reddish-pink. It is a refreshing cold drink for summer heat and complements a spicy meal.

Soju

The best-known alcoholic drink made in Korea is *soju*. This colourless drink is rather like vodka, and was originally made from rice or other grains, but it is now often made from sweet potatoes. It is a strong liquor, and a favourite with Koreans.

Wines

Following hard on the heels of *soju* in terms of popularity comes Korean wine, produced either as a blend of Korean grapes with wines from abroad or based on local fruit supplies. These traditional fruit-flavoured wines are made from locally

Above: Tea is served in a variety of flavours and at different temperatures to reflect the seasons.

available produce, fruits including plum, quince, pomegranate and cherry, and even herbal wines made of ginseng, which are believed to have excellent health benefits. Wines are also produced from flowers such as wild roses, peach blossom, acacia, chrysanthemums and honeysuckle.

Rice wine

Koreans have their own version of rice wine (also called *sake*), because rice is such a staple food. Both refined (*yakju*) and unrefined (*takju*) rice liquor are made. The unrefined is most popular with agricultural and rural workers, who love its thick texture, its milky appearance and its intense alcoholic strength.

Right: Rice wine (sake) is a very popular drink.

KIMCHI

No Korean meal is complete without the national dish of kimchi,
in which vegetables are seasoned, sealed in an airtight container and left to
ferment, creating a notable flavour with the fiery kick of red chilli. Hints
of garlic permeate the vegetables, which have a softened texture and yet
retain their crunch to the bite. Korea boasts more than a hundred
types of kimchi, *which are all rich in vitamins and minerals.*
A ubiquitous favourite when cold, kimchi *is also regularly blended*
into cooked dishes in order to capitalize on its unique flavour.

CLASSIC CABBAGE KIMCHI

Made with Chinese leaves, this is the classic variety of kimchi and the one most likely to be found at any meal. The spiciness of the chilli contrasts with the fish sauce and a hint of tangy spring onion. This dish takes a minimum of two days to prepare.

SERVES TEN

INGREDIENTS
1 head Chinese leaves (Chinese cabbage), about 2kg/4¹/₂lb
salt
For the marinade
50g/2oz/¹/₄ cup coarse sea salt
75ml/5 tbsp water
30ml/2 tbsp table salt
For the seasoning
2 oysters (optional)
¹/₂ Chinese white radish, about 500g/1¹/₄lb, peeled and thinly sliced
25g/1oz Korean chives
25g/1oz *minari*, watercress or rocket (arugula)
5 garlic cloves
15g/¹/₂oz fresh root ginger, peeled
¹/₂ onion
¹/₂ Asian pear, or ¹/₂ kiwi fruit
1 chestnut, sliced
3 spring onions (scallions), sliced
50g/2oz/¹/₄ cup Korean chilli powder
120ml/4fl oz/¹/₂ cup Thai fish sauce
5ml/1 tsp sugar
1 red chilli, sliced

1 Make a deep cut across the base of the head of Chinese leaves and split it in two. Repeat this with the two halves, splitting them into quarters. Then place the quartered head in a bowl and cover it with water, adding 30ml/2 tbsp salt. Leave the quarters to soak for around 2 hours.

2 Drain the cabbage and sprinkle with the sea salt for the marinade, making sure to coat between the leaves. Leave to stand for 4 hours.

3 Hold an oyster with the rounded shell up. Push the tip of a short-bladed knife into the hinge and twist to prise the shell open.

4 Cut the muscles of the oyster inside. Run the blade between the shells to open them. Cut the oyster away from the flat shell. Repeat with the other oyster. Season with a pinch of salt.

5 Cut the radish slices into fine strips. Cut the chives and *minari*, watercress or rocket into 5cm/2in lengths. Finely chop the garlic, ginger, onion and Asian pear or kiwi fruit. Combine the seasoning ingredients with 120ml/4fl oz/¹/₂ cup water.

6 Rinse the softened quarters of Chinese leaves in cold running water. Place in a large bowl and coat with the seasoning mixture, ensuring that the mixture gets between the leaves and that no leaf is left uncovered.

7 The outermost leaf of each quarter of cabbage will have softened. This can be wrapped tightly around the other leaves to help the seasoning permeate throughout the whole.

8 Place the Chinese leaves in an airtight container. Leave to stand at room temperature for 5 hours, then leave in the refrigerator for 24 hours.

COOK'S TIP
Kimchi can be stored for up to 5 months in the refrigerator. The flavour may, by then, be too pungent for the vegetable pickle to be eaten raw, but at this stage it can be used to flavour cooked dishes. If the *kimchi* is to be stored for a long period, use a covered container and wash it well with sterilizing fluid.

Per portion Energy 73kcal/303kJ; Protein 3.6g; Carbohydrate 13.5g, of which sugars 12.9g; Fat 0.6g, of which saturates 0.1g; Cholesterol 0mg; Calcium 121mg; Fibre 5.1g; Sodium 383mg.

WHITE KIMCHI

THIS STUFFED CABBAGE VERSION MAY BE MORE TIME-CONSUMING AND AMBITIOUS TO PREPARE THAN MOST KIMCHI, BUT IT IS NEVERTHELESS A FIRM FAVOURITE. WITH AN ELEGANT APPEARANCE AND A SUBTLE REFINED FLAVOUR, THIS DISH IS REGARDED AS A LUXURIOUS ACCOMPANIMENT TO ANY MEAL.

SERVES FOUR

INGREDIENTS
  1 white cabbage (Chinese cabbage)
  100g/3³/₄oz salt
  1 sheet dried kelp
  ¹/₂ white onion, finely grated or puréed
  1 apple, thinly sliced
  1 Asian pear, thinly sliced
  1 red date, thinly sliced
  20g/³/₄oz/2 tbsp pine nuts, ground
For the stuffing
  2 red chillies, seeded and sliced
  2 green chillies, seeded and sliced
  200g/7oz Chinese white radish,
    peeled and finely sliced
  50g/2oz spring onions (scallions),
    roughly chopped
  15ml/1 tbsp grated fresh root ginger
  2 red dates, seeded and sliced
  40g/1¹/₂oz watercress or Korean
    minari, roughly chopped
  15ml/1 tbsp fermented shrimps,
    finely chopped
  scant 5ml/1 tsp sugar
  5 garlic cloves, crushed

1 Cut the cabbage in half lengthways and place on a large dish. Sprinkle the salt over the cut surface. Spray the cabbage with water, then leave for 5 hours until the leaves have softened and lost their crispness.

2 Meanwhile bring 2.5 litres/4 pints/ 10 cups water to the boil in a pan and add the kelp. Reduce the heat slightly and simmer for 10 minutes, then strain the stock into a bowl and set it aside. Stir the onion, apple, Asian pear, red date and a pinch of salt into the kelp stock.

3 For the stuffing, mix the red and green chillies, radish, spring onions, ginger, red dates and watercress in a bowl. Add the fermented shrimps, sugar and garlic. Then mix all the ingredients until they are thoroughly combined.

4 Rinse the cabbage and drain the leaves. Push the stuffing mixture in between the leaves, then place the stuffed halves into a bowl and pour over the kelp stock. Leave the cabbage to soak for a day at room temperature.

5 Remove the cabbage from the stock and slice each piece lengthways into quarters. Transfer to a bowl, cover and chill lightly. Garnish with pine nuts before serving.

Per portion Energy 107kcal/446kJ; Protein 4.3g; Carbohydrate 13.8g, of which sugars 13.1g; Fat 4g, of which saturates 0.3g; Cholesterol 0mg; Calcium 122mg; Fibre 5.2g; Sodium 384mg.

DICED WHITE RADISH KIMCHI

WHITE RADISH KIMCHI IS TRADITIONALLY EATEN AS THE AUTUMN EVENINGS START TO DRAW IN, AS IT HAS A SPICINESS THAT FORTIFIES AGAINST THE COLD. THE PUNGENT AROMAS AND TANGY FLAVOURS MAKE THIS ONE OF THE MOST POPULAR VARIETIES OF KIMCHI.

SERVES FOUR

INGREDIENTS
   1.5kg/3¹/₂lb Chinese white radish,
     peeled
   225g/8oz/2 cups coarse sea salt
For the seasoning
   5ml/1 tsp sugar
   75ml/5 tbsp Korean chilli
     powder
   1 garlic clove, crushed
   ¹/₂ onion, finely chopped
   3 spring onions (scallions), finely
     sliced
   15ml/1 tbsp sea salt
   5ml/1 tsp Thai fish sauce
   5ml/1 tsp fresh root ginger, peeled
     and finely chopped
   22.5ml/4¹/₂ tsp light muscovado
     (brown) sugar

COOK'S TIP
Adjusting the seasoning makes a big difference to this dish. For extra kick, add a finely chopped red chilli to the seasoning, but be warned, this will make the dish extremely hot. Alternatively, blend half an onion in a food processor and add it to the seasoning to achieve a a tangier taste and a subtle sweetness.

1 Cut the radish into 2cm/³/₄in cubes. Place in a bowl and coat with the sea salt. Leave for 2 hours, draining off any water that collects at the bottom of the bowl. Drain well at the end of salting.

2 Combine all the ingredients for the seasoning and mix well with the salted radish. Place the radish in an airtight container and seal. Leave at room temperature for 24 hours and chill.

Per portion Energy 73kcal/302kJ; Protein 3.1g; Carbohydrate 14g, of which sugars 13.6g; Fat 0.8g, of which saturates 0.4g; Cholesterol 0mg; Calcium 81mg; Fibre 3.7g; Sodium 1203mg.

SPRING ONION KIMCHI

ALTHOUGH THIS KIMCHI DOES NOT HAVE THE SAME SPICINESS AS OTHER VARIETIES, THE SPRING ONIONS PROVIDE A UNIQUE PUNGENCY AND FLAVOUR. THE RICE MARRIES THE SPICY FLAVOURS AND SPRING ONIONS TOGETHER, WHILE THE SUGAR GIVES AN UNDERLYING HINT OF SWEETNESS.

SERVES SIX

INGREDIENTS
- 200g/7oz Chinese white radish, peeled
- 400g/14oz spring onions (scallions), trimmed
- 200ml/7fl oz/scant 1 cup dried anchovy stock
- 50g/2oz/⅓ cup sticky or pearl rice
- 115g/4oz Korean chilli powder
- 15ml/1 tbsp fermented shrimps, finely chopped
- 2 garlic cloves, crushed
- 120ml/4fl oz/½ cup anchovy sauce
- 7.5ml/1½ tsp sugar
- 5ml/1 tsp grated fresh root ginger

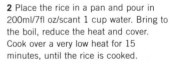

1 Cut the Chinese radish into bitesize pieces and place in a bowl with the spring onions. Pour over the anchovy stock and shuffle the vegetables down into it as far as possible. Cover and leave to soak in a cool place for 1 hour, then drain well.

2 Place the rice in a pan and pour in 200ml/7fl oz/scant 1 cup water. Bring to the boil, reduce the heat and cover. Cook over a very low heat for 15 minutes, until the rice is cooked.

3 In a large bowl, mix the chilli powder, fermented shrimps, garlic, anchovy sauce, sugar and ginger in a bowl.

4 Mix the cooked sticky rice and chilli mixture in a large bowl until well combined. Add the spring onions and turn them with the mixture by hand until thoroughly mixed. (Wear rubber gloves to protect your hands from the chilli powder.) Alternatively, use a spoon and fork to turn the spring onions carefully, taking care to avoid bruising or breaking them.

5 Take a bunch of 4–5 spring onions and use another spring onion to tie them in a bundle. Tie all the spring onions into bundles, keeping the sticky rice and seasoning coating on them. Replace the bundles in the bowl, cover and leave them to stand for a day at room temperature. Chill before serving.

Per portion Energy 77kcal/321kJ; Protein 7.4g; Carbohydrate 10.6g, of which sugars 3.8g; Fat 4.7g, of which saturates 0.3g; Cholesterol 7mg; Calcium 121mg; Fibre 1.3g; Sodium 652mg.

STUFFED CUCUMBER KIMCHI

A CLASSIC SUMMER VARIETY OF KIMCHI. THE REFRESHING NATURAL SUCCULENCE OF CUCUMBER IS PERFECT ON A HOT, HUMID DAY. THE SPICINESS OF THE CHILLI IS NEUTRALIZED BY THE MOISTNESS OF THE CUCUMBER AND THE COMBINED FLAVOURS INVIGORATE THE PALATE.

SERVES 4

INGREDIENTS
    15 small pickling cucumbers
    30ml/2 tbsp sea salt
    1 bunch Chinese chives
For the seasoning
    1 onion
    4 spring onions (scallions), thinly
      sliced
    75ml/5 tbsp Korean chilli powder
    15ml/1 tbsp Thai fish sauce
    10ml/2 tsp salt
    1 garlic clove, crushed
    7.5ml/1½ tsp grated fresh root ginger
    5ml/1 tsp sugar
    5ml/1 tsp sesame seeds

1 If the cucumbers are long, cut them in half widthways. Make two slits in a cross down the length of each cucumber or cucumber half, making sure not to cut all the way to the end. Coat thoroughly with salt and leave for 1 hour.

2 Cut the Chinese chives into 2.5cm/1in lengths, discarding the bulb.

3 Combine the onion and spring onions with the Chinese chives in a bowl. Add 45ml/3 tbsp of the chilli powder and add the Thai fish sauce, salt, garlic, ginger, sugar and sesame seeds. Mix the ingredients thoroughly by hand, using plastic gloves to prevent the chilli powder from staining your skin. Alternatively, use a spoon and fork to fold the ingredients together.

4 Lightly rinse the cucumbers to remove the salt crystals. Coat with the remaining chilli powder and press the seasoning into the slits. Put the cucumber into an airtight container and leave at room temperature for 12 hours before serving.

COOK'S TIPS
• Cucumber *kimchi* can be stored in the refrigerator, although it is best eaten within two days.
• Traditional British cucumbers are not the best choice for this recipe – large smooth-skinned gherkins or ridge cucumbers are better. They have a firmer texture, with less watery flesh and are used for all types of pickles in European recipes. They are delicious with the spicy *kimchi* seasoning and they retain a refreshingly crisp texture.

Per portion Energy 32kcal/131kJ; Protein 2.5g; Carbohydrate 3.9g, of which sugars 3.4g; Fat 2.1g, of which saturates 0.2g; Cholesterol 0mg; Calcium 88mg; Fibre 1.4g; Sodium 2067mg.

STUFFED GREEN CHILLI KIMCHI

THIS CRUNCHY, REFRESHING KIMCHI *IS A POPULAR SIDE DISH. IT IS NOT AS SPICY AS CLASSIC CABBAGE* KIMCHI *AND IT IS OFTEN SERVED AS A MILDER ACCOMPANIMENT TO GRILLED MEAT OR SEAFOOD. ITS HEAT CAN BE ADJUSTED BY THE USE OF MILD OR MORE POWERFUL CHILLIES.*

SERVES FOUR

INGREDIENTS
    30ml/2 tbsp salt, plus extra for
        seasoning
    20 mild green chillies
    45ml/3 tbsp chilli flakes
    500ml/17fl oz/generous 2 cups dried
        anchovy stock
    15ml/1 tbsp fermented shrimps,
        finely chopped
    ¹/₂ white onion, finely grated or puréed
For the stuffing
    2 onions, finely chopped
    ¹/₂ Chinese white radish, peeled and
        finely sliced
    5 red chillies, seeded and sliced
    5 garlic cloves, crushed
    15g/¹/₂oz fresh root ginger, peeled
        and grated

COOK'S TIPS
The dried chilli flakes in the stock and
the red chillies used in the stuffing
bring heat to the dish. For a milder
dish, use less pungent chillies.

1 Pour 1 litre/1³/₄ pints/4 cups water
into a bowl and then add the salt.
Slice the tops off the green chillies and
remove the seeds, while leaving the
pods whole.

2 Add the green chillies to the salt
water and leave them to soak for 30
minutes, drain thoroughly and set aside.

3 Tie the chilli flakes in a muslin
(cheesecloth) bag, place this in a bowl
and pour in 500ml/17fl oz/generous 2
cups water.

4 Set aside the bowl until the water
has taken on the colour and flavour
of the chillies, then remove the bag
and skim out any of the flakes that
have escaped.

5 Mix the anchovy stock with the chilli
water and add the fermented shrimps.
Add the grated or puréed onion.

6 Mix the onions, white radish, red
chillies, garlic and ginger for the
stuffing. Season with a pinch of salt
and blend thoroughly.

7 Stuff the mild green chillies with this
garlic and ginger mixture, packing it
in firmly but also taking care not to
break the chilli.

8 Place the stuffed chillies in the
bowl with the anchovy and chilli stock
and leave them to soak for a day at
room temperature.

9 Remove the chillies from the stock
and place them in a serving dish.
Drizzle over a little of the stock and
chill them well in the refrigerator before
serving at the table.

Per portion Energy 64kcal/268kJ; Protein 7.7g; Carbohydrate 4.5g, of which sugars 3.3g; Fat 1.8g, of which saturates 0.2g; Cholesterol 27mg; Calcium 115mg; Fibre 0.8g; Sodium 660mg.

PAK CHOI KIMCHI

THE PAK CHOI GREEN LEAVES THAT ORIGINATED IN CHINA HAVE BEEN ADOPTED ALL OVER ASIA. IN KOREA THEY ARE USED WIDELY IN MAKING KIMCHI. THIS VERSION IS EASY TO PREPARE, WITH PUMPKIN ADDING SWEETNESS AND HELPING TO MARRY THE OTHER FLAVOURS.

SERVES FOUR

INGREDIENTS
    8 small, white-stemmed pak choi
        (bok choi)
    15ml/1 tbsp sesame seeds, to garnish
For the stuffing
    250g/9oz pumpkin, peeled and
        seeded
    115g/4oz leeks, finely chopped
    1 garlic clove, crushed
    30ml/2 tbsp light soy sauce
    5ml/1 tsp grated fresh root ginger
    30ml/2 tbsp Korean chilli powder
    5ml/1 tsp sesame oil
    7.5ml/1½ tsp pine nuts, ground

1 Make sure the pak choi is fresh, crisp and bright. Reject any limp, bruised or broken pieces. Slice the pak choi in half lengthways. Rinse the pieces under running water, then drain and set aside.

2 Finely grate the pumpkin and place it in a bowl with the leeks and garlic.

3 Add the soy sauce, ginger, chilli powder, sesame oil, pine nuts and a pinch of salt. Mix thoroughly.

4 Place the pieces of pak choi in a serving bowl. Stuff the pumpkin mixture in between the leaves. Sprinkle any remaining stuffing over the top of the pak choi. Garnish with sesame seeds and serve.

COOK'S TIPS
• If pumpkin is not available, butternut squash can be used for this dish. To prepare the pumpkin or squash, discard the seeds, fibres and pith from the middle and cut off the thick peel. Then cut the flesh into chunks.
• A food processor can be used for speeding up preparation. Start by grinding the pine nuts as they are dry (a small bowl is ideal for this). Then chop the leeks, garlic and ginger together. Finally use the grating blade for the pumpkin – or cheat and chop the vegetable finely instead.

Per portion Energy 77kcal/317kJ; Protein 6.1g; Carbohydrate 4.6g, of which sugars 3.9g; Fat 5.5g, of which saturates 0.6g; Cholesterol 0mg; Calcium 284mg; Fibre 4.2g; Sodium 519mg.

SPICY KIMCHI STEW

THIS HEARTY PORK AND KIMCHI *DISH,* KIMCHI CHIGE, *IS A RICH STEW BUBBLING WITH FLAVOUR AND PIQUANCY AND IS TRADITIONALLY COOKED IN A HEAVY CLAY BOWL CALLED A* TUKBAEGE. *THE SLOW COOKING ALLOWS THE FLAVOURS TO MINGLE, CREATING COMPLEX, ENTICING TASTE COMBINATIONS.*

SERVES FOUR

INGREDIENTS
    4 dried shiitake mushrooms, soaked
        in warm water for about 30 minutes
    150g/5oz firm tofu
    200g/7oz boneless pork chop
    300g/11oz cabbage *kimchi* (see
        page 65)
    45ml/3 tbsp vegetable oil
    1 garlic clove, crushed
    15ml/1 tbsp Korean chilli powder
    750ml/1¼ pints/3 cups vegetable
        stock or water
    2 spring onions (scallions), finely
        sliced
    salt

1 When the shiitake mushrooms have reconstituted and become soft, drain and slice them, discarding the stems.

2 Dice the tofu into cubes approximately 2cm/¾in square.

3 Dice the pork into bitesize cubes with a sharp knife and then slice the *kimchi* into similar sized pieces. Squeeze out any excess liquid from the *kimchi* until it ceases to drip.

4 Pour the vegetable oil into a pan or wok and place over a medium heat. Add the pork and garlic and sauté until it is crisp and brown.

5 Once the pork has turned dark brown add the *kimchi* and chilli powder, and stir-fry for another 60 seconds, tossing the ingredients together.

6 Add the vegetable stock or water and bring to the boil. Add the tofu, mushrooms and spring onions, cover and simmer for 10–15 minutes. Season with salt and serve the mixture hot and bubbling from the pan.

VARIATIONS
• Create a lighter dish by substituting drained canned tuna for the pork.
• Alternatively, fresh tuna steak can be used and cut up in the same way as the pork chop. Use fish stock to emphasize the flavour.

COOK'S TIP
This recipe is better suited to firm tofu, rather than soft tofu, because it is less likely to break up during cooking. The majority of supermarkets sell firm tofu in long-life packs (usually as well as the fresh varieties in the chiller cabinets). The long-life packs provide a good kitchen standby.

Per portion Energy 185kcal/770kJ; Protein 15.1g; Carbohydrate 4.2g, of which sugars 4g; Fat 12.1g, of which saturates 1.9g; Cholesterol 32mg; Calcium 234mg; Fibre 1.8g; Sodium 534mg.

STIR-FRIED KIMCHI

ALTHOUGH KIMCHI IS CHARACTERISTICALLY A COLD DISH, THIS STIR-FRIED VERSION GIVES THE VEGETABLES A LIGHT QUALITY AND SUBTLE FLAVOUR. THE PUNGENCY OF THE RAW KIMCHI IS KNOCKED BACK DURING THE COOKING PROCESS, AND IS REPLACED BY A DELICIOUS NUTTY SWEETNESS.

1 Slice the cabbage *kimchi* into 2cm/³/₄in lengths and roughly chop the pork into similar sized pieces.

2 Coat a pan with the vegetable oil and stir-fry the garlic until lightly browned. Add the pork and stir-fry until it is golden. Add the *kimchi* and stir-fry.

3 Continue to stir-fry until the *kimchi* has darkened. Add the spring onion, soy sauce, sesame seeds, sesame oil and sugar, and quickly stir-fry. Ensure that all the ingredients are completely mixed.

4 Serve immediately with an accompaniment of steamed rice or a dish of noodles in broth.

VARIATIONS
• Peeled raw prawns (shrimp) can be used in place of the pork.
• Prepared squid rings (the tender body sac) are also delicious cooked in this recipe instead of the pork.
• For a vegetarian *kimchi*, leave out the meat. Firm tofu can be added to make a more substantial version.

SERVES FOUR

INGREDIENTS
    150g/5oz cabbage *kimchi* (see page 65)
    50g/2oz pork
    15ml/1 tbsp vegetable oil
    2 garlic cloves, finely chopped
    1 spring onion (scallion), sliced
    5ml/1 tsp dark soy sauce
    2.5ml/¹/₂ tsp sesame seeds
    5ml/1 tsp sesame oil
    2.5ml/¹/₂ tsp sugar
    steamed rice or noodles in broth,
      to serve

Per portion Energy 84kcal/348kJ; Protein 4.7g; Carbohydrate 2.9g, of which sugars 2.9g; Fat 6g, of which saturates 0.9g; Cholesterol 11mg; Calcium 36mg; Fibre 1.3g; Sodium 135mg.

TOFU AND STIR-FRIED KIMCHI

THE MILD FLAVOURS OF STIR-FRIED CABBAGE KIMCHI ARE A PERFECT COMPLEMENT TO THE DELICATE TASTE OF BLANCHED TOFU. THE HINT OF SWEETNESS AND UNDERLYING SPICINESS IN THE KIMCHI CONTRASTS WITH THE SMOOTH, CREAMY TEXTURE AND SOYA BEAN NUTTINESS OF THE TOFU.

SERVES THREE TO FOUR

INGREDIENTS

90g/3¹/₂oz cabbage *kimchi* (see page 65)
50g/2oz pork
15ml/1 tbsp vegetable oil
1 garlic clove, thinly sliced
5ml/1 tsp salt
5ml/1 tsp sugar
5ml/1 tsp sesame seeds
5ml/1 tsp sesame oil
1 block firm tofu

1 Slice the *kimchi* into 2cm/³/₄in lengths, and roughly chop the pork into similar sized pieces.

2 Coat a pan or wok with the vegetable oil and stir-fry the pork and garlic until crisp and golden. Season to taste with the salt.

3 Stir in the *kimchi* and quickly stir-fry the mixture over a high heat until it has become dark brown.

4 Add the sugar, sesame seeds and sesame oil to the stir-fried *kimchi*. Combine well and continue to stir-fry for a further 30 seconds. Then remove the pan from the heat and cover it with a lid while slicing the tofu.

5 Meanwhile, place the whole block of tofu into a pan of boiling water, ensuring that it is covered. Boil for 3–4 minutes, making sure that the water is not bubbling too rapidly, and then remove. Drain the tofu, and blot any excess water with kitchen paper.

6 Cut the tofu into slices about 1cm/¹/₃in thick. Arrange the warm tofu slices on a large plate or on individual dishes and place the pork and *kimchi* mixture in the middle. Serve warm.

COOK'S TIP
A pasta pan, with an integral strainer, is good for lowering delicate tofu into hot water and for draining it at the end of the cooking process.

Per portion Energy 98kcal/407kJ; Protein 7g; Carbohydrate 2.5g, of which sugars 2.3g; Fat 6.7g, of which saturates 1g; Cholesterol 8mg; Calcium 257mg; Fibre 0.6g; Sodium 504mg.

STREET SNACKS
& QUICK BITES

Snacks eaten on the street are commonplace throughout Korea and in the

big cities there are vendors to satisfy every desire of busy urban dwellers.

A popular snack both on the street and at home in the colder months

is the tasty matang, *or Sweet Potato with Almond Syrup.*

Light and crunchy Vegetable Fritters are a favourite as an appetizer.

Other tempting traditional snacks include crispy Pan-fried

Kimchi Fritters, sticky Stir-fried Rice Cake and Vegetables, and

spicy Steamed Tofu and Chive Dumplings.

VEGETABLE FRITTERS

THESE LIGHT AND CRUNCHY VEGETABLE FRITTERS ARE EQUALLY GOOD AS AN APPETIZER OR AS A QUICK SNACK ON THE GO. SIMPLE TO PREPARE AND EASY TO COOK, THEY ARE WONDERFULLY APPEALING AS THEY EMERGE GOLDEN BROWN FROM THE FRYING PAN.

SERVES FOUR

INGREDIENTS
  1 potato, thinly sliced
  1 small carrot, thinly sliced
  ½ small white onion, sliced
  ½ courgette (zucchini), thinly sliced
  1 red chilli, seeded and sliced
  salt and ground black pepper
  vegetable oil, for cooking
For the batter
  115g/4oz/1 cup plain (all-purpose)
    flour
  45ml/3 tbsp cornflour (cornstarch)
  1 egg, beaten
  5ml/1 tsp salt
For the dip
  30ml/2 tbsp dark soy sauce
  15ml/1 tbsp fish stock
  15ml/1 tbsp Chinese white radish,
    grated
  5ml/1 tsp vinegar
  5ml/1 tsp sesame seeds

1 To make the batter, sift the flour and cornflour into a bowl. Make a well in the middle and add the beaten egg with 250ml/8fl oz/1 cup water.

2 Blend the egg, water and salt with a wire whisk until smooth. Then gradually work in the flour mixture until it combines in a smooth batter. The batter should be thick enough to hold the vegetables together but it should still pour slowly from a ladle.

3 Place the potato, carrot, onion, courgette and chilli in a bowl. Mix them together well, then pour in the batter and mix it into the vegetables, adding a small amount of seasoning.

4 For the dip, mix the soy sauce, stock, white radish, vinegar and sesame seeds. Then set this aside to allow the flavours to mingle.

5 Heat a little vegetable oil in a frying pan or wok over a medium heat. Ladle three or four small portions of the fritter mixture into the pan (depending on the size of pan) and cook until they are set and golden brown underneath. Turn and cook the fritters on the second side until they are golden.

6 Drain the fritters on kitchen paper and keep hot in a warm oven or grill (broiler) compartment. Cook the remaining mixture in the same way.

7 Divide the dipping sauce among four small individual dishes. Serve the hot fritters on platters with the dishes of dipping sauce.

Per portion Energy 317kcal/1330kJ; Protein 6.7g; Carbohydrate 45.5g, of which sugars 5.3g; Fat 13.3g, of which saturates 1.9g; Cholesterol 48mg; Calcium 77mg; Fibre 2.7g; Sodium 1063mg.

PAN-FRIED KIMCHI FRITTERS

A CLASSIC APPETIZER AND POPULAR SNACK, THESE FRITTERS HAVE A CRISP GOLDEN COATING. THE CONTRAST OF THE CRUNCHY EXTERIOR AND SMOOTH FILLING MAKES FOR A DELICIOUS JUXTAPOSITION OF TEXTURES AND THE DISH IS SERVED WITH A ZESTY SOY DIP TO HELP BRING OUT THE FLAVOURS.

SERVES TWO

INGREDIENTS
90g/3½oz cabbage *kimchi* (see page 65), finely chopped
1 potato
a little milk (optional)
50g/2oz firm tofu, squeezed to remove excess water
25g/1oz/¼ cup plain (all-purpose) flour
1 egg, beaten
5ml/1 tsp crushed garlic
15ml/1 tbsp vegetable oil
salt and ground black pepper
For the dip
45ml/3 tbsp light soy sauce
2.5ml/½ tsp sesame oil
5ml/1 tsp lemon juice

1 Gently squeeze the *kimchi* to remove any excess liquid. Boil the potato and mash it, adding a little milk if required.

2 Crumble the tofu into a bowl. Add the *kimchi*, potato, flour, egg, garlic and seasoning. Mix well and form spoonfuls of mixture into small round patties.

3 Coat a frying pan or wok with the oil and place over a medium heat. Add the patties and fry until golden brown on both sides. Drain on kitchen paper.

4 For the dip, mix the soy sauce, sesame oil and lemon juice, and then serve with the fritters.

Per portion Energy 206kcal/863kJ; Protein 8.4g; Carbohydrate 20.9g, of which sugars 3.8g; Fat 10.5g, of which saturates 1.8g; Cholesterol 105mg; Calcium 188mg; Fibre 1.9g; Sodium 583mg.

STEAMED TOFU AND CHIVE DUMPLINGS

The slight spiciness and delicate texture of Korean chives make them a wonderful ingredient to add to these stuffed, paper-thin steamed dumplings, called MANDU. *Here the succulent filling is made with tofu, combined with beef and rice wine.*

SERVES FOUR

INGREDIENTS
    30 dumpling skins
    1 egg, beaten
    spinach leaves to line steamer
For the filling
    3 spring onions (scallions),
        finely chopped
    3 garlic cloves, crushed
    5ml/1 tsp finely grated fresh
        root ginger
    5ml/1 tsp mirin or rice wine
    90g/3½oz/scant ½ cup minced
        (ground) beef
    90g/3½oz firm tofu
    90g/3½oz Korean chives, finely
        chopped
    ½ onion, finely chopped
    30ml/2 tbsp soy sauce
    30ml/2 tbsp sesame oil
    15ml/1 tbsp sugar
    15ml/1 tbsp salt
    10ml/2 tsp ground black pepper
For the dipping sauce
    60ml/4 tbsp dark soy sauce
    30ml/2 tbsp rice vinegar
    5ml/1 tsp Korean chilli powder

1 To make the dipping sauce, mix the soy sauce, rice vinegar and chilli powder in a small serving bowl.

2 For the filling, combine the chopped spring onions, garlic, grated ginger, mirin or rice wine and minced beef into a bowl. Leave to marinate for 15 minutes.

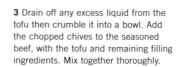

3 Drain off any excess liquid from the tofu then crumble it into a bowl. Add the chopped chives to the seasoned beef, with the tofu and remaining filling ingredients. Mix together thoroughly.

4 Take a dumpling skin and brush with a little beaten egg. Place a spoonful of the stuffing in the middle.

5 Fold into a half-moon shape, crimping the edges firmly to seal. Repeat with the other dumpling skins.

6 Cook over a pan of boiling water in a steamer lined with spinach leaves for 6 minutes. Alternatively, cook them in boiling water for 3 minutes. Arrange on a serving dish and serve with soy dipping sauce.

VARIATIONS
Almost any ingredient can be adapted for *mandu* fillings: beansprouts, minced pork, chopped prawns (shrimp), courgettes (zucchini) and cabbage *kimchi* (see page 65) are favourites.

COOK'S TIPS
• Asian stores often stock dumpling skins and these are quick to use, but they are not difficult to make if you have time. For 8 dumpling skins, sift 115g/4oz/1 cup plain (all-purpose) flour and 30ml/2 tbsp cornflour (cornstarch) together in a bowl and add 2.5ml/½ tsp salt. Pour in 50ml/2fl oz/¼ cup warm water and knead well until a smooth, elastic dough has formed. Cover the bowl with a damp dish towel and leave for 10 minutes. Place on a lightly floured surface and roll out the dough until paper-thin. Use a floured pastry (cookie) cutter or a sharp knife to cut the dough into circles roughly 7.5cm/3in in diameter.
• Dumplings can be cooked in a variety of ways. Steaming is the most popular, but grilling (broiling) and shallow-frying until golden brown also produce delicious results.

Per portion Energy 235kcal/982kJ; Protein 9.9g; Carbohydrate 26.1g, of which sugars 6.5g; Fat 10.8g, of which saturates 2.5g; Cholesterol 14mg; Calcium 208mg; Fibre 2.2g; Sodium 1054mg.

MUNG BEAN SOUFFLÉ PANCAKES

THESE MUNG BEAN PANCAKES, CALLED BINDAETUK, *ARE DELICIOUSLY LIGHT. FILLED WITH A COMBINATION OF MEAT AND VEGETABLES, THE FLAVOURS OF RICE WINE AND GARLIC IN THE MARINADE ARE COMPLEMENTED BY THE SHARPNESS OF THE SOY AND VINEGAR IN THE DIPPING SAUCE.*

SERVES TWO TO THREE

INGREDIENTS
  375g/13oz/2 cups mung beans,
    soaked overnight in cold water
  15ml/1 tbsp pine nuts
  30ml/2 tbsp sweet rice flour
  75g/3oz beef flank, sliced
  200g/7oz prawns (shrimp), peeled
    and finely chopped
  15ml/1 tbsp vegetable oil, plus extra
    for shallow-frying
  1 button (white) mushroom, thinly
    sliced
  ½ onion, thinly sliced
  ½ cucumber, seeded and sliced
  ½ cup cabbage *kimchi* (see page
    65), thinly sliced
  3 spring onions (scallions), thinly
    sliced
  1 red chilli, shredded
  salt and ground black pepper
For the marinade
  5ml/1 tsp mirin or rice wine
  2.5ml/½ tsp grated fresh root ginger
  5ml/1 tsp dark soy sauce
  1 garlic clove, crushed
  2.5ml/½ tsp sesame seeds
  5ml/1 tsp sesame oil
  ground black pepper
For the dipping sauce
  60ml/4 tbsp dark soy sauce
  10ml/2 tsp rice vinegar
  1 spring onion (scallion), finely
    chopped

1 Drain the mung beans and return them to the bowl (without any water). Roll the beans between the palms of your hands to remove the skins. Add plenty of water and the skins will float. Skim off and discard these skins. Rinse the beans thoroughly.

2 Place the peeled beans in a food processor or blender with the pine nuts and pour in 120ml/4fl oz/½ cup water. Blend well until the mixture becomes a thick, coarse milky paste.

3 Transfer the bean paste to a large bowl and then add the rice flour and 5ml/1 tsp salt. Gradually mix the flour and salt into the bean paste until it is thoroughly incorporated.

4 Put the beef into a large bowl. Pour over the mirin or rice wine. Add the ginger, soy sauce, garlic, sesame seeds and oil for the marinade, with black pepper to taste. Mix well to coat all the pieces of beef. Cover, refrigerate and leave to marinate for about 20 minutes, to allow the beef to absorb and develop all the flavours.

5 Season the prawns with salt and pepper and set aside. Combine all the dipping sauce ingredients in a small serving bowl and set aside.

6 Coat a frying pan with vegetable oil and heat over a medium heat. Add the beef, mushroom and onion, and stir-fry until the meat has browned. Next, add the cucumber, cabbage *kimchi* and spring onions. Toss the ingredients in the pan and remove from the heat.

7 Heat a little oil in a frying pan and add a spoonful of the bean paste, spreading it into a small pancake. Spoon a little of the beef mixture on to the middle of the pancake, with some shredded chilli and a spoonful of chopped prawns. Use a spatula to press the ingredients flat on to the pancake, and fry until golden underneath. Turn and cook until golden on the second side.

8 Make pancakes until the batter and topping mixtures are finished. Arrange the fritters on a large serving platter and serve with the soy dipping sauce.

Per portion Energy 492kcal/2070kJ; Protein 38.2g; Carbohydrate 55.4g, of which sugars 6.9g; Fat 14.2g, of which saturates 2.2g; Cholesterol 108mg; Calcium 175mg; Fibre 11.7g; Sodium 1867mg.

SEAFOOD AND SPRING ONION PANCAKE

THIS PANCAKE MAKES A GREAT APPETIZER. TENDER SQUID AND SCALLOPS ARE ACCOMPANIED BY THE CRUNCH AND PIQUANCY OF SPRING ONIONS. VEGETABLES AND SEAFOOD STUD THE CRISP SURFACE OF THE PANCAKE, WHILE THE CENTRE IS AMAZINGLY LIGHT AND MOIST.

SERVES FOUR

INGREDIENTS
90g/3½oz squid
2 oysters
5 clams
5 small prawns (shrimp), shelled
3 scallops, removed from
    the shell
15ml/1 tbsp vegetable oil
5 spring onions (scallions), sliced
    into thin strips
½ red chilli, seeded and cut into thin
    strips
½ green chilli, seeded and cut into
    thin strips
50g/2oz enoki mushrooms, caps
    removed
1 garlic clove, thinly sliced
salt and ground black pepper
For the batter
    115g/4oz/1 cup plain
        (all-purpose) flour
    40g/1½oz/⅓ cup cornflour
        (cornstarch)
    5ml/1 tsp salt
    5ml/1 tsp sugar
    2 eggs, beaten
For the dipping sauce
    90ml/6 tbsp light soy sauce
    22.5ml/4½ tsp rice vinegar
    1 spring onion (scallion), finely
        shredded
    1 red chilli, finely shredded
    1 garlic clove, crushed
    5ml/1 tsp sesame oil
    5ml/1 tsp sesame seeds

1 To make the batter, sift the flour and cornflour into a large bowl. Add the salt and sugar. Make a well in the middle. Add the eggs and 200ml/7fl oz/scant 1 cup iced water and whisk lightly, mixing in the flour mixture until smooth.

2 Wash the squid carefully, rinsing off any ink that remains on the body. Holding the body of the squid firmly, pull away the head and tentacles. If the ink sac is still intact, remove it and discard. Pull out all the innards including the long transparent pen. Peel off and discard the thin purple skin on the body, but keep the two small side fins. Slice the head across just under the eyes, severing the tentacles. Discard the rest of the head. Squeeze the tentacles at the head end to push out the round beak in the centre and discard. Rinse the pouch and tentacles well. (Your fishmonger will prepare squid for you, if you prefer.)

3 Chop the cleaned squid into small pieces and place in a bowl.

4 Open the oysters, Cover your hand with a thick folded cloth and take care when using an oyster knife. Hold the flat shell on top. Push the tip of an oyster knife or heavy, short-bladed knife into the hinge of the oyster and twist to prise the shell open. Cut the two muscles inside. Run the blade between the shells to open them. Discard the top shell. Cut the oyster away from the flat shell. Repeat with the remaining oyster. Add to the squid in the bowl.

5 Open the clam shells and tip each clam into the bowl. Add the prawns and scallops to the bowl. Season the mixture with salt and pepper, and leave to stand for 10 minutes.

6 Make the dipping sauce by combining all the ingredients in a small bowl.

7 Coat a large frying pan with vegetable oil and place over a medium heat. Pour one third of the batter into the pan, ensuring that it is a roughly consistent thickness across the base.

8 Place the spring onions, chillies, mushrooms and garlic on to the pancake and then add the seafood, distributing the ingredients evenly. Pour over the remaining batter and tilt the pan to form an even layer. Cook until the pancake is set and browned underneath, then turn it over and cook briefly to brown the top so that the pancake is golden brown on both sides.

9 Slice the pancake into bitesize pieces and serve it on a plate with the dipping sauce.

Per portion Energy 255kcal/1077kJ; Protein 16.5g; Carbohydrate 33.7g, of which sugars 1.9g; Fat 7.1g, of which saturates 1.4g; Cholesterol 232mg; Calcium 80mg; Fibre 1.4g; Sodium 613mg.

RICE ROLLS WITH BEEF AND SESAME

SIMILAR TO A MAKI ROLL, THIS KOREAN ALTERNATIVE AVOIDS THE USE OF VINEGAR WHEN COOKING THE RICE, RESULTING IN A DISH THAT IS LESS SOUR THAN ITS JAPANESE COUNTERPART. THE FRESH, CRUNCHY VEGETABLES ARE COMPLEMENTED BY THE SUBTLE FLAVOUR OF THE FISHCAKE.

SERVES FOUR

INGREDIENTS
50g/2oz beef, finely chopped
150g/5oz/¾ cup short grain rice, cooked (400g/14oz/4 cups when cooked)
1 Asian fishcake or Japanese *surimi*, thinly sliced
2 eggs, beaten
75g/3oz carrot, cut into strips
25g/1oz spinach
a little soy sauce
a little sesame oil
pinch of sugar
4 sheets dried seaweed paper or Japanese *nori*
75g/3oz pickled Chinese white radish, thinly sliced
15ml/1 tbsp sesame seeds
salt and ground black pepper
vegetable oil, for cooking
For the marinade
5ml/1 tsp soy sauce
2.5ml/½ tsp sugar
2.5ml/½ tsp sesame oil
1 garlic clove, crushed
Seasoning for the rice
2.5ml/½ tsp sugar
2.5ml/½ tsp rice vinegar
1.25ml/¼ tsp soy sauce
1.25ml/¼ tsp sesame oil
1.25ml/¼ tsp sesame seeds
Seasoning for the fishcake
2.5ml/½ tsp soy sauce
2.5ml/½ tsp sugar
30ml/2 tbsp sesame oil
15ml/1 tbsp sesame seeds

1 Place the beef in a bowl. Add the marinade ingredients and salt and pepper. Mix and leave for 10 minutes.

2 Mixing the sugar, rice vinegar, soy sauce, sesame oil and sesame seeds. Add the rice and mix well.

3 Mix the soy sauce, sugar, sesame oil and seeds, and black pepper. Cut the fish cake into thin slices and turn them in the seasoning until evenly coated.

4 Place a frying pan over a medium heat and add a little vegetable oil. Pour in the beaten eggs, tilting the pan to make a thin omelette. Slide the omelette out on to a plate and cut into 5mm/¼in slices.

5 Stir-fry the carrots in the pan, adding oil if necessary, and a pinch of salt. When slightly softened, remove and set aside.

6 Add the fishcake and stir-fry gently for 1 minute, trying not to break up the slices. Remove them and set aside. Add the beef and its marinade to the pan and stir-fry for 2–3 minutes. Remove the beef from the pan and set it aside.

7 Bring about 250ml/8fl oz/1 cup water to the boil in a pan. Add the spinach and bring back to the boil. Drain and rinse the spinach under cold water, then drain again. Place the spinach in a bowl and add a splash of soy sauce, a little sesame oil and a pinch of sugar.

8 Place a sheet of seaweed on a bamboo sushi mat. Spread an even layer of rice over about half the seaweed, keeping the rice about 5mm/¼in deep.

9 Across the centre of the rice, arrange a few strips of pickled radish (reserve about half for serving) and a quarter each of the carrot, spinach, omelette, fishcake and beef. Drizzle with a little sesame oil and sprinkle with a quarter of the sesame seeds. Dampen the uncovered edge of the seaweed.

10 Using the bamboo mat as a guide, slowly roll up the ingredients from the rice end, rolling the mat over and tucking in the end of the seaweed and rice to start a neat roll. Continue rolling with medium pressure – the wet seaweed should seal the end of the roll. Repeat with the remaining ingredients.

11 Use a sharp knife to slice the seaweed rolls into 2cm/¾in pieces. Wipe the knife clean after each cut and rinse it under cold water to prevent the mixture from sticking to it.

12 Arrange the slices on a platter and serve with the reserved pickled radish.

Per portion Energy 268kcal/1115kJ; Protein 12.3g; Carbohydrate 33g, of which sugars 2.9g; Fat 9.5g, of which saturates 2g; Cholesterol 127mg; Calcium 79mg; Fibre 1.1g; Sodium 1060mg.

STIR-FRIED RICE CAKE AND VEGETABLES

HEARTY KOREAN RICE CAKE IS A VERSATILE INGREDIENT USED IN MANY DIFFERENT RECIPES. HERE THE STICKY TEXTURE OF THE RICE CAKE IS COMPLEMENTED BY THE CRUNCH OF VEGETABLES AND A RICH TASTE OF BEEF. THE REFINED FLAVOURS REFLECT THE SNACK'S ORIGINS AS A ROYAL COURT SNACK.

SERVES FOUR

INGREDIENTS
1 long Korean rice cake
5ml/1 tsp sesame oil
2 dried shiitake mushrooms, soaked
    in warm water for about 30 minutes
    until softened
50g/2oz carrot
¼ cucumber
50g/2oz beef, thinly sliced
30ml/2 tbsp vegetable oil
¼ onion, finely sliced
For the seasoning
60ml/4 tbsp dark soy sauce
15ml/1 tbsp sugar
2.5ml/½ tsp ground white pepper
5ml/1 tsp sesame seeds
15ml/1 tbsp sesame oil
2 spring onions (scallions), finely
    chopped
30ml/2 tbsp mirin or rice wine
2 garlic cloves, crushed

1 Slice the rice cake into 4cm/1½in lengths and blanch these in salted boiling water for 2 seconds. Drain and rinse in cold water, then drain well again and transfer to a bowl. Coat the pieces of rice cake with the sesame oil and set aside.

2 When the soaked shiitake mushrooms have reconstituted and become soft, drain and thinly slice them, discarding the tough stem.

3 Cut the carrot into thin strips. Seed the cucumber and cut into thin strips.

4 Combine the soy sauce, sugar, pepper, sesame seeds and oil for the seasoning in a bowl. Add the beef and then turn the slices to coat them well with the seasoning. Cover and set aside for 15 minutes so that the beef absorbs the flavours.

5 Combine the spring onions with the mirin or rice wine and crushed garlic in a small bowl.

6 Coat a frying pan or wok with the vegetable oil and place over a medium heat. When the pan is hot, add the onion and seasoned beef. Stir-fry until the beef is browned and the onion lightly cooked. Then add the mushrooms, rice cake, carrot and cucumber to the pan.

7 Continue stir-frying until the vegetables have softened slightly. Then pour in the spring onion mixture. Reduce the heat and cook, stirring frequently, until the liquid has formed a sticky glaze to coat the ingredients. Transfer the mixture to a shallow serving dish and serve immediately.

VARIATION
A classic and considerably spicier version of this dish can be achieved by adding *gochujang* chilli paste to the seasoning instead of soy sauce. This version of the rice cakes traditionally omits the mushrooms.

Per portion Energy 369kcal/1538kJ; Protein 10.2g; Carbohydrate 35.3g, of which sugars 14.4g; Fat 21.9g, of which saturates 3.6g; Cholesterol 15mg; Calcium 50mg; Fibre 1.5g; Sodium 1806mg.

RICE SEAWEED ROLL WITH SPICY SQUID

This Korean favourite, CHUGMU KIMBAP, *is influenced by Japanese* MAKI, *although the seaweed rolls are served separately. The fluffy texture and mild taste of the rice roll are nicely set off by the crunch of the radish and the kick of the chilli and garlic.*

SERVES TWO

INGREDIENTS
    400g/14oz/4 cups cooked rice
    rice vinegar, for drizzling
    sesame oil, for drizzling
    150g/5oz squid
    90g/3½oz Chinese white radish,
        peeled and diced
    3 large sheets dried seaweed
        or nori
For the squid seasoning
    22.5ml/4½ tsp Korean chilli powder
    7.5ml/1½ tsp sugar
    1 garlic clove, crushed
    5ml/1 tsp sesame oil
    2.5ml/½ tsp sesame seeds
For the radish seasoning
    15ml/1 tbsp sugar
    30ml/2 tbsp rice vinegar
    22.5ml/4½ tsp Korean
        chilli powder
    15ml/1 tbsp Thai fish sauce
    1 garlic clove, crushed
    1 spring onion (scallion), finely
        chopped

1 Put the cooked rice in a bowl and drizzle over some rice vinegar and sesame oil. Mix well, then set aside.

2 Wash the squid carefully, rinsing off any ink that remains. Holding the body firmly, pull away the head and tentacles. If the ink sac is still intact, remove it and discard. Pull out all the innards including the long transparent pen or quill. Peel off and discard the thin purple skin on the body, but keep the two small side fins. Slice the head across just under the eyes, severing the tentacles. Discard the rest of the head.

3 Squeeze the tentacles at the head end to push out the round beak in the centre and discard. Rinse the pouch and tentacles. (The fishmonger will prepare squid if you prefer.) Use a sharp knife to score the squid with a crisscross pattern. Cut into pieces about 5cm/2in long and 1cm/⅓in wide.

4 Bring a pan of water to the boil over a high heat. Blanch the squid for 3 minutes, stirring constantly, then drain under cold running water.

5 Combine all the squid seasoning ingredients in a bowl, and then coat the squid. Set aside to absorb the flavours.

6 Put the radish in a bowl, then drizzle over some rice vinegar. Leave for 15 minutes. Drain the radish and transfer to a bowl. Add the radish seasoning ingredients, mix well and chill.

7 Place a third of the rice on to one of the sheets of seaweed, roll into a long cylinder and wrap it tightly. Then slice the cylinder into bitesize pieces. Repeat with the remaining seaweed sheets.

8 Arrange the finished rolls on a serving plate and serve with the seasoned squid and the radish.

COOK'S TIP
When cutting rice rolls, use a sharp damp knife and clean it with a damp cloth after each cut.

Per portion Energy 195kcal/830kJ; Protein 8.8g; Carbohydrate 36.2g, of which sugars 4.8g; Fat 2.8g, of which saturates 0.6g; Cholesterol 84mg; Calcium 32mg; Fibre 0.4g; Sodium 312mg.

FISHCAKE KEBABS IN SEAWEED SOUP

FISHCAKES ARE WIDELY EATEN AS STREET SNACKS AS THEY ARE HEARTY, FLAVOURSOME AND EASY TO COOK. THIS JAPANESE-STYLE DISH IS A CLASSIC EXAMPLE, WITH THE TENDER FISHCAKE COOKED ON SKEWERS IN A RICH, SEAWEED-FLAVOURED SOUP. PERFECT FOR A QUICK BITE.

SERVES FOUR

INGREDIENTS
    16 fishcake slices
        or fish balls
    16 wooden skewers
For the soup
    400g/14oz Chinese
        white radish, peeled
    3 sheets dried seaweed
    10ml/2 tsp Thai fish sauce
    10ml/2 tsp light soy sauce
    salt and ground black pepper
For the soy dip
    60ml/4 tbsp dark soy sauce
    5ml/1 tsp sesame seeds
    5ml/1 tsp wasabi
        paste, or to taste

1 Pierce each slice of fishcake or fish ball with a wooden skewer and then set them to one side.

2 To make the dip, mix the dark soy sauce and sesame seeds in a small dish, adding the wasabi paste to taste.

3 To make the soup, put the radish in a pan with the seaweed and 2 litres/3½ pints/8 cups water. Bring to the boil and add the Thai fish sauce and soy sauce.

4 Lay the fishcake kebabs in the liquid and boil for 20 minutes, or until the soup has thickened. Season with salt and pepper.

5 Pour a little soup into each bowl and add four fishcake kebabs. Serve with the spicy soy dip.

COOK'S TIP
You will find fishcake in large pieces or slices and fish balls are available at most Asian food stores.

Per portion Energy 104kcal/435kJ; Protein 6.4g; Carbohydrate 13.1g, of which sugars 3.1g; Fat 3.2g, of which saturates 0.5g; Cholesterol 13mg; Calcium 105mg; Fibre 1g; Sodium 1468mg.

SEAFOOD FRITTERS WITH PEAR AND SOY DIP

SUCCULENT PRAWNS, MOIST COD FILLET AND TASTY SEASONED CRAB ARE ALL BATTERED AND LIGHTLY SAUTÉED IN THESE CRISPY BITESIZE FRITTERS. THE PRAWN FRITTERS HAVE A MUSHROOM AND CHILLI STUFFING AND ALL ARE SERVED WITH A PEAR AND SOY SAUCE DIP.

SERVES FOUR

INGREDIENTS

2 eggs, beaten
vegetable oil, for frying
salt and ground black pepper

For the prawn fritters
5 medium-size prawns (shrimp)
juice of ½ lemon
30ml/2 tbsp white wine
2.5ml/½ tsp sesame oil
1 dried shiitake mushroom, soaked in warm water for about 30 minutes until softened
1 green chilli, finely chopped
45ml/3 tbsp plain (all-purpose) flour for dusting

For the crab fritters
75g/3oz crab meat
3 oyster mushrooms, finely sliced
1/2 green (bell) pepper, finely chopped
25g/1oz Korean chives, finely sliced
1 garlic clove, thinly sliced
2 eggs, beaten
45ml/3 tbsp plain (all-purpose) flour
Extra flour for dusting

For the cod fritters
300g/11oz cod fillet
7.5ml/1½ tsp dark soy sauce
5ml/1 tsp white wine
2.5ml/½ tsp sesame oil
45ml/3 tbsp plain (all-purpose) flour for dusting

For the dipping sauce
45ml/3 tbsp light soy sauce
45ml/3 tbsp sugar
1 garlic clove, crushed
10ml/2 tsp pear juice
2.5ml/½ tsp lemon juice
1.5ml/¼ tsp Korean chilli powder

1 Combine all the ingredients for the dipping sauce in a small serving bowl.

2 To make the prawn fritters, gently pull off the tail shell. Twist off the head. Peel away the soft body shell and the small claws beneath. Rinse well and season with salt, pepper, lemon juice, white wine and a dash of sesame oil.

3 When the soaked shiitake mushroom has reconstituted and become soft, drain and finely chop it, discarding the tough stem. Mix with the chilli, season with a dash of sesame oil and salt, and dust with a little flour. Set this mushroom stuffing aside. Dust the prawns with flour and then coat them with beaten egg. Set aside.

4 To make the crab fritters, season the crab meat with salt and pepper and place in a bowl. Add the mushrooms, pepper and chives. Then stir in the garlic, eggs and flour, and set the mixture aside.

5 For the cod fritters, cut the fillet into bitesize pieces and season with soy sauce, white wine and sesame oil. Set aside for 20 minutes. Dust with flour, coat in beaten egg and set aside.

6 Coat a large frying pan or wok with vegetable oil and place over a medium heat. Add the prawn and cod fritters, with spoonfuls of the crab mixture.

7 Fry until lightly browned and then add a little of the mushroom mixture to each prawn fritter. When all the fritters are golden on both sides transfer them to a platter. Serve with the dipping sauce.

Per portion Energy 294kcal/1227kJ; Protein 29.3g; Carbohydrate 9.1g, of which sugars 6.1g; Fat 15.3g, of which saturates 2.8g; Cholesterol 287mg; Calcium 103mg; Fibre 1.1g; Sodium 671mg.

STUFFED SQUID WITH SOY DIPPING SAUCE

THIS MUCH-LOVED SNACK IS SERVED ON THE STREET CORNERS OF KOREA. THE STEAMED SQUID HAS A SILKEN TEXTURE WHILE THE STUFFING MIXES A VIBRANT RANGE OF FLAVOURS MORE USUALLY FOUND IN DUMPLINGS. THIS DISH IS A DELICIOUS EXAMPLE OF TRADITIONAL MARKET FOOD.

SERVES TWO TO THREE

INGREDIENTS
    2 squid
    115g/4oz lean frying steak, finely
        chopped
    15ml/1 tbsp soy sauce
    5ml/1 tsp sugar
    5ml/1 tsp sesame oil
    ½ block firm tofu
    50g/2oz/¼ cup beansprouts
    1 green chilli, seeded and
        chopped
    1 fresh red chilli, seeded and
        chopped
    1 spring onion (scallion), finely
        chopped
    90g/3½oz/½ cup short grain rice,
        cooked
    plain (all-purpose) flour, for
        dusting
For the dipping sauce
    1 garlic clove, crushed
    45ml/3 tbsp dark soy sauce
    5ml/1 tsp sesame oil
    salt
    ground black pepper

1 To clean the squid, pull out the head and tentacles from the body. Discard the ink sac if it is intact. Then cut off and reserve the tentacles. Discard the head along with the other parts. Discard the long pen or quill from the body and wash the sac, rubbing off the purple skin.

2 Rinse and drain the squid and dry it well on kitchen paper. Then chop the squid tentacles.

3 Place the beef in a bowl and mix in the soy sauce, sugar and sesame oil. Cover and leave to marinate for about 10 minutes.

4 Meanwhile, squeeze the tofu to remove some of the liquid, then crumble it into a bowl. Bring a pan of water to the boil, add the beansprouts, bring the water back to the boil and drain immediately. Finely chop the beansprouts and add to the tofu.

5 Add the chillies and spring onion to the tofu mixture. Add the chopped squid tentacles. Stir in the cooked rice and the beef with its marinade, and mix to thoroughly combine the ingredients.

6 Dust the insides of the squid with flour, then stuff with the tofu mixture. Use bamboo skewers to close the squid and place them in a steamer. Steam over boiling water for about 20 minutes, until the squid is cooked and tender.

7 For the dipping sauce, mix the garlic, soy sauce and sesame oil, adding salt and pepper to taste. Transfer the mixture to a small serving dish.

8 Remove the stuffed squid from the steamer and cut them into slices, then serve with the dipping sauce.

Per portion Energy 335kcal/1414kJ; Protein 39.1g; Carbohydrate 15.9g, of which sugars 3.8g; Fat 11.5g, of which saturates 2.2g; Cholesterol 555mg; Calcium 87mg; Fibre 1.8g; Sodium 432mg.

SOUPS &
BROTHS

Korean soups are versatile food, eaten as snacks, as accompaniments to main meals and as nourishing dishes in themselves. Often using doenjang soya bean paste, the typically light, clear soups are characterized by flavourings such as seaweed and white radish. Cold Radish Kimchi Soup and Wheat Noodles in Soya Bean Soup are examples of dishes that can be eaten either chilled during the warmer months or piping hot on colder days. Another Korean classic is a rich broth using meat or fish to make a heartier meal during the winter.

RICE CAKE SOUP

TRADITIONALLY EATEN BY FAMILIES ON NEW YEAR'S DAY, THIS CEREMONIAL SOUP IS SIMPLE AND SATISFYING. A TRADITIONAL KOREAN NEW YEAR'S GREETING BETWEEN FRIENDS IS TO ASK IF THE OTHER PERSON HAS EATEN A BOWL OF RICE CAKE SOUP YET.

SERVES FIVE

INGREDIENTS

15g/½oz dried anchovies
200g/7oz beef sirloin, thinly
    sliced
1 garlic clove, crushed
30ml/2 tbsp salt
15ml/1 tbsp light soy sauce
1kg/2¼lb rice cake
½ leek, roughly chopped
2 eggs
vegetable oil, for cooking
dried seaweed paper or Japanese
    nori
ground black pepper

1 Bring 1 litre/1¾ pints/4 cups water to the boil in a wok or pan and add the dried anchovies. Boil over a high heat for 15 minutes. Remove and discard the anchovies. Set the stock aside.

2 Place the beef in a wok or pan over a medium heat. Add the garlic and a little ground pepper and cook gently, turning the slices, for 2 minutes. Add 1 litre/ 1¾ pints/4 cups water and bring to the boil. Simmer for 10 minutes, then strain the stock into a jug (pitcher) and set the beef aside.

3 Combine the anchovy and beef stocks in a wok or large pan. Add the salt and soy sauce and bring to the boil.

4 Slice the rice cake into bitesize pieces and add these to the boiling stock with the leeks. Bring the stock back to the boil, if necessary, and keep it boiling. Cook the rice cake for about 10 minutes, until tender.

5 Meanwhile, separate the eggs. The yolks are not needed: set them aside for another use. Whisk the whites lightly to break them up. Heat a little oil in a frying pan and add the egg whites, tilting the pan so that they run evenly over the pan. Cook until browned and set into a paper-thin crêpe. Transfer to a plate and leave to cool.

6 Roll up the cooled egg-white omelette and cut into 3cm/1¼in slices. Shake out the slices into strips. Slice the dried seaweed into strips.

7 Season the soup and ladle it into serving bowls. Divide the beef, seaweed and omelette strips among the bowls of soup, piling them up attractively in the middle of each one. Serve immediately.

Per portion Energy 431kcal/1817kJ; Protein 18.3g; Carbohydrate 63.2g, of which sugars 1.1g; Fat 13.4g, of which saturates 3.3g; Cholesterol 101mg; Calcium 68mg; Fibre 1.1g; Sodium 374mg.

SOYA BEANSPROUT SOUP

This gentle broth, kongnamul, is easy to make and easy on the palate, with just a hint of spiciness and a refreshing nutty flavour. It is reputed to be the perfect solution for calming the stomach after a heavy drinking session.

SERVES FOUR

INGREDIENTS

200g/7oz/generous 2 cups soya beansprouts
1 red or green chilli
15 dried anchovies
1 spring onion (scallion), finely sliced
3 garlic cloves, chopped
salt

1 Wash the soya beansprouts, and trim off the tail ends.

2 Seed the chilli and cut it diagonally into thin slices.

3 Boil 750ml/1¼ pints/3 cups water in a wok or pan and add the dried anchovies. After boiling for 15 minutes remove the anchovies and discard.

4 Add the soya beansprouts and boil for 5 minutes, ensuring the lid is kept tightly on. Add the spring onion, chilli and garlic, and boil for a further 3 minutes. Finally, add salt to taste, ladle the soup into bowls and serve.

COOK'S TIPS
• Soya beansprouts and dried anchovies are available at some Asian stores. If you are unable to find dried anchovies, then 5ml/1 tsp Thai fish sauce can be used as a substitute.
• The soup can be made using sprouted mung beans, but they should not be boiled for as long as the soya beansprouts – allow about 2 minutes to heat them and retain their texture.

VARIATION
To make a spicier version of this soup simply add 5ml/1 tsp of chilli powder to each bowl. The result is hotter and said to be great for curing a cold.

Per portion Energy 41kcal/173kJ; Protein 4.6g; Carbohydrate 2.7g, of which sugars 1.2g; Fat 1.4g, of which saturates 0.2g; Cholesterol 7mg; Calcium 46mg; Fibre 1g; Sodium 445mg.

WHEAT NOODLES IN SOYA BEAN SOUP

STRANDS OF THIN WHEAT NOODLES TASTE GREAT IN A MILD AND DELICIOUSLY NUTTY CHILLED SOUP, MAKING AN IDEAL DISH FOR A HOT SUMMER'S DAY. THE ICED BROTH IS TOPPED WITH SUCCULENT STRIPS OF CUCUMBER AND WEDGES OF TOMATO.

SERVES FOUR

INGREDIENTS

185g/6½oz/1 cup soya beans
30ml/2 tbsp sesame seeds
300g/11oz thin wheat noodles
salt
1 cucumber, cut into thin strips
   and 1 tomato, cut into wedges,
   to garnish

VARIATION
For a quick and easy version of this dish use 250ml/8fl oz/1 cup unsweetened soya milk rather than the soaked soya beans. Simply add the ground sesame seeds to the soya milk and chill to make the soup.

COOK'S TIP
To separate the skins and rubbed beans, place them in a bowl of cold water: the skins will float and can be skimmed off.

1 Soak the soya beans overnight. Rinse in cold water and remove the skins.

2 Gently toast the sesame seeds in a dry pan until they have lightly browned. Place the peeled soya beans and the sesame seeds in a food processor. Add 1 litre/1³/4 pints/4 cups water and process until fine. Strain through muslin (cheesecloth), collecting the liquid in a jug (pitcher). Chill the soya and sesame milk in the refrigerator.

3 Bring a pan of water to the boil and cook the noodles, making sure they are well covered. When they are cooked, drain them and rinse them well in cold water.

4 Place a portion of the wheat noodles in each soup bowl, and pour over the chilled soya and sesame liquid. Garnish the bowls with strips of cucumber and tomato wedges, then season with salt and serve.

Per portion Energy 268kcal/1121kJ; Protein 20.1g; Carbohydrate 17.9g, of which sugars 3.4g; Fat 13.3g, of which saturates 1.7g; Cholesterol 0mg; Calcium 174mg; Fibre 8.7g; Sodium 6mg.

NOODLE SOUP <u>WITH</u> OYSTER MUSHROOMS

COLLOQUIALLY KNOWN AS "MARKETPLACE NOODLES", THIS DISH HAS LONG BEEN ENJOYED AS A QUICK AND SIMPLE LUNCH. THE OYSTER MUSHROOMS GIVE THE MILD BROTH AN APPETIZING RICHNESS. SERVE WITH AN ACCOMPANIMENT OF RADISH KIMCHI AND A BOWL OF STEAMED RICE.

SERVES TWO

INGREDIENTS
  75g/3oz beef
  30ml/2 tbsp light soy sauce
  2 eggs, beaten
  45ml/3 tbsp vegetable oil
  4 oyster mushrooms
  75g/3oz courgette (zucchini)
  sesame oil, for drizzling
  115g/4oz plain noodles
  1 spring onion (scallion),
    finely chopped
  1 dried red chilli, thinly sliced
  2 garlic cloves, crushed
  salt and ground white pepper
  sesame seeds, to garnish

1 Pour 500ml/17fl oz/2¼ cups water into a pan and bring to the boil. Add the beef and cook until tender, about 20 minutes. Remove the meat and slice into thin strips.

2 Strain the cooking liquid through a sieve (strainer) into a jug (pitcher). Then add the light soy sauce to the stock and set to one side.

3 Season the beaten eggs with a pinch of salt. Coat a frying pan with 10ml/2 tsp vegetable oil and heat over a medium heat. Add the beaten eggs, swirling the pan to coat it evenly, and make a thin omelette. Cook until set and lightly browned on each side.

4 Slide the omelette from the pan on to a board and roll it up, then slice it thinly and shake out the slices into thin strips.

5 Cut the oyster mushrooms and courgette into thin strips. Sprinkle both with a little salt. Pat dry with kitchen paper after 5 minutes.

6 Heat the remaining vegetable oil in a wok over a medium heat. Quickly stir-fry the mushrooms and drizzle with sesame oil before setting them aside. Add and lightly fry the courgette until it softens, then remove. Finally, stir-fry the beef until lightly browned, and set aside.

7 Bring a pan of water to the boil. Add the plain noodles and bring back to the boil. Cook for 3–5 minutes, or according to the packet instructions, until just tender. Drain the noodles and rinse in cold water. Leave to drain again. Quickly reheat the reserved beef stock.

8 Place the noodles at the base of a soup dish or divide between two individual bowls. Cover with the mushrooms, courgette and sliced beef. Top with the spring onion, chilli and garlic, then pour over the beef stock until roughly one third of the ingredients are covered. Finally, sprinkle with sesame seeds before serving.

COOK'S TIP
Spare egg yolks can be used for mayonnaise. To freeze, lightly whisk them with sugar, noting the weight of sugar and number of yolks on the label.

Per portion Energy 492kcal/2059kJ; Protein 23.1g; Carbohydrate 40.4g, of which sugars 3.3g; Fat 27.7g, of which saturates 4.9g; Cholesterol 213mg; Calcium 60mg; Fibre 2.3g; Sodium 1167mg.

DUMPLING SOUP

THE SUCCULENT DUMPLINGS TASTE FANTASTIC IN THIS CLEAR SOUP. AS READY-TO-EAT DUMPLINGS ARE WIDELY AVAILABLE, THIS DISH IS REALLY SIMPLE TO MAKE AND A DELIGHT TO EAT.

SERVES TWO

INGREDIENTS
    750ml/1¼ pints/3 cups beef stock
    16 frozen dumplings
    1 spring onion (scallion), sliced
    ¼ green chilli, sliced
    1 garlic clove, crushed
    15ml/1 tbsp light soy sauce
    salt and ground black pepper

1 Place the stock in a pan and bring to the boil. Add the frozen dumplings, cover, and boil for 6 minutes.

2 Add the spring onion, chilli, garlic and soy sauce, and boil for 2 minutes. Season with salt and black pepper.

Per portion Energy 106kcal/445kJ; Protein 2g; Carbohydrate 12.6g, of which sugars 0.6g; Fat 6.1g, of which saturates 3.4g; Cholesterol 5mg; Calcium 30mg; Fibre 0.5g; Sodium 842mg.

WHITE RADISH AND BEEF SOUP

THE SMOKY FLAVOURS OF BEEF ARE PERFECTLY COMPLEMENTED BY THE TANGINESS OF CHINESE WHITE RADISH IN THIS MILD AND REFRESHING SOUP WITH A SLIGHTLY SWEET EDGE.

SERVES FOUR

INGREDIENTS
    200g/7oz Chinese white radish, peeled
    50g/2oz beef
    15ml/1 tbsp sesame oil
    ½ leek, sliced
    15ml/1 tbsp light soy sauce
    salt and ground black pepper

1 Slice the white radish and cut the pieces into 2cm/¾in squares. Roughly chop the beef into bitesize cubes.

2 Heat the sesame oil in a large pan, and stir-fry the beef until golden brown. Add the white radish and briefly stir-fry.

3 Add 750ml/1¼ pints/3 cups water. Boil, then simmer, covered, for 7 minutes. Add the leek, soy sauce and sesoning. Simmer for 2 minutes. Serve.

Per portion Energy 60Kcal/247kJ; Protein 3.7g; Carbohydrate 2g, of which sugars 1.8g; Fat 4.1g, of which saturates 1g; Cholesterol 7mg; Calcium 17mg; Fibre 1g; Sodium 281mg.

COLD RADISH KIMCHI SOUP

THIS ICE-COLD SOUP IS NORMALLY SERVED AS AN ACCOMPANIMENT TO A HOT DISH, SUCH AS GRILLED OR BARBEQUED MEAT. THE SPICY SEASONING CONTRASTS DELICIOUSLY WITH THE CHILLED BROTH.

SERVES EIGHT

INGREDIENTS

   1 Chinese leaves (Chinese cabbage)
   150g/5oz Chinese white radish, peeled and diced
   50g/2oz/¼ cup salt
   50g/2oz Korean chilli flakes
   1 Asian pear, peeled and diced
   2 cucumbers, finely sliced
   75g/3oz watercress
   75g/3oz spring onions (scallions), roughly sliced
   10 garlic cloves, crushed
   25g/1oz fresh root ginger, finely sliced
   25g/1oz/3 tbsp pine nuts, to garnish

1 Slice the cabbage and cut the radish into cubes measuring about 3cm/1¼in. Place the vegetables in a large bowl. Add 250ml/8fl oz/1 cup water and the salt, and leave to stand for 1 hour.

2 Pour 2 litres/3½ pints/8¾ cups water into a very large large bowl. Tie the chilli flakes in a muslin (cheesecloth) bag, and then put it in the water.

3 Cover the bowl and set it aside until the water has taken on the colour and flavour of the chilli. Then remove the bag and skim out any flakes that may have escaped from the bag and are left in the water.

4 Drain the cabbage and radish and add them to the chilli water. Leave to stand for 30 minutes.

5 Add a further 2 litres/3½ pints/8¾ cups water. Stir in the Asian pear, cucumbers, watercress, spring onions, garlic and ginger. Set the soup aside for 30 minutes to allow the flavours to develop and mingle.

6 Season the soup with a little salt, if required, then serve garnished with the pine nuts.

Per portion Energy 92kcal/382kJ; Protein 3.4g; Carbohydrate 8g, of which sugars 5.7g; Fat 5.4g, of which saturates 0.5g; Cholesterol 0mg; Calcium 67mg; Fibre 2.2g; Sodium 15mg.

WINTER KIMCHI SOUP

THE SPICY FLAVOURS OF CHILLI AND GINGER IN THIS CHILLED SOUP ARE UNIQUELY WARMING ON A COLD WINTER'S NIGHT. TRADITIONALLY, THE SOUP WAS SERVED WITH SWEET POTATOES, WHICH WOULD HAVE BEEN BAKED IN THE EMBERS OF THE HOUSEHOLD FIRE.

SERVES FOUR

INGREDIENTS

3 Chinese white radishes, peeled
115g/4oz/½ cup salt
4 spring onions (scallions), shredded
1 garlic clove, sliced
115g/4oz fresh root ginger, sliced
2 red chillies, seeded and sliced
3 green chillies, seeded and sliced
1 Asian pear, peeled and diced
sugar syrup, to taste
10g/¼oz/1 tbsp pine nuts, to garnish

COOK'S TIP
To make a light sugar syrup, dissolve 225g/8oz/1 cup sugar in 600ml/ 1 pint/2½ cups water in a pan over a medium heat, stirring occasionally. Bring to the boil and boil for 2–3 minutes, until the syrup has reduced slightly. Take care not to allow the sugar to burn. Leave the syrup to cool. Store the syrup in an airtight jar in the refrigerator, where it will keep for up to 2 weeks. Alternatively, freeze the syrup in 50ml/2fl oz/¼ cup containers.

1 Place the Chinese white radishes in a bowl. Pour in 3.5 litres/6 pints/15 cups water and the salt, and leave them to soak overnight.

2 The next day, add the spring onions to the radishes in salt water and leave them to stand for 30 minutes.

3 Tie the garlic and ginger in a muslin (cheesecloth) bag and add to the radishes and spring onion with the red and green chillies. Cover and leave to stand for another day in the refrigerator.

4 Remove the radishes from the mixture, cut them into bitesize dice and then return the pieces to the soup. Remove and discard the garlic and ginger.

5 Add the pear to the soup, adding a little sugar syrup if it is too salty. Serve garnished with pine nuts.

COOK'S TIP
Peeled radishes are milder than unpeeled ones. To prepare a radish, slice off the roots and leaves, wash under cold running water and drain.

Per portion Energy 48kcal/198kJ; Protein 1.7g; Carbohydrate 5.9g, of which sugars 5.8g; Fat 2.1g, of which saturates 0.2g; Cholesterol 0mg; Calcium 37mg; Fibre 2g; Sodium 28mg.

SPICY POTATO AND COURGETTE SOUP

THIS KOREAN TAKE ON A TYPICAL WESTERN SOUP IS SEASONED WITH SPICES FOR A LIVELY KICK. THE GOCHUJANG CHILLI PASTE ALSO HELPS TO THICKEN THE SOUP AND GIVE IT A SILKY TEXTURE. THE ADDITION OF POTATOES AND BEEF MAKE IT A REALLY HEARTY AND FILLING MEAL IN A BOWL.

SERVES TWO

INGREDIENTS
    5ml/1 tsp salt
    400g/14oz baby new potatoes,
        peeled
    5ml/1 tsp sesame oil
    15ml/1 tbsp Korean chilli powder
    5ml/1 tsp *gochujang* chilli paste
    1 garlic clove, crushed
    115g/4oz minced (ground) beef,
        finely chopped
    1 small courgette (zucchini), halved
        and sliced
    1 red chilli, seeded and thinly sliced
    ½ small leek, thinly sliced
    5ml/1 tsp sake
    1 spring onion (scallion), shredded,
        to garnish

1 Bring 750ml/1¼ pints/3 cups water to the boil in a large pan. Add the salt and the potatoes.

2 Mix the sesame oil, chilli powder, *gochujang* paste and garlic with the beef until well combined. Add the seasoned beef mixture to the pan and boil for 5 minutes.

3 Add the courgette and boil for a further 3 minutes. Then add the chilli, leek and sake and boil for 2 minutes. Garnish with the spring onion.

COOK'S TIP
Chopping minced beef breaks it down into very fine pieces. Shape the meat in a neat block and chop it in both directions using a large knife.

Per portion Energy 371kcal/1552kJ; Protein 18.6g; Carbohydrate 38.2g, of which sugars 5.6g; Fat 17.1g, of which saturates 5.3g; Cholesterol 35mg; Calcium 70mg; Fibre 4.1g; Sodium 73mg.

COLD SUMMER CUCUMBER SOUP

NATURALLY COOL AND REFRESHING CUCUMBER IS SHARPENED WITH CIDER VINEGAR IN THIS CHILLED SOUP, WHICH IS PERFECT FOR COOLING EVERYONE DOWN AT LUNCH ON A HOT SUMMER DAY. IT MAKES A GREAT APPETIZER FOR ANY HOT NOODLE OR BARBECUE DISH.

SERVES FOUR

INGREDIENTS
    2 cucumbers, peeled, halved and seeded
    1 garlic clove, crushed
    50g/2oz spring onions (scallions), sliced
    30ml/2 tbsp cider vinegar
    30ml/2 tbsp sugar syrup (see page 104)
    salt

1 Slice the cucumbers into thin strips, add salt and leave for 10 minutes.

2 Combine 500ml/17fl oz/2 generous cups water with the garlic, spring onions, vinegar and syrup. Add the cucumber before ladling into bowls.

Per portion Energy 40kcal/166kJ; Protein 0.8g; Carbohydrate 9.2g, of which sugars 9.1g; Fat 0.2g, of which saturates 0g; Cholesterol 0mg; Calcium 20mg; Fibre 0.6g; Sodium 30mg.

POLLACK AND EGG SOUP

POPULAR AS A RESTORATIVE AFTER A NIGHT OUT, THIS DISH IS MOST COMMONLY SERVED FOR BREAKFAST. MADE WITH DRIED FISH AND FRESH EGG AND SERVED WITH A BOWL OF RICE AND A DISH OF KIMCHI, IT ALSO MAKES A PERFECT LUNCH OR LIGHT SUPPER.

SERVES SIX

INGREDIENTS
    115g/4oz dried pollack
    25g/1oz/¼ cup plain (all-purpose) flour
    7.5ml/1½ tsp sesame oil
    200g/7oz Chinese white radish, peeled and diced
    1 garlic clove, crushed
    7.5ml/1½ tsp salt
    1 spring onion (scallion), shredded
    1 egg

1 Shred the pollack and rinse, drain and toss in the flour. Heat the sesame oil, add the fish, radish and garlic, then stir-fry.

2 Add 2 litres/3½ pints/8¾ cups water and boil. Reduce, cover and simmer for 15 minutes. Skim off the surface film. Stir in the salt and spring onion. Crack the egg in the pan and stir until set. Serve.

Per portion Energy 107kcal/450kJ; Protein 18g; Carbohydrate 3.9g, of which sugars 0.8g; Fat 2.3g, of which saturates 0.5g; Cholesterol 61mg; Calcium 29mg; Fibre 0.5g; Sodium 216mg.

SPICY SEAFOOD NOODLE SOUP

JAMPONG IS A SPICY, GARLIC-INFUSED SEAFOOD STEW. THICK JAPANESE UDON NOODLES ARE ADDED TO THE RICH BROTH, WHICH IS FLAVOURED WITH CHARACTERISTICALLY KOREAN SEASONINGS, TO CREATE AN ENTICING FUSION DISH. ADD A BOWL OF STEAMED RICE FOR THE PERFECT QUICK LUNCH.

SERVES TWO

INGREDIENTS
50g/2oz pork loin
50g/2oz mussels
50g/2oz prawns (shrimp)
90g/3½oz squid
15ml/1 tbsp vegetable oil
1 dried chilli, sliced
½ leek, sliced
2 garlic cloves, finely sliced
5ml/1 tsp grated fresh
   root ginger
30ml/2 tbsp Korean
   chilli powder
5ml/1 tsp mirin or rice wine
50g/2oz bamboo shoots, sliced
½ onion, roughly chopped
50g/2oz carrot, roughly chopped
2 Chinese leaves (Chinese cabbage),
   roughly chopped
750ml/1¼ pints/3 cups beef
   stock
light soy sauce, to taste
300g/11oz udon or flat
   wheat noodles
salt

1 Slice the pork thinly, put it on a plate and set aside.

2 Prepare the seafood. Scrub the mussels with a stiff brush and rinse them under cold running water. Discard any that remain closed after being sharply tapped. Scrape off any barnacles from the shells and remove the "beards" with a small knife. Rinse well. Hold each prawn between two fingers and gently pull off the tail shell. Twist off the head. Peel away the soft body shell and the small claws beneath. Rinse well.

3 Wash the squid. Holding the body, pull away the head and tentacles. Remove and discard the ink sac, if intact. Pull out the innards including the long transparent pen. Discard the thin purple skin, but keep the two small side fins. Slice off the head just under the eyes (discard it), severing the tentacles.

4 Squeeze the tentacles at the head end to push out the round beak in the centre and discard. Rinse the pouch and tentacles. Score the flesh of the body sac in a crisscross pattern, and slice into 2cm/¾in pieces.

5 Coat a pan with the vegetable oil and place over high heat. When hot, add the chilli, leek, garlic and ginger. Stir-fry until the garlic has lightly browned and add the sliced pork. Stir-fry quickly. Then add the chilli powder and mirin or rice wine, and stir to coat the ingredients thoroughly.

6 Add the bamboo shoots, onion and carrot, and stir-fry until soft.

7 Add the seafood and cabbage and cook over a high heat for 30 seconds. Pour in the beef stock and bring to the boil. Reduce the heat. Season with salt and soy sauce, then cover and simmer for 3 minutes. Discard any closed mussels.

8 Cook the udon or wheat noodles in a pan of boiling water until soft, then drain and rinse with cold water. Place a portion of noodles in each soup bowl, ladle over the soup and serve.

Per portion Energy 778Kcal/3288kJ; Protein 39.5g; Carbohydrate 122.8g, of which sugars 9.4g; Fat 17.7g, of which saturates 1.4g; Cholesterol 176mg; Calcium 104mg; Fibre 6.9g; Sodium 734mg.

SPICY POLLACK SOUP

THIS SOUP HAS A WONDERFUL REFRESHING SPICINESS AND IS OFTEN ENJOYED AS AN AUTUMNAL DISH. THE MINARI *CONTRIBUTES A PEPPERY FLAVOUR THAT COMPLEMENTS THE DELICATE FLAVOUR OF THE POLLACK BUT WATERCRESS MAKES AN EQUALLY GOOD ALTERNATIVE.*

SERVES FOUR

INGREDIENTS

600g/1lb 6oz pollack fillet
15ml/1 tbsp sake
5ml/1 tsp sesame oil
15ml/1 tbsp Korean chilli powder
5ml/1 tsp *gochujang* chilli paste
2 garlic cloves, crushed
115g/4oz Chinese white radish,
   peeled
10g/¼oz dried anchovies
5ml/1 tsp dark soy sauce
5ml/1 tsp light soy sauce
¼ block firm tofu, cubed
10g/¼oz leek, thinly sliced
1 red chilli, seeded and thinly sliced
10g/¼oz enoki mushrooms
20g/¾oz chrysanthemum leaves
20g/¾oz watercress or Korean
   minari
salt and ground black pepper

1 Remove any bones from the pollack fillet and cut it diagonally into strips. Place the fish in a bowl with the sake, sesame oil and a pinch of salt, and toss the strips to coat them in seasoning. Place in the refrigerator for 1 hour.

2 Drain off the liquid, leaving the fish in the bowl. Add the chilli powder, *gochujang* paste and garlic and toss gently, coating the fish with the mixture. Leave to stand for 10 minutes.

3 Cut the radish into 3cm/1¼in cubes. Bring 1 litre/1¾ pints/4 cups water to the boil in a large pan and add the dried anchovies. Boil for 2 minutes, then remove and discard the anchovies.

4 Add the radish, dark and light soy sauces, and boil for a further 2 minutes.

5 Add the pollack and simmer the soup gently for 3 minutes, until the fish is just cooked.

6 Finally, add the tofu, leek, red chilli, enoki mushrooms, chrysanthemum leaves and watercress. Stir the ingredients into the soup gently to avoid breaking them up. Simmer the soup for a further 3 minutes.

7 Add seasoning, if required, then ladle into bowls and serve immediately.

VARIATIONS
• Any thick-filleted white fish can be used in this soup as a substitute for the pollack. For example, cod, haddock, hake or hoki are all suitable. Thin fish fillets will disintegrate.
• The soup can also be made with a mixture of seafood, such as prepared squid, prawns and mussels instead of the white fish.
• Alternatively, use half white fish and half seafood.

Per portion Energy 175kcal/733kJ; Protein 31.1g; Carbohydrate 2.3g, of which sugars 0.8g; Fat 3.7g, of which saturates 0.5g; Cholesterol 71mg; Calcium 162mg; Fibre 0.4g; Sodium 372mg.

SPINACH AND CLAM SOUP

THE LEAFY FLAVOUR OF THE FRESH SPINACH MARRIES PERFECTLY WITH THE NUTTY TASTE OF THE DOENJANG SOYA BEAN PASTE TO MAKE THIS MOUTHWATERING SOUP WITH CLAMS.

SERVES THREE

INGREDIENTS
  9 clams
  90g/3½oz spinach
  2 spring onions (scallions)
  40g/1½oz/scant ¼ cup minced
    (ground) beef
  15ml/1 tbsp *doenjang* soya bean paste
  15ml/1 tbsp crushed garlic
  salt

1 Scrub the clams in cold water, and rinse the spinach. Cut the spring onions lengthways and then into 5cm/2in strips.

2 Stir the beef and soya bean paste over a medium heat until they are cooked.

3 Pour in 750ml/1¼ pints/3 cups water and boil. Add the clams and spinach and simmer for 5 minutes.

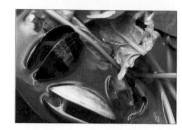

4 When the clams have opened, add the spring onions and garlic. Discard any closed clams. Season and serve.

Per portion Energy 90kcal/377kJ; Protein 11.1g; Carbohydrate 4.7g, of which sugars 3.8g; Fat 3.1g, of which saturates 1.1g; Cholesterol 30mg; Calcium 119mg; Fibre 2.2g; Sodium 1471mg.

SEAWEED SOUP

SEAWEED SOUP IS SAID TO DETOXIFY THE BODY AND HELP CIRCULATION. THIS RICH KOREAN BROTH IS PACKED WITH RIBBONS OF SEAWEED. A CHILLED VERSION CAN BE SERVED AS A SUMMER SIDE DISH.

SERVES FOUR

INGREDIENTS
  25g/1oz dried seaweed
  40g/1½oz beef, diced
  37.5ml/7½ tsp sesame oil
  3 garlic cloves, finely chopped
  45ml/3 tbsp light soy sauce
  salt and ground black pepper

1 Soak the seaweed for 20 minutes. Drain and cut into 2.5cm/1in lengths.

2 Season the beef with 15ml/1 tbsp of the sesame oil and pepper and leave for 10 minutes. Stir-fry the beef and seaweed in a pan with the remaining sesame oil. When the meat is cooked, add 750ml/ 1¼ pints/3 cups water, cover and boil.

3 Add the garlic and soy sauce. Cover and boil until it has turned slightly milky in colour. Season before serving.

Per portion Energy 77kcal/318kJ; Protein 2.5g; Carbohydrate 0.7g, of which sugars 0.6g; Fat 7.2g, of which saturates 1.3g; Cholesterol 6mg; Calcium 3mg; Fibre 0.1g; Sodium 274mg.

CLEAR COD SOUP

THIS QUICK SOUP IS A POPULAR DAILY DISH, OFTEN MADE AS A FAMILY EVENING MEAL. IT IS SPICY AND PACKED WITH DELICIOUS INGREDIENTS. A GLASS OF SOJU IS THE PERFECT ACCOMPANIMENT.

SERVES FOUR

INGREDIENTS
 25g/1oz dried anchovies
 600g/1lb 6oz cod fillet, skinned and
   cut into wide strips
 225g/8oz Chinese white radish,
   peeled and diced
 2 garlic cloves, crushed
 2 spring onions (scallions), roughly
   sliced
 ½ leek, finely sliced
 ½ block firm tofu, cubed
 ½ hot red chilli, seeded and
   sliced
 50g/2oz enoki mushrooms
 50g/2oz watercress
 salt and ground black pepper

1 Bring 1.5 litres/2½ pints/6¼ cups water to the boil in large pan and add the dried anchovies. Boil for 10 minutes over a high heat. At the end of this time use a slotted spoon to remove the anchovies. Discard the anchovies and retain the stock.

2 Add the cod and radish. Simmer the soup for about 4 minutes, until the fish is opaque and just cooked.

3 Stir in the garlic, spring onions and leek. Add the tofu and let the soup simmer for a further 10 minutes, but do not stir or the tofu will break up.

COOK'S TIPS
• For an especially spicy soup, increase the quantity of hot chilli and use one or more chillies to taste.
• Spicy soups are suitable in the hottest months, when perspiration has a cooling effect, or to combat the cold of winter.
• For a milder version, use a plump, mild variety with one seeded and sliced chilli.

4 Add the enoki mushrooms, watercress, chilli and salt. Increase the heat and boil for 2 minutes. Add pepper and serve.

Per portion 164kcal/687kJ; Protein 32.3g; Carbohydrate 1.7g, of which sugars 1.5g; Fat 3.1g, of which saturates 0.5g; Cholesterol 73mg; Calcium 196mg; Fibre 1g; Sodium 350mg.

OCTOPUS AND WATERCRESS SOUP

THIS REFRESHING SEAFOOD SOUP HAS A WONDERFULLY RESTORATIVE QUALITY. DELICIOUS OCTOPUS IS COOKED IN A RICH VEGETABLE BROTH, WITH WHITE RADISH AND WATERCRESS ADDING A DISTINCTIVE FLAVOUR THAT IS QUINTESSENTIALLY KOREAN.

SERVES TWO TO THREE

INGREDIENTS
    1 large octopus, cleaned
    150g/5oz Chinese white radish,
      peeled
    1/2 leek, sliced
    20g/3/4oz kelp or spinach leaves
    3 garlic cloves, crushed
    1 red chilli, seeded and sliced
    15ml/1 tbsp light soy sauce
    75g/3oz watercress or rocket
      (arugula)
    salt and ground black pepper

VARIATION
For a spicier version of this soup try adding a teaspoon of Korean chilli powder. This gives the dish a really tangy kick.

COOK'S TIP
The sweet root of white radish is not the only part which is eaten. The radish leaves, rich in iron, calcium and vitamin C, can be sautéed or eaten raw in salad.

1 Rinse the octopus in salted water and cut into pieces about 2.5cm/1in long.

2 Then prepare the peeled white radish by dicing it finely.

3 Pour 750ml/1 1/4 pints/3 cups water into a large pan and bring to the boil. Reduce the heat and then add the radish, leek, kelp or spinach, and crushed garlic.

COOK'S TIP
It is possible to cook Chinese white radish for a long time without it losing its taste and texture. It can also be grated and is a crisp and juicy addition to a salad.

4 Simmer the contents of the pan over a medium heat until the radish softens and becomes clear. Discard the kelp and leek and then add the sliced chilli.

5 Add the prepared pieces of octopus, increase the heat and boil for 5 minutes. Season with soy sauce, salt and pepper, and then add the watercress or rocket.

6 Remove the pan from the heat, cover and leave to stand for 1 minute while the leaves wilt into the liquid. Ladle into bowls and serve.

Per portion Energy 106kcal/449kJ; Protein 19.9g; Carbohydrate 2.6g, of which sugars 2.3g; Fat 1.9g, of which saturates 0.5g; Cholesterol 48mg; Calcium 108mg; Fibre 1.7g; Sodium 386mg.

BLUE CRAB CASSEROLE

The perfect centrepiece for any meal, this rich and hearty soup is traditionally shared between the whole family. Although live blue crabs are not always readily available and can be substituted with European crab, they do give this casserole unsurpassed flavour.

SERVES FOUR

INGREDIENTS
2 live blue crabs
7.5ml/1½ tsp sesame oil
15ml/1 tbsp Korean chilli powder
2 garlic cloves, crushed
300g/11oz Chinese white radish, peeled and diced
300g/11oz courgette (zucchini), thinly sliced
50g/2oz green chilli, seeded and sliced
20g/¾oz red chilli, seeded and sliced
5ml/1 tsp light soy sauce
5ml/1 tsp dark soy sauce
5ml/1 tsp salt
5ml/1 tsp sugar
275g/10oz leeks, roughly sliced
50g/2oz chrysanthemum leaves
50g/2oz watercress or Korean *minari*
15ml/1 tbsp *doenjang* soya bean paste
15ml/1 tbsp sake

1 Put the crabs in iced water for at least 5 minutes to stun them. Remove their top shells and small legs (set these aside). Remove the entrails, gills and mouth parts. Slit the crabs down the middle on a heavy board, using a heavy knife and a meat mallet or rolling pin to give four pieces. See also cook's tips below.

2 Place the crab shells and legs in a large pan. Pour in 1.5 litres/2½ pints/6¼ cups water and bring to the boil. Reduce the heat and simmer for 1 hour, skimming occasionally to remove any scum, if necessary. Strain the stock, discarding the shells and legs.

3 Heat a large pan over a low heat and add 50ml/2fl oz/¼ cup of the crab stock. Stir in the sesame oil, half the chilli powder and the garlic. Bring to the boil, then reduce the heat and simmer the mixture briefly.

4 Pour in the rest of the stock, stirring to mix it with the chilli-flavoured stock and add the radish. Bring the stock back to the boil, then reduce the heat and simmer for 10 minutes.

5 Add the crabs, courgette and green and red chillies, and boil for a further 10 minutes, until the crab turns bright orange. Add the remaining chilli powder, the light and dark soy sauces, salt and sugar. Bring the soup back to the boil.

6 The final stage is to add the leeks, chrysanthemum leaves, watercress or *minari*, *doenjang* soya bean paste and sake. Remove the pan from the heat and cover it, then leave the soup to stand for 2 minutes. To serve, ladle the soup into bowls, including a piece of the crab in each.

COOK'S TIPS
• Blue crab is a popular American species providing mainly body meat. If it is not readily available, the common or European crab can be used. These crabs have meaty legs, which should be used rather than discarded.
• An alternative way of preparing a live crab is to place it in a freezer, pre-set at the fast-freeze setting, for a few hours. This is a more humane way of killing the crab before cutting it up.

Per portion Energy 168kcal/700kJ; Protein 20.5g; Carbohydrate 7g, of which sugars 6.3g; Fat 6.4g, of which saturates 0.9g; Cholesterol 63mg; Calcium 57mg; Fibre 3.4g; Sodium 1055mg.

HOT AND SPICY FISH SOUP

THIS SOUP, A FIRM FAVOURITE TO ACCOMPANY A GLASS OF SOJU, HAS A DELICIOUS SPICY KICK.
HALIBUT OR SEA BASS CAN BE USED JUST AS WELL AS COD. THE WHITE FISH FLAKES HAVE THE BITE
OF RED CHILLI, AND THE WATERCRESS AND SPRING ONIONS ADD A REFRESHING ZESTY QUALITY.

SERVES THREE TO FOUR

INGREDIENTS

1 cod, filleted and skinned, head
   separate
225g/8oz Chinese white radish,
   peeled and cut into 2cm/¾in cubes
½ onion, chopped
2 garlic cloves, crushed
22.5ml/4½ tsp Korean chilli
   powder
5ml/1 tsp *gochujang* chilli
   paste
2 spring onions (scallions), roughly
   sliced
1 block firm tofu, cubed
90g/3½oz watercress or rocket
   (arugula)
salt and ground black pepper

1 Slice the cod fillets into three or four
large pieces and set the head aside.

2 Bring 750ml/1¼ pints/3 cups water to
the boil and add the fish head, radish,
onion, crushed garlic, a pinch of salt.
the chilli powder and *gochujang* chilli
paste. Boil for 5 minutes more.

3 Remove the fish head and add the
sliced fillet to the pan. Simmer until the
fish is tender, about 4 minutes.

4 Add the spring onions, tofu, and
watercress or rocket. Simmer the soup
without stirring for 2 minutes more.
Season with salt and pepper and serve.

Per portion Energy 132kcal/554kJ; Protein 23.4g; Carbohydrate 2.8g, of which sugars 2.3g; Fat 3g, of which saturates 0.5g; Cholesterol 46mg; Calcium 300mg; Fibre 1.1g; Sodium 80mg.

SUMMER SOUP WITH GINSENG AND RED DATES

TRADITIONALLY EATEN ON THE HOTTEST DAY OF SUMMER, SAMGYETANG IS A SMOOTH CHICKEN BROTH WITH A REVITALIZING QUALITY. THE COMBINATION OF RED DATES AND GINSENG MAKES A MEMORABLE DISH. SAMGYETANG IS TRADITIONALLY SERVED WITH A SMALL SERVING OF SALT AND GROUND PEPPER.

SERVES TWO

INGREDIENTS

200g/7oz/1 cup short grain or
    pudding rice
800g/1¾lb whole small chicken or
    poussin
4 chestnuts, peeled
4 garlic cloves, peeled
2 red dates
2 fresh ginseng roots
4 ginkgo nuts
salt and ground black pepper
finely shredded spring onions
    (scallions), to garnish

1 Soak the rice in a bowl of cold water for 20 minutes. Meanwhile, remove the wing tips and neck from the chicken, clean it thoroughly and sprinkle with salt.

2 Drain the rice and combine with the chestnuts and garlic to make a stuffing. Pack the stuffing into the neck end of the body cavity and pull down the skin before trussing the chicken.

COOK'S TIPS
• Ginkgo nuts, from the *ginkgo biloba* tree, are also popular in Chinese and Japanese cooking. Along with red dates, they are often sold in healthfood stores.
• If you cannot find ginseng root, sprinkle in a sachet of Korean ginseng tea (available from healthfood stores) instead. Be careful to buy "pure" ginseng tea and not one that includes fruit or other ingredients.
• A good quality chicken will make all the difference to the flavour of this soup.

3 Put the chicken into a heavy pan and then add cold water to cover the chicken. Bring to the boil.

4 Once the water is boiling add the red dates, ginseng roots and ginkgo nuts. Reduce the heat and simmer the soup for 1 hour, or until it thickens.

5 Transfer to a bowl and serve garnished with spring onions.

Per portion Energy 630kcal/2654kJ; Protein 56.3g; Carbohydrate 93.1g, of which sugars 12.3g; Fat 3.6g, of which saturates 0.8g; Cholesterol 140mg; Calcium 60mg; Fibre 2.2g; Sodium 128mg.

CHICKEN SOUP WITH HAND-MADE NOODLES

THE HAND-MADE WHEAT NOODLES IN THIS DISH ARE IMPRESSIVE, YET THEY ARE REMARKABLY EASY TO MAKE. THE NOODLES ARE BATHED IN A HOT CHICKEN BROTH AND TOPPED WITH VEGETABLE STRIPS, SEASONED CHICKEN SHREDS AND A DASH OF SPICY SAUCE TO MAKE A REALLY SATISFYING DISH.

SERVES TWO

INGREDIENTS
½ whole chicken, about 500g/1¼lb
2 leeks
4 garlic cloves, peeled
40g/1½oz fresh root ginger, peeled
8 dried shiitake mushrooms, soaked
  in warm water for about 30 minutes
  until softened
115g/4oz carrot
1 courgette (zucchini)
30ml/2 tbsp vegetable oil
1 onion, finely chopped
10ml/2 tsp sesame oil
light soy sauce, to taste
½ dried chilli, finely chopped
salt and ground white pepper
For the seasoning
10ml/2 tsp dark soy sauce
2 spring onions (scallions), finely
  chopped
2 garlic cloves, crushed
30ml/2 tbsp sesame oil
30ml/2 tbsp sesame seeds
For the noodles
225g/8oz/2 cups plain
  (all-purpose) flour
6 eggs, beaten
For the sauce
30ml/2 tbsp light soy sauce
2 spring onions (scallions), finely
  chopped
2 garlic cloves, crushed
10ml/2 tsp Korean chilli powder
10ml/2 tsp sesame seeds
15ml/1 tbsp sesame oil

1 Slice the chicken into large pieces and place in a pan. Add the leeks, garlic, root ginger and water to cover. Bring to the boil over a medium heat and boil for 20 minutes, or until the chicken is tender. Remove the chicken and strain the liquid into a jug (pitcher).

2 Skin and bone the chicken and tear the meat into thin strips. Mix the seasoning ingredients in a bowl with salt and pepper. Add the chicken, coat with seasoning and set aside.

3 To make the noodles, sift the plain flour into a bowl with a pinch of salt and add the beaten eggs and a splash of water. Mix together by hand and knead the dough until it is smooth and elastic.

4 Place the dough on a lightly floured surface and roll out to about 3mm/⅛in thick. The dough will be firm and slightly sticky. Fold it three times and then slice it into thin noodles.

5 Drain the shiitake mushrooms and slice them, discarding the stems. Cut the carrot and courgette into strips.

6 Heat the vegetable oil in a frying pan and lightly stir-fry the mushrooms, courgette, carrot and onion. Season with sesame oil and salt and set aside.

7 Combine all the sauce ingredients in a dish, adding a little water if required.

8 Bring the chicken stock to the boil with the light soy sauce, salt and pepper. Add the noodles and cook for 4 minutes. Transfer the noodles to a bowl and ladle the broth over them. Top with the chicken, vegetables and a little dried chilli. Stir in the sauce before eating.

Per portion Energy 1138kcal/4767kJ; Protein 94.1g; Carbohydrate 70.4g, of which sugars 11.4g; Fat 55.6g, of which saturates 10.5g; Cholesterol 746mg; Calcium 392mg; Fibre 10.1g; Sodium 739mg.

OXTAIL SOUP

GINGER AND GARLIC GIVE THIS SOUP A DISTINCTIVELY ASIAN FLAVOUR, WHILE OXTAIL GIVES IT AN INCOMPARABLE RICHNESS. SLOW COOKING IS ESSENTIAL, NOT ONLY FOR TENDER MEAT, BUT ALSO TO BRING OUT THE FLAVOURS AND ALLOW THEM TO MINGLE UNTIL THE MEAT IS TRULY SUCCULENT.

SERVES FOUR

INGREDIENTS

600g/1lb 6oz oxtail, cut into 5cm/2in
   pieces
3 small onions, quartered
115g/4oz leeks, roughly chopped
150g/5oz Chinese white radish,
   peeled and diced
115g/4oz fresh root ginger, sliced
10 garlic cloves, peeled
salt and ground black pepper
115g/4oz spring onions (scallions),
   finely shredded, to garnish

1 Soak the oxtail in plenty of cold water for 2 hours. Drain and repeat this process four or five times to remove the blood from the meat. Drain the meat and trim off any fat.

2 Bring 1.5 litres 2½ pints/6¼ cups water to the boil in a large pan. Add the oxtail, onions, leeks, radish, ginger and garlic, then bring back to the boil. Reduce the heat, cover and simmer gently for about 5 hours without stirring. Top up the water, if necessary. The soup should turn milky white in colour.

3 Strain the soup into a large serving bowl and add the pieces of oxtail. Discard the vegetables. Season with salt and pepper, then garnish with spring onions and serve.

Per portion Energy 212kcal/886kJ; Protein 20.7g; Carbohydrate 14.5g, of which sugars 10.8g; Fat 8.4g, of which saturates 0.1g; Cholesterol 0mg; Calcium 82mg; Fibre 3.8g; Sodium 137mg.

HOT <u>AND</u> SPICY BEEF SOUP

YUKGEJANG IS ONE OF THE MOST TRADITIONAL KOREAN SOUPS. THE SMOKY TASTE OF FERN FRONDS GIVES IT ITS UNIQUE FLAVOUR AND RED CHILLI POWDER PROVIDES A FIERCE KICK AND FIERY COLOUR. YUKGEJANG MAKES A PERFECT LUNCH DISH WHEN SERVED WITH RICE AND ACCOMPANIED BY KIMCHI.

SERVES TWO

INGREDIENTS
    75g/3oz dried fern fronds
    250g/9oz beef flank
    10ml/2 tsp sesame oil
    30ml/2 tbsp chilli powder
    1 garlic clove, finely chopped
    15ml/1 tbsp vegetable oil
    75g/3oz/1/2 cup beansprouts, trimmed
    1 leek, sliced
    1 spring onion (scallion), sliced
    75g/3oz small mushrooms, trimmed
    salt

1 Boil the dried fern fronds for about 3 minutes. Drain and rinse with cold water. Cut the fronds into thirds and discard the tougher stem pieces.

2 Place the beef flank in a medium pan and cover it with water. Bring the pan to the boil, cover and then cook over a high heat for 30 minutes. Skim the surface and remove any fat and foam.

3 Remove the beef from the pan and strain the stock into a jug (pitcher).

4 Cut the beef into thin strips and place in a bowl. Add the sesame oil, chilli powder and chopped garlic, and coat the meat.

5 Heat the vegetable oil in a large pan. Add the meat with the ferns, beansprouts, leek and spring onion. Stir-fry for 2 minutes, reduce the heat and pour in the beef stock. Cover and cook for 30 minutes or so until tender.

6 Add the mushrooms and simmer for a further 2 minutes. Add salt to taste and serve.

VARIATION
If ferns are not available, the best alternative is an equivalent amount of shiitake mushrooms.

Per portion Energy 225kcal/935kJ; Protein 21.5g; Carbohydrate 3g, of which sugars 2g; Fat 14.1g, of which saturates 4g; Cholesterol 48mg; Calcium 28mg; Fibre 2.3g; Sodium 59mg.

BEEF BROTH WITH BUCKWHEAT NOODLES

THE REFRESHING PROPERTIES OF THIS CHILLED BROTH, NAENGMYUN, MAKE IT A POPULAR SUMMER DISH. THE BUCKWHEAT NOODLES FLOAT IN A TRADITIONAL SOUP WHICH IS DISTINCTIVELY FLAVOURED WITH MUSTARD AND RICE VINEGAR AND TOPPED WITH MATCHSTICKS OF CRUNCHY CHINESE RADISH.

SERVES TWO

INGREDIENTS
    90g/3½oz beef shank
    1 leek, roughly chopped
    ½ onion, peeled and roughly chopped
    10g/¼oz fresh root ginger, peeled
        and roughly chopped
    4 garlic cloves, peeled and chopped
    ¼ Chinese white radish, peeled
    ½ cucumber
    1 Asian pear
    90g/3½oz *naengmyun* buckwheat
        noodles
    1 hard-boiled egg, sliced in half
    ice cubes, to serve
For the seasoning
    15ml/1 tbsp rice vinegar
    15ml/1 tbsp sugar
    ready-made English (hot) mustard,
        sugar, rice vinegar and salt, for
        seasoning at the table

1 Place the beef in a bowl of cold water. Soak for 30 minutes, then drain. Pour 1 litre/1¾ pints/4 cups water into a pan and bring to the boil. Add the beef and reduce the heat. Simmer for 1 hour, skimming the fat from the surface.

2 Add the leek, onion, root ginger and garlic, and cook for another 20 minutes. Remove the meat and cut into thin slices.

3 Strain the soup into a jug (pitcher). Cool and chill in the refrigerator.

4 Cut the radish into thin strips. Seed the cucumber and cut into thin strips. Peel and core the pear and cut into strips.

5 Place the radish strips in a bowl and add the rice vinegar and sugar and a pinch of salt. Coat the radish and leave it to chill.

6 Prepare a large pan of boiling water, and cook the noodles for 5 minutes. Drain and rinse two or three times in cold water until the water runs clear. Chill in the refrigerator.

7 Pour the chilled broth into two individual bowls, adding a couple of ice cubes to each. Add a portion of noodles and divide the beef, pear, cucumber and seasoned radish between them both. Top with half an egg.

8 Place the mustard, sugar, rice vinegar and salt in small serving dishes and serve with the soup for seasoning at the table. Stir the seasonings into the broth to taste: start with 5ml/1 tsp of vinegar and 2.5ml/½ tsp mustard, with a pinch of salt and sugar.

COOK'S TIP
For a perfect hard-boiled egg, put the egg in cold water and bring quickly to the boil. Reduce the heat and simmer gently for 8 minutes. Drain, crack the shell and cool under cold running water.

Per portion Energy 403kcal/1698kJ; Protein 22.2g; Carbohydrate 57.5g, of which sugars 22.9g; Fat 10.9g, of which saturates 2.8g; Cholesterol 131mg; Calcium 100mg; Fibre 6.8g; Sodium 87mg.

RICE & NOODLES

Rice and noodles form the backbone of every meal in Korea. Rice, or bap, is preferred in the sticky short and medium grain varieties and is traditionally cooked on its own, although additions such as beans, chestnuts and soya beansprouts are also popular. It is used to make delicious savoury porridge, such as Abalone Porridge and sweet dishes such as Pumpkin Congee, a type of rice porridge. Hot and cold noodle dishes are favourites — ranging from hearty noodle dishes such as Stir-fried Udon Noodles to chilled noodle salads such as Spicy Buckwheat Noodles.

GINSENG AND RED DATE RICE

THE MIXTURE OF RICE AND GRAINS IN THIS DISH CREATES A PLEASING APPEARANCE AND DELICIOUSLY COMPLEX FLAVOUR. THE MEDICINAL PROPERTIES OF GINSENG HAVE LONG BEEN VALUED IN KOREA AND THIS TRADITIONAL CEREMONIAL DISH IS RENOWNED FOR INCREASING STAMINA AND VITALITY.

SERVES FOUR

INGREDIENTS

    115g/4oz/⅔ cup mixed grains
    50g/2oz/¼ cup short grain rice or
      pudding rice
    50g/2oz/¼ cup glutinous, sticky or
      pearl rice
    50g/2oz/¼ cup brown rice
    10 aduki or red beans
    5 red dates
    10 chestnuts, cooked and peeled
    fresh ginseng root
    salt

VARIATION

For a different combination, use short grain rice with the mixed grain selection.

1 Combine the grains, the three types of rice and the aduki or red beans in a bowl. Pour in cold water to cover and leave to soak for 2 hours. Drain the rice mixture through a sieve (strainer) and rinse thoroughly under cold water. Transfer the rice and beans to a large pan.

2 Discard the seeds from the dates and slice the dates into small pieces. Halve the chestnuts and slice the ginseng root into two pieces (do not slice the ginseng if it is a small piece).

3 Add the dates, chestnuts and ginseng to the rice and mix together thoroughly. Pour in water to cover the ingredients by about 1cm/½in. Add a pinch of salt. Bring to the boil and cook for five minutes, then reduce the heat and simmer for a further 15 minutes or until all the water has evaporated. Stir thoroughly and serve.

COOK'S TIPS
• Mixed grain rice is made from a mixture of brown rice, sweet rice, wild rice, barley, hulled millet, green peas, yellow peas, black-eyed beans (peas), kidney beans and red beans. It is available from Korean or Japanese food stores.
• Glutinous rice is a sticky rice. There are many types of short grain rice, including Western pudding and risotto rice. Pearl rice sometimes refers to short, or round, grain rice. Asian and wholefood stores stock many varieties.

Per portion Energy 383kcal/1609kJ; Protein 8.3g; Carbohydrate 84.4g, of which sugars 2.1g; Fat 1.5g, of which saturates 0.2g; Cholesterol 0mg; Calcium 33mg; Fibre 2.1g; Sodium 4mg.

TOBIKO AND VEGETABLE RICE

THE SHIMMERING, TRANSLUCENT YELLOW GLOBES OF FLYING FISH ROE MAKE A DAZZLING ADDITION TO THIS RICE DISH AND A MIXTURE OF VEGETABLES PROVIDE CRISP TEXTURE AND A FRESH TASTE. IT IS POPULAR DURING THE SUMMER EITHER FOR LUNCH OR AS A LIGHT SUPPER.

SERVES FOUR

INGREDIENTS
    400g/14oz/2 cups sticky rice, freshly
        cooked
    2 leaves from a round (butterhead)
        lettuce, finely sliced
    2 red cabbage leaves, finely sliced
    ½ cucumber, deseeded and finely
        sliced lengthways
    25g/1oz carrot, finely sliced
        lengthways
    25g/1oz Chinese white radish, peeled
        and finely sliced lengthways
    60ml/4 tbsp sushi ginger or Japanese
        gari, finely sliced
    50g/2oz/4 tbsp flying fish roe or
        Japanese *tobiko*
    30ml/2 tbsp sesame oil
For the garnish
    20g/¾oz cress
    30ml/2 tbsp sesame seeds
For the vinegar dressing
    45ml/3 tbsp cider vinegar
    60ml/4 tbsp sugar
    salt

1 For the dressing, heat a small pan over a low heat and add the vinegar, sugar and a pinch of salt. Once the mixture has started to bubble, remove the pan from the heat and set it aside for a few minutes to allow the vinegar to evaporate.

COOK'S TIP
To add a finishing touch, drizzle the rice, vegetables and fish roe with a little sesame oil. Garnish with cress and sesame seeds before serving.

2 Combine the dressing with the cooked rice in a large bowl, mixing thoroughly. A flat wooden spatula or special rice paddle is ideal for turning the rice, mixing it without damaging the grains.

3 Mix the lettuce, red cabbage, cucumber, carrot and white radish. Spoon the rice into four bowls and top with the vegetables. Add the ginger and finish with fish roe or *tobiko* on top.

Per portion Energy 341kcal/1432kJ; Protein 8.8g; Carbohydrate 53g, of which sugars 21.9g; Fat 11.7g, of which saturates 1.8g; Cholesterol 41mg; Calcium 148mg; Fibre 3.4g; Sodium 31mg.

SOYA BEANSPROUT RICE

BLENDED THROUGH THE RICE, SOYA BEANSPROUTS IMPART A PLEASING CRUNCHINESS AND REFRESHING FLAVOUR, WHICH IS ENHANCED BY GARLIC, CHILLIES AND SPRING ONION. THIS DISH HAS THE REPUTATION OF BEING IRRESISTIBLE – IT IS IMPOSSIBLE TO REFUSE A SECOND HELPING.

SERVES FIVE

INGREDIENTS
   200g/7oz/1 cup short grain rice
   450g/1lb/2 cups soya
      beansprouts
   1 garlic clove, crushed
   5ml/1 tsp light soy sauce
   15ml/1 tbsp sesame oil
   salt
For the sauce
   1 garlic clove, crushed
   2.5ml/½ tsp grated fresh root
      ginger
   7.5ml/1½ tsp seeded and sliced
      jalapeño pepper
   15ml/1 tbsp seeded and sliced red
      chilli
   2.5ml/½ tsp sugar
   45ml/3 tbsp light soy sauce
   30ml/2 tbsp sesame seeds
   1 spring onion (scallion), finely
      chopped
   7.5ml/1½ tsp Korean chilli
      powder
   45ml/3 tbsp finely chopped button
      (white) mushrooms

1 Soak the rice in cold water for 30 minutes, drain in a sieve (strainer) and then rinse it well.

2 Bring 750ml/1¼ pints/3 cups water to the boil in a pan and then add a pinch of salt.

3 Add the soya beansprouts to the pan and boil for 3 minutes. Drain the sprouts, reserving the cooking liquid and rinse.

4 Place the soya beansprouts in a bowl. Add the garlic, soy sauce, sesame oil and a pinch of salt. Mix and set aside.

5 Place the rice in a pan and pour in enough of the reserved cooking liquid to cover the rice by about 1cm/½in. Bring to the boil and cook for 5 minutes.

6 Add the soya beansprouts, reduce the heat and cook for a further 12 minutes, until all the water has evaporated.

7 Using a small dish, thoroughly combine the garlic, ginger, jalapeño pepper, chilli, sugar, soy sauce, sesame seeds, spring onion, chilli powder and button mushrooms.

8 To serve, divide the rice among serving bowls and top with the ginger and sesame seed sauce.

COOK'S TIP
Beans are easily sprouted at home. Mung beans are particularly simple and quick, as are soya beans and chickpeas. You simply need to soak them in water overnight, and then drain them and place in a jar. Cover with a cloth and keep in a shaded place at room temperature. Rinse twice a day to keep the beans moist and fresh.

Per portion Energy 233kcal/974kJ; Protein 7.2g; Carbohydrate 36.6g, of which sugars 3g; Fat 6.4g, of which saturates 0.9g; Cholesterol 0mg; Calcium 70mg; Fibre 1.9g; Sodium 860mg.

STIR-FRIED KIMCHI AND RICE

UBIQUITOUS KOREAN KIMCHI IS NORMALLY ENJOYED AS AN APPETIZER OR ACCOMPANIMENT BUT THIS DISH TURNS IT INTO A MAIN COURSE. STIR-FRYING THE KIMCHI BRINGS OUT ITS NATURAL SWEETNESS, WHILE THE INCLUSION OF RICE BALANCES SOME OF THE CHILLI SPICINESS.

2 Add the cooked rice and mix it with the *kimchi* before adding the green pepper and sesame oil. Stir-fry for a further 5 minutes.

3 Divide the rice between two bowls and garnish with the chopped chives and a sprinkle of sesame seeds.

COOK'S TIP
Use scissors to chop chives and spring onions instead of a knife. Hold them in a bunch over a bowl and snip tiny slices.

SERVES TWO

INGREDIENTS
   45ml/3 tbsp vegetable oil
   5ml/1 tsp Korean chilli powder
   500g/1¼lb *kimchi*, cut into
     bitesize pieces
   200g/7oz/1 cup sticky rice, cooked
   ½ small green (bell) pepper, seeded
     and finely chopped
   15ml/1 tbsp sesame oil
For the garnish
   30ml/2 tbsp chopped chives
   15ml/1 tbsp sesame seeds

1 Heat a wok over a medium heat. Add the vegetable oil, chilli powder and *kimchi*. Stir-fry until lightly browned.

Per portion Energy 697kcal/2900kJ; Protein 13.2g; Carbohydrate 98g, of which sugars 17.6g; Fat 27.7g, of which saturates 3.5g; Cholesterol 0mg; Calcium 200mg; Fibre 7.3g; Sodium 23mg.

SASHIMI RICE

WHILE JAPANESE SASHIMI RICE IS ACCOMPANIED EXCLUSIVELY BY WASABI AND SOY SAUCE, THIS KOREAN VARIATION INCLUDES VEGETABLES AND IS SERVED WITH A SPICY, SOUR SAUCE. ACCOMPANIED BY A BOWL OF MISO SOUP, THIS IS WIDELY POPULAR AS A QUICK, YET SATISFYING, LUNCH DISH.

SERVES FOUR

INGREDIENTS
115g/4oz Chinese white radish, peeled
115g/4oz *sangchi* green leaves, shredded
50g/2oz perilla or *shiso* leaves, thinly sliced
½ cucumber, thinly sliced
4 garlic cloves, crushed
4 green chillies, seeded and sliced
45ml/3 tbsp sesame oil
250g/9oz tuna steak
400g/14oz/2 cups sticky rice, freshly cooked

For the sauce
115g/4oz *gochujang* chilli paste
100ml/3½fl oz/scant ½ cup cider vinegar
45ml/3 tbsp sugar
3 garlic cloves, crushed
30ml/2 tbsp sesame seeds
30ml/2 tbsp sake
30ml/2 tbsp sesame oil

1 Prepare the sauce: mix the *gochujang* chilli paste, cider vinegar, sugar, garlic, sesame seeds, sake and sesame oil in a bowl. Mix well, then set aside to allow the flavours to mingle.

2 Cut the radish into short lengths, then finely slice these and cut the slices into short fine strips.

3 Soak the radish strips in cold water for 15 minutes, then drain them and place in a bowl.

4 Add the *sangchi* green leaves, perilla or *shiso*, cucumber, garlic and chillies to the radish. Pour in 1 tablespoon of the sesame oil and toss the ingredients.

5 Slice the tuna into bitesize pieces, about 1 x 2cm/½ x ¾in.

6 Place the tuna in a bowl. Add 1 tablespoon of the sesame oil and mix gently to coat the fish.

7 Mix the remaining sesame oil with the rice and divide it among four bowls.

8 Place the vegetables on top of the rice and then lay the tuna mixture over the vegetables. Pour the sauce into side dishes and serve with the rice.

COOK'S TIP
Make a point of buying tuna from a good fishmonger for this dish. As it is served raw you should be sure that it is extremely fresh and that it has not previously been frozen.

Per portion Energy 457kcal/1915kJ; Protein 21.1g; Carbohydrate 44.7g, of which sugars 13.7g; Fat 22.8g, of which saturates 3.7g; Cholesterol 18mg; Calcium 158mg; Fibre 1.9g; Sodium 80mg.

OYSTER RICE

This dish is a seafood classic. The distinctive flavour of oysters infuses this recipe and is complemented by a subtle hint of ginger. Sake adds an almost imperceptible sweetness, while flakes of dried seaweed complete the seafood seasoning.

SERVES FOUR

INGREDIENTS

300g/11oz/1½ cups short grain rice
3cm/1¼in fresh root ginger, peeled
   and finely sliced
10 oysters, shucked, rinsed and
   drained
15ml/1 tbsp light soy sauce
30ml/2 tbsp sake
salt
dried seaweed paper or Japanese
   nori, shredded, to garnish

COOK'S TIP
Use a short, blunt but tough, oyster knife
for opening oysters (see page 87).

1 Soak the rice for 30 minutes, then drain in a sieve (strainer) and rinse well. Soak the ginger in cold water for 10 minutes to remove some of its heat, then drain.

2 Bring 500ml/17fl oz/generous 2 cups water to the boil in a pan. Add the oysters, soy sauce, sake and a pinch of salt. Boil for 3 minutes, then drain the oysters and ginger, reserving the cooking liquid.

3 Place the rice in a pan and pour in enough oyster stock to cover the rice by about 1cm/½in. Bring to the boil and cook for 5 minutes. Add the oysters and ginger, reduce the heat and cook for 15 minutes, until the water has evaporated.

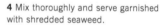

4 Mix thoroughly and serve garnished with shredded seaweed.

Per portion Energy 320kcal/1338kJ; Protein 11g; Carbohydrate 61.4g, of which sugars 0.2g; Fat 1g, of which saturates 0.1g; Cholesterol 29mg; Calcium 85mg; Fibre 0g; Sodium 433mg.

STIR-FRIED UDON NOODLES

UDON NOODLES ORIGINATED IN JAPAN BUT QUICKLY BECAME POPULAR IN KOREA. THE MEDLEY OF SEAFOOD, MEAT AND VEGETABLES IN THIS STIR-FRY IS DELICIOUSLY ENHANCED BY THE SWEET, SALTY FLAVOURS IN THE SAUCE. THIS IS AN IDEAL LUNCH DISH.

SERVES FOUR

INGREDIENTS

200g/7oz squid, cleaned and
    skinned
350g/12oz *udon* noodles
8 tiger prawns (shrimp), shelled
4 mussels, shucked
30ml/2 tbsp vegetable oil
115g/4oz beef sirloin, cut into
    strips
½ onion, finely sliced
1 green (bell) pepper, seeded and
    finely sliced
1 carrot, finely sliced
50g/2oz oyster mushrooms, sliced
½ lettuce, shredded
15ml/1 tbsp chilli oil
salt and ground black pepper
For the sauce
15ml/1 tbsp oyster sauce
10ml/2 tsp sugar
30ml/2 tbsp sake
45ml/3 tbsp dark soy sauce

3 Bring 1 litre/1¾ pints/4 cups water to the boil in a large pan and add a pinch of salt. Add the squid, prawns and mussels to the pan, bring the water back to the boil, and then drain and set aside.

4 For the sauce, mix the oyster sauce, sugar, sake and soy sauce in a bowl. Set the sauce aside, to allow the flavours to mingle.

5 Heat the vegetable oil in a wok over a high heat and add the beef, then stir-fry for 3 minutes. Continue stir-frying, add the onion, pepper, carrot, mushrooms and lettuce, and stir-fry for 2 more minutes.

6 Add the blanched seafood. Add the noodles and sauce, and stir-fry until the seafood is reheated and cooked and all the ingredients are coated. Season with chilli oil and black pepper, and serve.

1 Score diagonal cuts across the squid flesh with a sharp knife, taking great care not to cut right through, and then cut the sacs into strips of about 2cm/¾in.

2 Bring a pan of water to the boil and add the udon noodles. Boil them for 3 minutes and then drain the noodles. Rinse the cooked noodles under cold water and set aside.

VARIATION
For a quick dish, use prepared mixed seafood that is already blanched.

Per portion Energy 594kcal/2502kJ; Protein 36g; Carbohydrate 76g, of which sugars 10.1g; Fat 18.1g, of which saturates 2.4g; Cholesterol 232mg; Calcium 85mg; Fibre 3.8g; Sodium 1072mg.

PO JANG MA CHA STREET NOODLES

SOLD BY MOBILE VENDORS ON BUSTLING STREET CORNERS, THESE NOODLES ARE A POPULAR, FILLING SNACK. THE FISHCAKE AND SEAWEED PERFECTLY COMPLEMENT EACH OTHER AND CREATE A LIGHT, NOURISHING DISH, WHICH IS ALSO QUICK AND EASY TO PREPARE AT HOME.

SERVES THREE

INGREDIENTS
    300g/11oz *somyun* thin wheat
        noodles
    150g/5oz fishcake, sliced, or fish balls
    2 sheets dried tofu or Japanese *yuba*,
        sliced
    dried seaweed paper or Japanese
        nori, shredded
    2 spring onions (scallions), shredded
    5ml/1 tsp sesame seeds
    5ml/1 tsp Korean chilli powder
For the stock
    dried seaweed paper or japanese *nori*
    50g/2oz Chinese white radish
    10g/¼oz dried anchovies
    1 leek, sliced
    3 garlic cloves, peeled
    ½ white onion, sliced
    30ml/2 tbsp dark soy sauce
    salt and ground black pepper

1 First make the stock. Bring 2 litres/3½ pints/8¾ cups water to the boil in a large pan. Add the dried seaweed paper, radish, dried anchovies, leek, garlic, onion and soy sauce.

2 Bring back to the boil, reduce the heat slightly and boil the stock steadily for 15 minutes. Strain the stock, discarding the flavouring ingredients. Sample the stock and season to taste.

3 Bring a pan of water to the boil and add the *somyun* noodles. Simmer for about 1 minute, then drain. Place a portion of noodles into each of three soup bowls.

4 Bring the stock to the boil. Add the fishcake or fish balls and dried tofu or *yuba*. Boil for 10 minutes, until the tofu is tender.

5 Pour the soup over the noodles in the bowls. Garnish with the seaweed, spring onions and sesame seeds and sprinkle with chilli powder before serving.

VARIATION
Fresh tofu can be used as an alternative to dried tofu, but it should not be boiled for 10 minutes. At step 4, add the fishcake or fish balls and simmer for 5 minutes, then add the fresh tofu in one piece and simmer for a further 5 minutes. Use a large spatula or flat draining spoon to lift the tofu carefully from the soup. Slice it and divide it among the bowls, adding it to the noodles. Then pour in the soup. This way the tofu will not disintegrate.

Per portion Energy 505kcal/2133kJ; Protein 16.2g; Carbohydrate 82.2g, of which sugars 3.7g; Fat 14.7g, of which saturates 1.2g; Cholesterol 25mg; Calcium 77mg; Fibre 3.7g; Sodium 767mg.

SPICY BUCKWHEAT NOODLES

THIS CHILLED NOODLE SALAD, CALLED BIBIM NAENGMYUN, *IS IDEAL FOR A SUMMER LUNCH DISH AND IS NOT TIME-CONSUMING TO MAKE. THE COOL TEMPERATURE OF THE BUCKWHEAT NOODLES CONTRASTS WITH THE SPICINESS OF THE DRESSING, AND ASIAN PEAR ADDS A DELICIOUS SWEETNESS.*

SERVES TWO

INGREDIENTS
- 90g/3½oz *naengmyun* buckwheat noodles
- 1 hard-boiled egg
- ½ cucumber
- ½ Asian pear
- ice cubes, to serve

For the sauce
- 30ml/2 tbsp *gochujang* chilli paste
- 5ml/1 tsp Korean chilli powder
- 30ml/2 tbsp sugar
- 10ml/2 tsp sesame oil
- 1 garlic clove, finely chopped
- 2.5ml/½ tsp soy sauce
- 5ml/1 tsp sesame seeds

1 Cook the noodles in a large pan of boiling water for 5 minutes. Drain them, and then rinse two or three times in cold water until the water runs clear. Chill for 30 minutes.

2 Slice the hard-boiled egg in half. Seed the cucumber and slice it into long, thin matchstick strips. Peel and core the Asian pear and slice it into fine matchstick strips.

COOK'S TIP
Be sure to use a large pan with plenty of water when cooking *naengmyun* noodles, as they contain a lot of starch so will stick to the pan and each other easily. Add a few drops of oil while cooking to help prevent the water from frothing up and boiling over; this also helps to keep the noodles separate when they are first drained.

3 In a large bowl combine all the ingredients for the sauce and blend them together well. Arrange the noodles in the centre of a large serving platter. Pour over the sauce and then sprinkle with the pear and cucumber strips. Place the egg on the top and add ice cubes to the plate before serving.

Per portion Energy 337kcal/1421kJ; Protein 9.4g; Carbohydrate 58.3g, of which sugars 25.1g; Fat 9g, of which saturates 1.3g; Cholesterol 105mg; Calcium 52mg; Fibre 3.3g; Sodium 133mg.

ABALONE PORRIDGE

THE UNIQUE FLAVOUR OF ABALONE MAKES IT A PRIZED INGREDIENT IN KOREAN COOKING AND THE PREPARATION TIME IS WELL WORTH THE EFFORT. AS PART OF TRADITIONAL KOREAN MEALS, WHICH OFTEN INCLUDE NINE COURSES, THIS DISH IS CONSIDERED A SOPHISTICATED APPETIZER.

5 Thinly slice the abalone and pound each slice to tenderize it. Mix the abalone slices with the sesame oil, sake, soy sauce and salt and pepper.

6 Heat a wok or frying pan over a high heat. Add the abalone and seasoning, and cook the slices for 30 seconds on each side, then remove from the heat.

SERVES TWO

INGREDIENTS
115g/4oz/⅔ cups short grain rice or pudding rice
300g/11oz fresh abalone, shelled
½ small leek, chopped
½ small onion, chopped
1 oyster mushroom
15ml/1 tbsp sesame oil
5ml/1 tsp sake
5ml/1 tsp light soy sauce
salt and ground white pepper
For the garnish
a little vegetable oil
10g/¼oz enoki mushrooms
20g/¾oz cress
soy sauce

1 Soak the rice in cold water for 30 minutes. Drain in a sieve (strainer) and rinse really well, then grind coarsely in a food processor.

2 Trim the black skin from around the outside of the abalone and set aside the flesh from the centre. Place the black skin in a pan.

3 Add the leek, onion, oyster mushroom and 120ml/4fl oz/½ cup water to the pan. Bring to the boil and simmer for 10 minutes.

4 Strain the stock through a sieve, then pour it into a jug (pitcher) and discard the flavouring ingredients.

7 Bring the rice and stock to the boil. Reduce the heat to low, add the abalone and its cooking juices, and simmer until smooth and creamy. Heat a little oil in the wok. Add the enoki mushrooms and cook for a few seconds. Spoon the porridge into bowls and garnish with mushrooms, cress and soy sauce.

Per portion Energy 407kcal/1702kJ; Protein 25.5g; Carbohydrate 54.7g, of which sugars 3.9g; Fat 9.4g, of which saturates 1.6g; Cholesterol 62mg; Calcium 108mg; Fibre 3.6g; Sodium 974mg.

VEGETABLE PORRIDGE

*WITH A TEXTURE SIMILAR TO RISOTTO, THIS DISH MAKES A POPULAR, FORTIFYING BREAKFAST.
BECAUSE IT USES SESAME OIL RATHER THAN BUTTER, IT IS LIGHTER THAT ITS ITALIAN EQUIVALENT
AND IS WIDELY REGARDED AS A NUTRITIOUS OPTION BY HEALTH-CONSCIOUS KOREANS.*

SERVES TWO

INGREDIENTS

115g/4oz/⅔ cup short grain rice or
  pudding rice
1 dried shiitake mushroom
15ml/1 tbsp sesame oil
1 spring onion (scallion), finely
  chopped
1 small carrot, finely chopped
750ml/1¼ pints/3 cups vegetable or
  fish stock
salt and ground black pepper

For the garnish
2 quail's egg yolks
sesame seeds

1 Soak the rice in cold water for 30
minutes, then drain and rinse well.

2 Soak the shiitake mushroom in warm
water for about 15 minutes, or until soft,
then chop finely, discarding the stalk.

3 Coat a pan with the sesame oil and
place on medium heat. Add the spring
onion, carrot, mushroom and a pinch of
salt and stir-fry briefly. Add the rice and
stir-fry for 1 minute to coat the grains.

4 Pour in the stock. Reduce the heat
when the stock simmers. Simmer the
mixture, stirring gently, until the porridge
has thickened to a smooth consistency.
Season with salt and pepper.

5 Spoon the porridge into bowls.
Garnish each portion with a quail's egg
yolk and a sprinkling of sesame seeds.

COOK'S TIP
Instead of the quail's egg yolk, finish the
porridge with a halved boiled egg, if
preferred. The result is different –
stirring in the uncooked yolk enriches the
porridge as the yolk lightly cooks in the
hot mixture – but it still tastes good.

VARIATION
For a more meat-based variation of
vegetable porridge, use chicken stock
instead of vegetable and fish stock.

Per portion Energy 310kcal/1292kJ; Protein 6.1g; Carbohydrate 57.8g, of which sugars 8.4g; Fat 6.1g, of which saturates 0.8g; Cholesterol 0mg; Calcium 49mg; Fibre 2.1g; Sodium 5mg.

PUMPKIN CONGEE

THE NATURAL SWEETNESS OF PUMPKIN IS EXCELLENT IN THIS POPULAR AUTUMNAL SNACK, WHICH IS SUITABLE BOTH AS AN ACCOMPANIMENT TO SAVOURY DISHES AND AS A DESSERT. DESPITE ITS HUMBLE ORIGINS AS A FARMER'S STAPLE, THIS CONGEE IS ENJOYED THROUGHOUT KOREAN SOCIETY.

SERVES TWO TO THREE

INGREDIENTS
   600g/1lb 6oz pumpkin, seeded,
     peeled and cut into chunks
   75g/3oz/²⁄₃ cup sweet or glutinous
     rice flour
   30g/1¼oz/2 tbsp sugar
   5 chestnuts, cooked, peeled
     and crushed
   salt
For the garnish
   1 red date, seeded and finely sliced
   6 pine nuts

COOK'S TIP
Canned pumpkin pieces or purée can be used in this recipe. Cooked, puréed pumpkin freezes very well and is ideal for making dishes such as this one.

1 Place the pumpkin in a large pan and add just enough water to cover the pieces. Bring to the boil and simmer until the pumpkin is soft, then drain, reserving the cooking liquid. Cool the pumpkin slightly before blending it to a smooth paste in a food processor, adding a little of the reserved cooking water if it is very thick. Set aside.

2 Place the rice flour in a pan and stir in 200ml/7fl oz/scant 1 cup water. Cook over medium heat, stirring, until boiling and thickened.

3 Gradually stir in the pumpkin and sugar with a pinch of salt. Add the chestnuts. Simmer the congee briefly, stirring until it is smooth and creamy.

4 Ladle the congee into glass dishes or bowls and serve decorated with sliced red date and pine nuts.

Per portion Energy 185kcal/781kJ; Protein 3.4g; Carbohydrate 41g, of which sugars 15g; Fat 1g, of which saturates 0.3g; Cholesterol 0mg; Calcium 77mg; Fibre 3.2g; Sodium 4mg.

MIUM CONGEE

ORIGINATING IN CHINA, THIS RICE PORRIDGE IS POPULAR ALL OVER ASIA. AS A MEDICINAL DISH, SERVED TO RESTORE STAMINA, MIUM IS TRADITIONALLY MADE USING ONLY RICE; HOWEVER, THE OTHER INGREDIENTS BRING AN UNFORGETTABLE FLAVOUR, ESPECIALLY WHEN FINISHED WITH A SWIRL OF SOY SAUCE.

SERVES ONE

INGREDIENTS
  50g/2oz/¼ cup short grain rice or
    pudding rice
  1 small piece ginseng root, halved
  25g/1oz dried seaweed
  1 dried shiitake mushroom
  2 red dates
  3 chestnuts, cooked and peeled
  30g/1¼oz leeks

1 Soak the rice in cold water for 30 minutes, then drain and rinse. Place the rice in a pan and add the ginseng, seaweed, shiitake mushroom, dates, chestnuts and leeks.

2 Pour in 1 litre/1¾ pints/4 cups water. Bring to the boil, reduce the heat and cover the pan.

3 Simmer for 20–30 minutes, stirring occasionally, until the rice has broken down and the congee is smooth and milky in consistency.

4 To serve, pour the mixture through a sieve (strainer) into a bowl and discard the flavouring ingredients.

COOK'S TIP
Try kelp or wakame seaweed – *dahima* or *miyuk* in Korean – in this dish. A dash of soy sauce makes a finishing touch.

Per portion Energy 238kcal/997kJ; Protein 4.9g; Carbohydrate 51.8g, of which sugars 2.8g; Fat 1.2g, of which saturates 0.2g; Cholesterol 0mg; Calcium 31mg; Fibre 1.9g; Sodium 4mg.

PINE NUT CONGEE

RICH AND NUTRITIOUS, PINE NUTS ARE VALUED IN KOREAN COOKING FOR THEIR DISTINCTIVE, SLIGHTLY FRAGRANT FLAVOUR. IN THIS DELICIOUS DISH THE PINE NUTS GIVE THE RICE A WOODY TASTE AND SUBTLE SWEETNESS AS WELL AS A PLEASING TEXTURE.

SERVES ONE

INGREDIENTS
  115g/4oz/⅔ cup short grain rice or
    pudding rice
  50g/2oz/⅓ cup pine nuts, ground,
    plus 6 pine nuts
  1 red date, seeded and thinly
    sliced, to garnish

1 Soak the rice in plenty of cold water for 30 minutes.

2 Drain the rice in a sieve (strainer) and rinse it well. Shake it thoroughly to get rid of excess water, then grind it to a powder in a food processor.

3 Place the ground pine nuts in a food processor. Pour in 200ml/7fl oz/ scant 1 cup water and process to a fine paste.

4 Place the ground rice in a pan with 750ml/1¼ pints/3 cups water and bring to the boil.

5 Reduce the heat, cover the pan and simmer for 20 minutes. The grains will break down and produce a milky congee.

6 Remove the pan from the heat and stir in the pine nuts. Serve garnished with the whole pine nuts and red date.

Per portion Energy 806kcal/3359kJ; Protein 16.1g; Carbohydrate 106.3g, of which sugars 14.5g; Fat 34.9g, of which saturates 2.3g; Cholesterol 0mg; Calcium 37mg; Fibre 1.7g; Sodium 3mg.

FISH &
SHELLFISH

Korea is surrounded by sea, and fish and shellfish are strongly evident in
the diet. Recipes range from chilled seafood salads with hot dressings, such as
Skate Salad with Mustard, Garlic and Soy Dressing to slow-cooked
casseroles full of seafood, such as Monkfish with Soya Beansprouts.
Alternatively, enjoy the combination of oily fish with the dry, clean taste
of rice wine in Braised Mackerel with White Radish, or the strong kick of
Fiery Octopus. Spices and chilli paste make frequent appearances, usually
complemented by milder ingredients such as watercress.

BRAISED MACKEREL <u>WITH</u> WHITE RADISH

OILY FISH SUCH AS MACKEREL IS A PERFECT MATCH FOR THE CLEAN, DRY TASTE OF SAKE. GARLIC AND CHILLI COMBINE WITH THE STRONGLY FLAVOURED FISH, WHILE THE DICED RADISH ABSORBS ALL THE FLAVOURS OF THE COOKING LIQUID FOR AN UNUSUAL AND DELICIOUS TASTE.

SERVES TWO TO THREE

INGREDIENTS
    1 large mackerel, filleted
    300g/11oz Chinese white radish,
      peeled
    120ml/4fl oz/½ cup light soy sauce
    30ml/2 tbsp sake or
      rice wine
    30ml/2 tbsp maple syrup
    3 garlic cloves, crushed
    10ml/2 tsp Korean chilli powder
    ½ onion, chopped
    1 red chilli, seeded
      and sliced
    1 green chilli, seeded
      and sliced

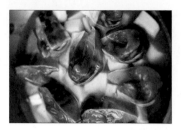

1 Slice the mackerel into medium-size pieces with a very sharp knife. Cut the radish into 2.5cm/1in cubes, and then arrange evenly across the base of a large pan. Cover the layer of radish cubes with a layer of mackerel.

2 Pour the soy sauce over the fish and add 200ml/7fl oz/ scant 1 cup water, the sake or rice wine, and the maple syrup. Sprinkle on the crushed garlic and chilli powder and gently stir, trying not to disturb the fish and radish. Add the onion and sliced chillies and cover.

3 Place over high a heat and bring the liquid to the boil. Reduce the heat and simmer for 8–10 minutes, or until the fish is tender, spooning the soy liquid over the fish as it cooks. Ladle into bowls and serve immediately.

VARIATION
If Chinese white radish is not available potatoes make a good alternative, and give a sweeter, more delicate flavour.

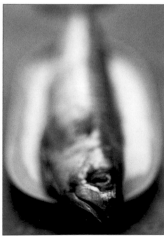

Per portion Energy 207kcal/861kJ; Protein 13.4g; Carbohydrate 11.4g, of which sugars 10.9g; Fat 11g, of which saturates 2.3g; Cholesterol 36mg; Calcium 33mg; Fibre 1.2g; Sodium 81mg.

BLACKENED HERRING <u>WITH</u> CHILLI SAUCE

GRILLING THE FISH UNTIL GENTLY BLACKENED IS A GREAT WAY TO PRESERVE THEIR DISTINCTIVE TASTE AND CREATES AN IMPRESSIVE APPEARANCE WHEN SERVED. THE CHILLI SAUCE IS FULL OF SWEET AND SPICY FLAVOURS AND ADDS A UNIQUELY KOREAN STYLE TO THIS FAMILIAR FISH.

SERVES TWO

INGREDIENTS
    4 small herring, gutted
    lemon wedges, to garnish
For the sauce
    15ml/1 tbsp *gochujang* chilli
      paste
    30ml/2 tbsp Korean chilli
      powder
    15ml/1 tbsp dark soy sauce
    15ml/1 tbsp lemon juice
    10ml/2 tsp sake
    30ml/2 tbsp maple syrup
    30ml/2 tbsp finely chopped spring
      onion (scallion)
    1 garlic clove, crushed

1 Wash the fish, dry with kitchen paper and score diagonally on both sides.

2 To prepare the *gochujang* sauce, mix the chilli paste and powder, soy sauce, lemon juice, sake, maple syrup, spring onion and garlic in a large shallow dish.

3 Add the herring and leave to marinate for 5 minutes, then turn the fish and leave for a further 5 minutes.

4 Heat a griddle pan or frying pan over a medium heat. Brush a little of the sauce over both sides of the fish before placing in the pan.

5 Cook for 10–15 minutes, turning once, until the fish has blackened slightly on each side but do not let them burn. Serve with lemon wedges.

Per portion Energy 499kcal/2085kJ; Protein 39.5g; Carbohydrate 23.1g, of which sugars 17.7g; Fat 28.6g, of which saturates 6.9g; Cholesterol 100mg; Calcium 168mg; Fibre 0.3g; Sodium 1371mg.

MONKFISH <u>WITH</u> SOYA BEANSPROUTS

*THIS DISH BLENDS THE FRAGRANT TASTE AND DELICATE TEXTURE OF MONKFISH WITH THE CRUNCHY,
NUTTY QUALITIES OF SOYA BEANSPROUTS. COATED WITH A FIERCE CHILLI SAUCE, THE HEAT GIVES WAY
TO A DELICIOUS COMBINATION OF DISTINCTIVELY KOREAN FLAVOURS.*

SERVES TWO TO THREE

INGREDIENTS
- 600g/1lb 6oz monkfish fillets
- 1 sheet dried kelp
- 30ml/2 tbsp vegetable oil
- 300g/11oz soya beansprouts
- 50g/2oz/7 tbsp cornflour (corn starch)
- 115g/4oz watercress or Korean *minari*, chopped
- ½ leek, sliced
- 1 green chilli, seeded and sliced
- 1 red chilli, seeded and sliced
- 15ml/1 tbsp sesame oil
- salt and ground black pepper
- 7.5ml/1½ tsp sesame seeds, to garnish

For the sauce
- 90ml/6 tbsp Korean chilli powder
- 2 garlic cloves, crushed
- 5ml/1 tsp grated fresh root ginger
- 30ml/2 tbsp sugar
- 15ml/1 tbsp sake or *mirin*
- 15ml/1 tbsp rice vinegar
- 5ml/1 tsp cider vinegar

1 Cut the monkfish into 5cm/2in strips. Sprinkle with a little salt and leave to stand for 2 hours.

2 For the sauce, mix the chilli powder, crushed garlic, grated ginger, sugar, sake or *mirin*, rice vinegar and cider vinegar in a jug (pitcher). Add a little salt and pepper and mix the ingredients well. Set aside to allow the flavours to mingle.

3 Bring 300ml/½ pint/1¼ cups water to the boil in a pan and add the dried kelp. Reduce the heat a little and cook for 10 minutes. Then you need to strain and reserve the stock, discarding the kelp.

4 Heat a pan over high heat and add the vegetable oil. Stir-fry the monkfish for 2 minutes and add the kelp stock. Simmer for 3 minutes. Add the soya beansprouts and cover. Simmer for 3 more minutes.

5 Mix the cornflour to a smooth paste with 50ml/2 fl oz/¼ cup warm water. Stir the sauce into the fish mixture. Reduce the heat before adding the watercress, leeks, chillies and cornflour paste. Simmer the mixture gently, stirring, until the sauce is thickened.

6 Spoon the monkfish and sauce on to plates, drizzle with sesame oil and garnish with sesame seeds before serving.

COOK'S TIP
Fresh monkfish should be kept cool at all times and should not be left unrefrigerated for long. As soon as you get the fish home, rinse it in cold water, and pat dry with kitchen paper. The best way to store it is on a cake rack in a shallow pan filled with crushed ice. Cover with cling wrap or foil and keep in the coldest part of the refrigerator. You can do this for up to two days.

Per portion Energy 421kcal/1775kJ; Protein 38.3g; Carbohydrate 36.4g, of which sugars 13.3g; Fat 15g, of which saturates 2.1g; Cholesterol 28mg; Calcium 136mg; Fibre 2.5g; Sodium 73mg.

SKATE SALAD <u>WITH</u> MUSTARD, GARLIC <u>AND</u> SOY DRESSING

THE SHARPNESS OF THE MUSTARD AND PUNGENCY OF THE GARLIC OFFSET THE FLAVOUR OF THE SKATE PERFECTLY IN THIS DISH. POPULAR AS AN APPETIZER, OR AS A LIGHT LUNCH IN THE SUMMER, THIS RECIPE BLENDS AN ARRAY OF GREEN LEAVES TO PROVIDE A REFRESHING SALAD.

2 Remove the skate flesh from the cartilage of the wing. Shred the flesh and set it aside.

3 For the dressing, mix the Asian pear, oil, vinegar, garlic, mustard and soy sauce. Season with salt and pepper and mix well.

4 Place the rocket, watercress, mixed leaves and diced tomatoes in a large serving bowl. Add the shredded skate and toss the ingredients together.

5 Pour the dressing over the salad, toss lightly and garnish with orange zest.

SERVES FOUR

INGREDIENTS
  800g/1¾lb skate
  15ml/1 tbsp white wine vinegar
  15 peppercorns
  1 thyme sprig
  115g/4oz rocket (arugula)
  115g/4oz watercress
  200g/7oz mixed salad leaves
  2 tomatoes, seeded and diced
  finely pared orange zest, to garnish
For the dressing
  30ml/2 tbsp grated Asian pear
  30ml/2 tbsp virgin olive oil
  30ml/2 tbsp white wine vinegar
  30ml/2 tbsp crushed garlic
  10ml/2 tsp English (hot) mustard
  5ml/1 tsp dark soy sauce
  salt and ground black pepper

1 Thoroughly rinse the skate in cold water. Bring a large pan of water to the boil and add the vinegar, peppercorns and thyme. Reduce the heat so that the water simmers. Add the skate and poach it for 7–10 minutes, or until the flesh is just beginning to come away from the cartilage. Do not overcook. Drain thoroughly.

Per portion Energy 219kcal/919kJ; Protein 33.6g; Carbohydrate 4.4g, of which sugars 4.2g; Fat 7.5g, of which saturates 1g; Cholesterol 0mg; Calcium 257mg; Fibre 2.8g; Sodium 637mg.

GRIDDLED SEA BREAM <u>WITH</u> ORANGE DIPPING SAUCE

THIS RECIPE SHOWCASES THE DELICACY OF THIS WONDERFUL FISH BY KEEPING THE SEASONING TO A MINIMUM AND GRILLING IT TO GIVE A SUBTLE SMOKY TASTE. THE SWEET SHARPNESS AND FRESH QUALITY OF THE ORANGE DIPPING SAUCE UNLOCK A MOUTHWATERING FLAVOUR.

SERVES TWO

INGREDIENTS

1 large sea bream, gutted and cleaned
30ml/2 tbsp white wine
5ml/1 tsp sesame seeds, ground
1 red chilli, seeded and sliced
1 garlic clove, crushed
5ml/1 tsp finely chopped fresh root ginger
5ml/1 tsp sesame oil
15ml/1 tbsp plain (all-purpose) flour
30ml/2 tbsp vegetable oil
salt
2 spring onions (scallions), finely sliced, to garnish

For the dipping sauce

15ml/1 tbsp sugar
20ml/4 tsp orange juice
45ml/3 tbsp dark soy sauce
1 garlic clove, crushed
5ml/1 tsp grated fresh root ginger
60ml/4 tbsp vegetable or kelp stock
7.5ml/1½ tsp rice vinegar

1 Make diagonal slashes on both sides of the sea bream, then place it in a dish and pour over the white wine. Leave to stand for 10 minutes.

2 Mix the ground sesame seeds with the chilli, garlic, ginger and sesame oil. Add a pinch of salt and mix well. Drain the wine off the fish and rub the sesame mixture into the slashes in the bream and also into the fish cavity. Leave to marinate for 30 minutes.

3 Meanwhile make the dipping sauce. Simmer the sugar and orange juice in a small pan over a low heat until reduced to a concentrated syrup.

4 Add the soy sauce, garlic, ginger and stock and simmer for 3 minutes, then strain the liquid into a jug (pitcher). Add the vinegar and stir well, then set aside.

5 Heat a griddle pan or frying pan over a medium heat and add the oil. Dust the bream with flour and wrap the tail in foil. Cook for 10 minutes, turning once, until the skin turns crisp and brown and the flesh is springy to the touch.

6 Place the fish on a warmed serving dish. Garnish with the spring onions and serve with the dipping sauce.

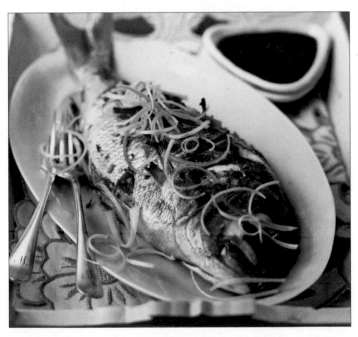

Per portion Energy 436kcal/1828kJ; Protein 45.7g; Carbohydrate 16.4g, of which sugars 10.5g; Fat 21.3g, of which saturates 1.8g; Cholesterol 95mg; Calcium 136mg; Fibre 0.5g; Sodium 1879mg.

SALMON TERIYAKI

JAPANESE DISHES ARE VERY POPULAR IN KOREA, AND THE TASTE OF THIS TRADITIONAL TERIYAKI SAUCE ECHOES THE FLAVOUR OF THE HUGELY POPULAR KOREAN DISH BULGOGI. THE MARINADE IS RICH AND COMPLEX, COMBINING THE SWEETNESS OF MAPLE SYRUP WITH THE SALTINESS OF SOY SAUCE.

2 Mix the sugar, sake or *mirin*, maple syrup and light soy sauce in a small jug (pitcher) until thoroughly combined.

3 Heat a frying pan or wok over a medium heat. Add the oil and then add the salmon, reserving the marinade. Cook the salmon, turning as necessary, until it is lightly browned on both sides.

4 Reduce the heat and pour over any reserved marinade and the sake mixture. Turn the salmon to ensure the pieces are evenly coated. Cook gently for a few minutes, until the juices form a sticky glaze on the fish.

5 Transfer the salmon to plates, garnish with sesame seeds and whole chives and serve.

COOK'S TIPS
• Dried ground ginger should not be substituted for fresh ginger.
• When buying fresh ginger, look for firm ginger with smooth skin (skin that is wrinkled means that the root is dry and will have less flavour).

SERVES FOUR

INGREDIENTS
1 garlic clove, crushed
5ml/1 tsp grated fresh root ginger
30ml/2 tbsp dark soy sauce
15ml/1 tbsp rice vinegar
400g/14oz salmon fillet, cut into
 4 portions
10ml/2 tsp sugar
15ml/1 tbsp sake or *mirin*
5ml/1 tsp maple syrup
30ml/2 tbsp light soy sauce
60ml/4 tbsp olive oil
For the garnish
5ml/1 tsp sesame seeds
whole chives

1 Combine the garlic, ginger, dark soy sauce and rice vinegar in a shallow dish large enough to hold the salmon. Mix well, then add the salmon portions and coat them with the marinade. Cover and leave to marinate for 1 hour.

Per portion Energy 239kcal/995kJ; Protein 24.8g; Carbohydrate 2.1g, of which sugars 1.7g; Fat 13.3g, of which saturates 2.3g; Cholesterol 58mg; Calcium 93mg; Fibre 0.3g; Sodium 323mg.

KING PRAWNS WITH PINE NUT DRESSING

THIS SEAFOOD DISH IS A SOPHISTICATED APPETIZER THAT HAS BEEN PASSED DOWN FROM THE ROYAL BANQUETING TABLES OF A BYGONE AGE. SUCCULENT STEAMED PRAWNS ARE MIXED WITH SHREDDED BEEF AND CRUNCHY BAMBOO SHOOTS, THEN COATED WITH A RICH DRESSING OF PINE NUTS.

SERVES TWO

INGREDIENTS
    6 large king prawns (jumbo shrimp)
    20g/¾oz fresh root ginger, peeled
      and sliced
    15ml/1 tbsp *mirin* or rice wine
    ½ cucumber
    75g/3oz bamboo shoots, sliced
    90g/3½oz beef flank
    15ml/1 tbsp vegetable oil
    salt and ground white pepper
For the dressing
    60ml/4 tbsp pine nuts
    10ml/2 tsp sesame oil
    salt and ground black pepper

1 Prepare a steamer over a pan of boiling water, with a bowl in place under the steamer to catch any liquid. Place the prawns in the steamer with the ginger, and pour over the mirin or rice wine. Steam for 8 minutes.

2 Seed the cucumber and slice it lengthways into thin strips. Sprinkle with salt, and then leave to stand for 5 minutes. Squeeze the cucumber gently to remove any liquid.　•

3 Remove the prawns from the steamer, discarding the ginger. Remove the bowl of liquid from beneath the steamer and set it aside.

4 Blanch the bamboo shoots in boiling water for 30 seconds. Remove, slice and sprinkle with salt. Add the beef to the boiling water and cook until tender. Drain and leave to cool.

5 Make a shallow cut down the centre of the back of each prawn. Pull out the black vein and then rinse the prawn thoroughly. Slice them into 2cm/½in pieces. Transfer to the refrigerator.

6 Slice the beef thinly, cut into bitesize pieces and chill in the refrigerator. Coat a frying pan or wok with the vegetable oil and quickly stir-fry the cucumber and bamboo shoots, then chill them.

7 To make the dressing, roughly grind the pine nuts in a mortar and pestle and then transfer to a bowl. Add 45ml/3 tbsp of the prawn liquid from the bowl and add the sesame oil with a pinch of salt and pepper. Mix well.

8 Set all the chilled ingredients on a platter and pour over the dressing before serving.

Per portion Energy 416kcal/1724kJ; Protein 24.7g; Carbohydrate 3.5g, of which sugars 2.7g; Fat 33.8g, of which saturates 4.3g; Cholesterol 124mg; Calcium 62mg; Fibre 1.5g; Sodium 619mg.

SEAFOOD SALAD ᴵᴺ MUSTARD DRESSING

The classic Korean ingredients of seafood, chestnuts and salad vegetables are given a new twist here with the addition of English mustard, giving the dish a pleasant heat. Simple to prepare, this is a perfect quick snack or appetizer.

SERVES TWO

INGREDIENTS

- 50g/2oz squid
- 50g/2oz king prawns (jumbo shrimp)
- 50g/2oz jellyfish (optional)
- 50g/2oz cooked whelks
- 90g/3½oz Asian pear
- ⅓ carrot
- ½ medium cucumber
- 25g/1oz Chinese leaves (Chinese cabbage), shredded
- 25g/1oz chestnuts, sliced
- 25g/1oz crab meat or seafood stick

For the dressing
- 15ml/1 tbsp ready-made English (hot) mustard
- 30ml/2 tbsp sugar
- 15ml/1 tbsp milk
- 45ml/3 tbsp cider vinegar
- 5ml/1 tsp chilli oil
- 2.5ml/½ tsp dark soy sauce
- 5ml/1 tsp salt

1 Wash the squid carefully, rinsing off any ink. Holding the body firmly, pull away the head and tentacles. If the ink sac is intact, remove it and discard. Pull out all the innards including the long transparent pen. Peel off and discard the thin purple skin on the body, but keep the two small side fins. Slice the head across just under the eyes, severing the tentacles. Discard the rest of the head.

2 Squeeze the tentacles at the head end to push out the round beak in the centre and discard. Rinse the pouch and tentacles well. (Your fishmonger will prepare squid for you if you prefer.) Score the squid with a crisscross pattern, and slice into strips about 2cm/½in wide.

3 Hold each prawn between two fingers and pull off the tail shell. Twist off the head. Peel away the soft body shell and the small claws. Make a shallow cut down the centre of the curved back of the prawn. Pull out the black vein with a cocktail stick (toothpick). Rinse well. Slice the prawns and jellyfish, if using, into similar sized pieces.

4 Bring a pan of lightly salted water to the boil and blanch the squid, prawns and jellyfish for 3 minutes, then drain. Thinly slice the whelks.

5 Peel the Asian pear. Cut the pear into thin strips and do the same with the carrot. Seed the cucumber and cut into thin strips.

6 Combine all the dressing ingredients in a bowl until they are well blended. Take a large serving platter and arrange the vegetable strips, Chinese leaves and chestnuts in rows, or fan them out around the centre of the plate.

7 Arrange the seafood on the platter, including the crab meat or seafood stick. Pour over the dressing and chill well in the refrigerator before serving.

COOK'S TIP

Although jellyfish makes an exotic component of this dish, it can be very difficult to find outside China, Japan and Korea. Selected specialist Asian stores may stock it, but outside the Far East it tends to be a rare delicacy.

Per portion Energy 206kcal/872kJ; Protein 18g; Carbohydrate 29.8g, of which sugars 23.9g; Fat 2.4g, of which saturates 0.6g; Cholesterol 230mg; Calcium 62mg; Fibre 2.4g; Sodium 1282mg.

PRAWN TEMPURA

KNOWN AS TUIGUIM IN KOREA, THIS DISH IS AN ADAPTATION OF A JAPANESE FAVOURITE. THE TRICK TO GREAT TEMPURA IS TO KEEP THE BATTER AS LIGHT AND CRISP AS POSSIBLE BY NOT STIRRING IT TOO VIGOROUSLY. BATTER MIXTURE IS AVAILABLE FROM ALL ASIAN GROCERS.

SERVES FOUR

INGREDIENTS
15 raw tiger prawns (shrimp)
5ml/1 tsp sesame oil
5ml/1 tsp sake
150g/5oz/1½ cups batter mix
50g/2oz/7 tbsp cornflour
(cornstarch)
ground black pepper
For the dipping sauce
5ml/1 tsp fish bouillon powder or
Japanese *hondashi*
50g/2oz Chinese white radish, peeled
and grated
5ml/1 tsp finely chopped fresh
root ginger
1 spring onion (scallion), finely
chopped
15ml/1 tbsp maple syrup
15ml/1 tbsp sugar
30ml/2 tbsp light soy sauce
30ml/2 tbsp lemon juice

1 Chill 250ml/8fl oz/1 cup water ready for the batter. Remove the heads and the shells from the prawns, leaving the tail intact.

2 With a sharp knife make a slit down the centre of the curved back of each prawn and remove the black vein with the point of the knife. Rinse under cold water and dry gently with kitchen paper.

3 Combine the sesame oil, sake and a little ground pepper in a bowl. Add the prawns and coat them in the mixture. Cover and place in the refrigerator for 15 minutes.

4 Meanwhile prepare the dipping sauce. Mix the bouillon powder with 100ml/ 3½fl oz/scant ½ cup warm water until it has fully dissolved.

5 Add the Chinese radish, ginger and spring onion. Thoroughly mix in the maple syrup, sugar, light soy sauce and lemon juice, then divide among four small dishes and chill.

6 Place the batter in a bowl and add the chilled water. Mix the batter gently without stirring too vigorously, as this will add air to the mixture and reduce the crispness.

7 Heat vegetable oil in a wok to 180°C/ 350°F or until a cube of day-old bread browns in 30–60 seconds. Meanwhile, place the cornflour in a bowl. Drain the prawns and coat them in the cornflour.

COOK'S TIP
To make a good fish batter yourself, combine 150g/5oz/1¼ cups yellow corn meal, ¼ tbsp black pepper, ¼ tbsp salt, ¼ tbsp paprika, ½ tbsp garlic powder and ½ tbsp garlic salt.

8 One at a time, shake the prawns lightly to remove any excess cornflour and dip them into the batter mix.

9 Deep-fry the prawns in the oil for 2 minutes, until crisp and golden. Drain on kitchen paper and serve immediately, with the dipping sauce.

Per portion Energy 221kcal/923kJ; Protein 14.1g; Carbohydrate 14.3g, of which sugars 3.5g; Fat 12.3g, of which saturates 1.5g; Cholesterol 146mg; Calcium 72mg; Fibre 0.3g; Sodium 688mg.

GRILLED TIGER PRAWNS

THIS MILDLY SPICED SEAFOOD DISH IS OFTEN ENJOYED DURING THE SUMMER AND CAN BE COOKED IN A GRIDDLE PAN OR THROWN ON THE BARBECUE. THE MARINADE ENHANCES THE FLAVOUR OF THE PRAWNS AND THE STIR-FRIED VEGETABLES ADD A BEAUTIFUL TOUCH TO THE PRESENTATION.

3 Score the skewered prawns on both sides and then place them in a bowl. Add the wine, sake and chilli oil. Season with salt and pepper, then toss the prawns to coat them evenly in the marinade and set aside for 15 minutes.

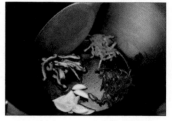

4 Meanwhile heat a wok over medium heat and add the sesame oil. One ingredient at a time, stir-fry the garlic, chillies and shiitake mushrooms, keeping them separate. Season with a pinch of salt and set aside.

SERVES TWO

INGREDIENTS
  6 raw tiger prawns (shrimp)
  10ml/2 tsp white wine
  15ml/1 tbsp sake
  2.5ml/½ tsp chilli oil
  7.5ml/1½ tsp sesame oil
  1 garlic clove, finely sliced
  ½ green chilli, seeded and sliced
  ½ red chilli, seeded and sliced
  ½ shiitake mushroom, finely sliced
  30ml/2 tbsp dark soy sauce
  a little lemon juice
  salt and ground black pepper
  finely pared lemon zest, to garnish

COOK'S TIPS
• If using wooden skewers, soak them in cold water for 15 minutes to prevent them from burning during cooking.
• This dish is well suited to the barbecue. Drizzle with marinade as the prawns cook.

1 Prepare six small skewers for the prawns. Remove the head and shell from the prawns, leaving the tail intact. Make a small slit with a sharp knife down the centre of the curved back of each prawn and remove the black vein with the point of the knife. Rinse in cold water and dry gently with kitchen paper.

2 Thread each prawn on to a skewer, piercing first through the tail and then through the head.

5 Heat a griddle pan or frying pan over medium heat and cook the prawns, brushing them with soy sauce as they cook to help prevent them from burning.

6 Grill (broil) the prawns for about 5 minutes, turning once, or until their flesh is opaque.

7 Remove the prawns from the skewers and arrange three on each plate. Add a little of the stir-fried vegetables and a squeeze of lemon juice. Garnish with a little lemon zest and serve.

Per portion Energy 142kcal/593kJ; Protein 13.4g; Carbohydrate 9g, of which sugars 8.7g; Fat 6g, of which saturates 0.7g; Cholesterol 146mg; Calcium 67mg; Fibre 0.2g; Sodium 144mg.

SPICY WHELK SALAD

THIS SALAD IS A POPULAR APPETIZER, OFTEN EATEN AS A SNACK WITH DRINKS. THE SALTINESS OF THE WHELKS MINGLES WITH THE HEAT OF THE CHILLI AND THE REFRESHING COOLNESS OF THE CUCUMBER, TO CREATE A CAPTIVATING COMBINATION OF TASTES AND TEXTURES.

SERVES TWO

INGREDIENTS
300g/11oz cooked whelks, drained
½ medium cucumber
1 carrot
2 spring onions (scallions)
1 red chilli, finely sliced
1 green chilli, finely sliced
½ onion, finely sliced
For the dressing
45ml/3 tbsp soy sauce
45ml/3 tbsp sugar
45ml/3 tbsp rice vinegar
30ml/2 tbsp Korean chilli powder
10ml/2 tsp garlic, crushed
5ml/1 tsp sesame seeds
2.5ml/½ tsp salt
2.5ml/½ tsp ground pepper
5ml/1 tsp sesame oil

1 Wash the whelks thoroughly to remove any grit and drain them well. Slice them into 1cm/½in pieces.

2 Seed the cucumber and then slice it along its length into long, thin matchstick strips. Then cut the carrot into thin strips and slice the spring onions into thin strips.

3 Blend all the ingredients for the dressing in a bowl, mixing them together thoroughly.

4 Combine the whelks with the cucumber, carrot, chillies, onion and spring onions in a large salad bowl. Pour over the dressing and toss the salad before serving.

Per portion Energy 215kcal/907kJ; Protein 25g; Carbohydrate 17g, of which sugars 14.1g; Fat 5.7g, of which saturates 1.1g; Cholesterol 338mg; Calcium 69mg; Fibre 1.8g; Sodium 1737mg.

SQUID AND SEAWEED WITH CHILLI DRESSING

THIS CHILLED SEAFOOD SALAD MAKES A GREAT APPETIZER AND REALLY DOES STIMULATE THE APPETITE. THE FLAVOURS OF CHILLI AND RICE VINEGAR ARE BALANCED BY SWEET MAPLE SYRUP, WITH THE KELP PROVIDING AN UNUSUAL AND TANTALIZING AROMA AND TASTE.

SERVES TWO

INGREDIENTS
  400g/14oz squid
  200g/7oz dried kelp, roughly
    chopped
  2 cucumbers, thinly sliced
  10ml/2 tsp sesame seeds
  6 spring onions (scallions), finely
    chopped
  2 dried red chillies, finely chopped
  salt
For the dressing
  30ml/2 tbsp rice vinegar
  2 garlic cloves, crushed
  60ml/4 tbsp *gochujang* chilli
    paste
  60ml/4 tbsp maple syrup
  15ml/1 tsp grated fresh
    root ginger

COOK'S TIP
If you can't find kelp, try spinach with a squeeze of lemon juice.

1 Wash the squid carefully, rinsing off any ink. Holding the body firmly, pull away the head and tentacles. If the ink sac is intact, remove it and discard. Pull out all the innards including the long transparent pen. Peel off and discard the thin purple skin on the body, but keep the two small side fins. Slice the head across just under the eyes, severing the tentacles. Discard the rest of the head. Squeeze the tentacles at the head end to push out the round beak in the centre and discard. Rinse the pouch and tentacles well. (Your fishmonger will prepare squid for you if you prefer.) Use a sharp knife to score the squid with a crisscross pattern, and slice into generous pieces about 4cm/1½in long.

2 Soak the kelp in cold water for 20 minutes and blanch in boiling water for 1 minute, draining it almost immediately to retain its texture and colour.

3 Squeeze any excess water from the leaves by hand. Roughly chop the kelp into bitesize pieces.

4 Put the cucumber in a colander and sprinkle with salt. Leave for 10 minutes, and pour away any excess liquid. Put the dressing ingredients in a large bowl.

5 Bring a pan of water to the boil. Blanch the squid for 3 minutes, stirring, then drain under cold running water.

6 Place the squid, cucumber and kelp on a platter and pour the dressing over the dish. Chill in the refrigerator and sprinkle with the sesame seeds, spring onions and chillies before serving.

Per portion Energy 321kcal/1354kJ; Protein 35.6g; Carbohydrate 30g, of which sugars 27.3g; Fat 7.3g, of which saturates 1.3g; Cholesterol 450mg; Calcium 247mg; Fibre 3.3g; Sodium 433mg.

SPICY STIR-FRY SQUID

THE SECRET TO THIS DISH IS TO STIR-FRY THE SQUID VERY BRIEFLY, RETAINING ITS CREAMY TEXTURE AND DISTINCTIVE FLAVOUR. THE SAUCE IS THICKENED WITH GOCHUJANG CHILLI PASTE, WHILE THE SAKE AND MAPLE SYRUP ADD A SUBTLE SWEETNESS WHICH OFFSETS THE FIERY DRESSING.

SERVES TWO TO THREE

INGREDIENTS

1 squid, cleaned and skinned
30ml/2 tbsp vegetable oil
65g/2½oz carrot, cut into fine
  strips
1 red chilli, seeded and sliced
1 green chilli, seeded and sliced
1 white onion, roughly chopped
2 cabbage leaves, roughly
  chopped
7.5ml/1½ tsp Korean chilli powder
1 garlic clove, crushed
30ml/2 tbsp sake
15ml/1 tbsp *gochujang* chilli paste
7.5ml/1½ tsp maple syrup
5ml/1 tsp sesame oil
5ml/1 tsp sesame seeds, to garnish

1 Score diagonal cuts across the squid flesh, taking care not to cut right through, and then cut the sacs into 2cm/¾in strips.

2 Heat a large pan or wok over a medium heat. Add the vegetable oil, carrot, red and green chillies, onion and cabbage and gently coat them in the oil.

3 Add the squid and the chilli powder, and toss the ingredients together until the squid has taken on the colour of the chilli powder.

4 Stir in the garlic, sake, chilli paste, maple syrup and sesame oil. Increase the heat and stir-fry until the squid is cooked and tender. Sprinkle with the sesame seeds, to garnish, and serve.

COOK'S TIP
Squid is widely available throughout the year, either fresh or frozen. The freezing and thawing process actually breaks down some of the tough muscle fibres so that the squid becomes more tender. Frozen squid is sold as tubes (bodies) and as tentacles. It has a long freezer life.

Per portion Energy 134kcal/562kJ; Protein 15.1g; Carbohydrate 4.8g, of which sugars 3.5g; Fat 6.2g, of which saturates 0.9g; Cholesterol 202mg; Calcium 23mg; Fibre 0.9g; Sodium 956mg.

FIERY OCTOPUS

Here octopus is stir-fried to give it a rich meaty texture, then smothered in a fiery chilli sauce, so the dish is an appealing medley of octopus absorbed with GOCHUJANG *spiciness and the zing of jalapeño chillies. Serve with steamed rice and a bowl of soup.*

SERVES TWO

INGREDIENTS

  2 small octopuses, cleaned and
    gutted
  15ml/1 tbsp vegetable oil
  ½ onion, sliced 5mm/¼in thick
  ½ carrot, thinly sliced
  ½ leek, thinly sliced
  75g/3oz jalapeño chillies,
    trimmed
  2 garlic cloves, crushed
  10ml/2 tsp Korean chilli powder
  5ml/1 tsp dark soy sauce
  45ml/3 tbsp *gochujang* chilli
    paste
  30ml/2 tbsp *mirin* or rice wine
  15ml/1 tbsp maple syrup
  sesame oil and sesame seeds, to
    garnish

COOK'S TIP
To make the octopus more tender, knead it with a handful of plain (all-purpose) flour and rinse in salted water.

1 Blanch the octopuses in boiling water to soften slightly, but do not leave them in too long. Drain them well, and cut into pieces that are approximately 5cm/2in long.

2 Heat the oil in a frying pan over a medium-high heat and add the onion, carrot, leek and jalapeño chillies. Stir-fry for 3 minutes.

3 Add the octopus and garlic and sprinkle over the chilli powder. Stir-fry for 3–4 minutes, or until the octopus is tender. Add the soy sauce, *gochujang* paste, *mirin* or rice wine, and maple syrup. Mix well and stir-fry for 1 minute more.

4 Transfer to a serving platter and garnish with a drizzle of sesame oil and a sprinkling of sesame seeds.

COOK'S TIPS
• If the taste is too fiery, mix some softened vermicelli noodles in with the stir-fry to dilute the chilli paste.
• Rice wine, also called *Shaoxing* rice wine, is used both for drinking and cooking, but when used for cooking it has a lower alcohol content. It is widely available in supermarkets as well as specialist Asian stores.

Per portion Energy 235kcal/988kJ; Protein 28.6g; Carbohydrate 13.2g, of which sugars 11.9g; Fat 8g, of which saturates 1.2g; Cholesterol 72mg; Calcium 76mg; Fibre 2.4g; Sodium 204mg.

SPICY SCALLOPS WITH ENOKI MUSHROOMS

FRAGRANT STEAMED SCALLOPS ARE HERE GIVEN A SPICY TWIST WITH SHREDS OF CHILLI PEPPER.
DELICATE ENOKI MUSHROOMS AND STRIPS OF SAUTÉED OMELETTE MATCH THE ELEGANT FLAVOURS OF
THE SEAFOOD, AND SHREDDED SEAWEED AND LEMON ZEST MAKE AN ATTRACTIVE GARNISH.

SERVES TWO

INGREDIENTS
    5 scallops, with shells
    30ml/2 tbsp vegetable oil
    10ml/2 tsp sesame oil
    2 egg yolks, beaten
    1 sheet dried seaweed
    1 red chilli, seeded and finely
      sliced
    ½ green (bell) pepper, finely
      sliced
    65g/2½oz enoki mushrooms
    salt and ground white
      pepper
    grated rind of 1 lemon, to
      garnish

1 First of all scrub the scallop shells. Then cut the hinge muscles at the scallop's base and lift off the rounded shell.

2 Scrape away the beard-like fringe, which is next to the white scallop with its orange coral, and remove the intestinal thread. Then you can ease the scallop and the coral right away from the shell.

3 Heat 15ml/1 tbsp vegetable oil in a wok and stir-fry the scallops until browned. Season with sesame oil, salt and pepper.

4 Place the scallop shells into a pan of boiling water and then drain. Add 10ml/2 tsp oil to the wok and heat it over a low heat.

5 Pour in the beaten egg yolks and add a pinch of salt. Cook to form a thin omelette. Once set, remove from the pan and slice into strips.

6 Cut the seaweed into thin strips. Add the chilli and the pepper to the pan, adding oil if required, and stir-fry with a pinch of salt.

7 Place the scallop shells in a steamer, and set one scallop on each shell. Place the pepper mixture, some omelette strips and some mushrooms on each shell, and steam for 4 minutes.

8 Garnish with the seaweed strips and a sprinkle of lemon rind.

COOK'S TIP
Enoki mushrooms have a mild flavour and a crunchy texture. They should be refrigerated in paper bags and can be stored for up to 14 days.

Per portion Energy 325kcal/1356kJ; Protein 27.2g; Carbohydrate 6.8g, of which sugars 3.1g; Fat 21.3g, of which saturates 3.8g; Cholesterol 249mg; Calcium 59mg; Fibre 1.2g; Sodium 193mg.

RAW BLUE CRAB <u>WITH</u> CHILLI DRESSING

This dish is unique to Korea, where the silken texture and delicate flavour of blue crab are highly prized. The chilli dressing gives the crab a delicious sweet and spicy taste, creating a dish that is perfect both as an accompaniment or as a main dish.

SERVES FOUR

INGREDIENTS
4 blue crabs, live
30ml/2 tbsp light soy sauce
50ml/2fl oz/¼ cup dark soy sauce
30ml/2 tbsp maple syrup
10ml/2 tsp sugar
60ml/4 tbsp Korean chilli powder
2 garlic cloves, crushed
5ml/1 tsp grated fresh root
  ginger
2 green chillies, seeded and
  sliced
1 red chilli, seeded and sliced
20g/¾oz watercress, chopped
2 spring onions (scallions), sliced
15ml/1 tbsp sesame seeds, to
  garnish
freshly cooked rice, to serve

1 Place the live crabs in iced water for 5 minutes to stun them, then remove and discard their top shells and small legs (these unwanted parts can be used to make stock, which can be frozen). Remove the entrails, gills and mouth parts and then split each crab into quarters with a heavy knife. Trim off the tips of the legs.

2 Place the pieces of crab in a bowl. Add the light and dark soy sauces. Cover and leave to marinate for about 30 minutes.

3 Remove the pieces of crab from the bowl, letting the sauce drip off. Stir the maple syrup, sugar and chilli powder into the sauce. Then add the garlic, ginger, chillies and watercress and mix together thoroughly.

4 Replace the crab and coat the pieces with the soy mixture. Cover and leave to marinate for 1 hour in the refrigerator.

5 Transfer the crab to a serving plate and pour over some of the marinade. Garnish with sesame seeds and serve with rice.

COOK'S TIP
Blue crab meat is delicious, but each crab has a small proportion of meat to body weight (only about 15 percent meat). The body meat is said to be tastier than claw meat, but both should be used to maximize the potential of each crab.

Per portion Energy 110kcal/464kJ; Protein 15.5g; Carbohydrate 3.7g, of which sugars 3.6g; Fat 3.9g, of which saturates 0.4g; Cholesterol 41mg; Calcium 32mg; Fibre 0.2g; Sodium 809mg.

CRAB MEAT SALAD <u>WITH</u> GARLIC DRESSING

THE COMBINATION OF ASIAN PEAR AND PINEAPPLE JUICE MAKES A LIGHT, REFRESHING COMPLEMENT TO THE SWEETNESS OF THE CRAB IN THIS RECIPE. WITH A ZESTY DRESSING CREATING A BALANCE OF FLAVOURS, THIS DISH MAKES A GREAT APPETIZER.

SERVES TWO TO THREE

INGREDIENTS
45ml/3 tbsp sugar
30ml/2 tbsp cider vinegar
30ml/2 tbsp pineapple juice
5ml/1 tsp grated fresh root ginger
1 cucumber, peeled, seeded and
  finely sliced
1 Asian pear, cored and finely sliced
10ml/2 tsp cornflour (cornstarch)
150g/5oz raw crab meat
20g/¾oz cress, to garnish
For the dressing
30ml/2 tbsp Dijon mustard
30ml/2 tbsp white wine vinegar
2 garlic cloves, crushed
15ml/1 tbsp pineapple juice
5ml/1 tsp dark soy sauce
5ml/1 tsp salt
30ml/2 tbsp sugar

1 Combine the sugar, cider vinegar, pineapple juice and ginger in a bowl. Add 1.5 litres/2½ pints/6¼ cups chilled water and stir gently until the sugar has dissolved. Add the Asian pear and cucumber and leave for 10 minutes, then drain and set aside.

2 Place the cornflour in a heatproof bowl that will fit in a steamer and add the crab meat. Mix together gently to coat the crab meat evenly.

3 Place a steamer over a pan of boiling water and put the bowl of crab meat inside it. Cover and steam for 10 minutes and then set the crab to one side to cool.

4 For the dressing, combine the mustard, vinegar, garlic, pineapple juice, soy sauce, salt and sugar, then stir in 50ml/2fl oz water.

5 Place the pear, cucumber and crab meat in a serving dish and pour over the dressing. Toss the salad and garnish with cress before serving.

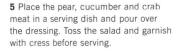

Per portion Energy 149kcal/630kJ; Protein 10.8g; Carbohydrate 21.2g, of which sugars 17.9g; Fat 2.9g, of which saturates 0.4g; Cholesterol 36mg; Calcium 34mg; Fibre 0.5g; Sodium 812mg.

CHICKEN
& PORK

Poultry marries well with sweet and spicy flavours and appears in many Korean dishes. Despite the growing popularity of deep-fried chicken, the traditional methods of griddling and stewing are still firm favourites. Spicy chicken dishes, such as the fiery sweet Gochujang Chicken Stew, are a welcome warming treat on cold nights. Pork — originally popular because it was so easily available and therefore cheap — still remains a favourite, with dishes such as Spicy Pork Stir Fry and Sweet and Sour Pork. Chilli paste is often added to pork dishes to set the tastebuds alight.

GOCHUJANG CHICKEN STEW

*THIS WARMING AUTUMN STEW IS FILLED WITH VEGETABLES AND SPICES TO WARD OFF THE COLD.
CHILLIES AND GOCHUJANG CHILLI PASTE SUPPLY A VIVID RED COLOUR AND GIVE THE CHICKEN
A FIERY QUALITY, AND A DELICIOUS HINT OF SWEETNESS OFFSETS THE PIQUANCY.*

SERVES FOUR

INGREDIENTS
  3 potatoes
  1 carrot
  2 onions
  1 chicken, about 800g/1¾lb
  30ml/2 tbsp vegetable oil
  2 garlic cloves, crushed
  3 green chillies, seeded and
    finely sliced
  1 red chilli, seeded and
    finely sliced
  15ml/1 tbsp sesame oil
  salt and ground black pepper
  2 spring onions (scallions), finely
    chopped, to garnish
For the marinade
  30ml/2 tbsp *mirin* or rice wine
  salt and ground black pepper
For the seasoning
  15ml/1 tbsp sesame seeds
  10ml/2 tsp light soy sauce
  30ml/2 tbsp *gochujang* chilli
    paste
  45ml/3 tbsp Korean chilli
    powder

1 Peel the potatoes and cut into
bitesize pieces. Soak them in cold
water for approximately 15–20 minutes
and then drain.

2 Peel the carrot and onions and cut
into medium-size pieces.

3 Divide up the whole of the chicken,
including the skin and bone. Then
cut it into bitesize pieces and place
in a dish.

4 Combine the marinade ingredients
and pour over the chicken. Stir to coat
thoroughly and leave for 10 minutes.

5 Heat 15ml/1 tbsp vegetable oil in a
frying pan or wok and quickly stir-fry
the crushed garlic. Add the chicken and
stir-fry, draining off any fat that comes
from the meat during cooking. When
lightly browned, place the chicken on
kitchen paper to remove any excess oil.

6 To make the seasoning, grind the
sesame seeds in a mortar and pestle.
Combine the soy sauce, *gochujang*
paste, chilli powder and the ground
sesame seeds in a bowl and mix
together thoroughly.

7 In a pan heat the remaining
vegetable oil and add the potatoes,
carrot and onions. Briefly cook over
a medium heat, stirring, then add
the chicken.

8 Pour over enough water so that
two-thirds of the meat and vegetables
are immersed in the water, and bring
the pan to the boil. Then add the
chilli seasoning and reduce the heat.
Stir the seasoning into the water and
simmer until the volume of liquid has
reduced by about one-third. Add the
sliced chillies.

9 Simmer for a little longer until the
liquid has thickened slightly.

10 Add the sesame oil, transfer the
contents to deep serving bowls and
garnish with the chopped spring onion
before serving.

COOK'S TIP
When selecting a chicken, always make
a point of using a good quality, or
preferably an organic, one as the results
are far tastier.

Per portion Energy 470kcal/1955kJ; Protein 27.4g; Carbohydrate 20.4g, of which sugars 4.7g; Fat 31.5g, of which saturates 7.5g; Cholesterol 128mg; Calcium 56mg; Fibre 2.3g; Sodium 296mg.

SWEET AND SPICY CHICKEN

THIS DEEP-FRIED CHICKEN DISH HAS A SPICY KICK, MELLOWED BY THE SWEETNESS OF PINEAPPLE AND MAPLE SYRUP. THE CRISP GOLDEN EXTERIOR ENVELOPS THE SOFT TEXTURE OF THE MEAT, AND CHILLI AND GARLIC GIVE THIS RECIPE A REALLY TANGY TASTE.

SERVES THREE

INGREDIENTS

675g/1½lb chicken breast fillets or
  boneless thighs
175g/6oz/1½ cups cornflour
  (cornstarch)
vegetable oil, for deep-frying
2 green chillies, sliced
2 dried red chillies, seeded and
  sliced
3 walnuts, finely chopped
salt and ground black pepper

For the marinade
15ml/1 tbsp white wine
15ml/1 tbsp dark soy sauce
3 garlic cloves, crushed
½ onion, finely chopped

For the sauce
15ml/1 tbsp chilli oil
2.5ml/½ tsp *gochujang* chilli paste
30ml/2 tbsp dark soy sauce
7.5ml/1½ tsp pineapple juice
15 garlic cloves, peeled
30ml/2 tbsp maple syrup
15ml/1 tbsp sugar

1 Slice the chicken into bitesize strips and season with the salt and pepper.

2 Combine all the marinade ingredients in a large bowl. Mix well and add the chicken, rubbing the mixture thoroughly into the meat. Leave to marinate for 20 minutes.

3 Sprinkle the marinated chicken with a thin coating of cornflour, covering the meat well and evenly. Fill a wok or medium heavy pan one-third full of vegetable oil and heat over a high heat to 170°C/340°F.

4 Add the chicken and deep-fry for 3–5 minutes, or until golden brown. Remove the chicken and drain on kitchen paper to remove any excess oil.

5 Blend all the sauce ingredients together in a large pan, adding the garlic cloves whole, and heat over a medium heat.

6 Once the sauce is bubbling, add the fried chicken and stir to coat the meat with the sauce.

7 Leave to simmer until the sauce has formed a sticky glaze over the chicken, and add the chillies. Transfer to a serving dish and garnish with the walnuts.

Per portion Energy 655kcal/2749kJ; Protein 56.4g; Carbohydrate 45.3g, of which sugars 14.4g; Fat 28.8g, of which saturates 3.5g; Cholesterol 158mg; Calcium 34mg; Fibre 0.4g; Sodium 1249mg.

CHICKEN AND VEGETABLES IN CHILLI SAUCE

WITH A MEDLEY OF CRUNCHY VEGETABLES FOR TEXTURE AND RICE CAKE TO HELP DIFFUSE SOME OF THE SPICINESS, THIS RECIPE IS ALWAYS A POPULAR FAVOURITE AT FAMILY GATHERINGS IN KOREA. THE DISH IS VERY PIQUANT, SO DON'T OFFER IT TO THE FAINTHEARTED.

SERVES FOUR

INGREDIENTS
    500g/1¼lb chicken breast fillet
    115g/4oz rice cake, sliced
    150g/5oz sweet potato, finely diced
    ½ white onion, thinly sliced
    1 carrot, thinly sliced
    4 cabbage leaves, thinly sliced
    50g/2oz *perilla* or *shiso* leaves, thinly
        sliced
    1 leek, finely sliced
    2 green chillies, seeded and sliced
    vegetable oil, for cooking
For the marinade
    45ml/3 tbsp *gochujang* chilli paste
    22.5ml/4½ tsp Korean chilli powder
    30ml/2 tbsp soy sauce
    30ml/2 tbsp maple syrup
    22.5ml/4½ tsp sugar
    30ml/2 tbsp sake or mirin
    3 garlic cloves, crushed
    22.5ml/4½ tsp grated fresh root
        ginger
    15ml/1 tbsp sesame oil
    15ml/1 tbsp sesame seeds
    7.5ml/1½ tsp Korean or Japanese
        curry powder

1 Prepare the marinade in a large bowl. Thoroughly mix the chilli paste and powder, soy sauce, maple syrup, sugar, sake or mirin, garlic, ginger, sesame oil and seeds, and curry powder.

2 Slice the chicken into bitesize pieces with a sharp knife and add them to the marinade. Coat the pieces thoroughly with the mixture and leave to stand for 1 hour.

3 Heat a little vegetable oil in a wok and add the rice cake and sweet potato. Stir-fry, then add the marinated chicken and stir-fry for a further 6 minutes.

4 Stir in the onion, carrot and cabbage and stir-fry for a further 3 minutes, then remove from the heat.

5 Add the perilla or shiso, leek and chillies. Toss the ingredients together and serve.

COOK'S TIP
The chicken is very spicy, so a bowl of rice, salad or water *kimchi* are the best accompaniments to the dish.

Per portion Energy 368kcal/1545kJ; Protein 32.8g; Carbohydrate 37.5g, of which sugars 19g; Fat 10.2g, of which saturates 1.6g; Cholesterol 88mg; Calcium 47mg; Fibre 3.3g; Sodium 1033mg.

FIERY SOY CHICKEN WITH NOODLES

THIS DISH IS A FAVOURITE FROM ANDONG, A PROVINCE IN THE SOUTH OF THE KOREAN PENINSULA WHICH IS FAMOUS FOR ITS FOOD AND DRINK. BRAISING MAKES THE CHICKEN WONDERFULLY TENDER, WHILE ALLOWING THE SOY SAUCE TO RELEASE ITS NUTTY FLAVOUR AND LOSE ITS SALTINESS.

SERVES FOUR

INGREDIENTS
1 chicken, about 800g/1¾lb
22.5ml/4½ tsp grated fresh root ginger
45ml/3 tbsp white wine
75g/3oz glass noodles
30ml/2 tbsp vegetable oil
2 dried red chillies, sliced
2 small green chillies, seeded and sliced
1 carrot, diced
150g/5oz potato, diced
½ cucumber, roughly chopped
½ cabbage
½ white onion, diced
1 leek, roughly chopped
For the sauce
100ml/3½fl oz/scant ½ cup soy sauce
75ml/5 tbsp brown sugar
45ml/3 tbsp maple syrup
75ml/5 tbsp sake or *mirin*
30ml/2 tbsp crushed garlic
7.5ml/1½ tsp grated fresh root ginger
15ml/1 tbsp sesame oil
5ml/1 tsp caramel
7.5ml/1½ tsp sesame seeds
ground black pepper

1 Cut the chicken, with skin and bone, into pieces about 4cm/1½in wide. Bring a pan of water to the boil. Add the chicken and boil for 3 minutes, then drain and place in a bowl.

2 Add the ginger and white wine to the chicken and mix thoroughly. Leave to stand for about 30 minutes.

3 Meanwhile place the noodles in a bowl and pour in warm water to cover, then set aside to soak for 10 minutes.

4 For the sauce, mix the soy sauce, sugar, maple syrup, sake or *mirin*, garlic, ginger, sesame oil, caramel and sesame seeds in a bowl. Mix well, adding pepper to taste.

5 Heat a wok or pan over a medium heat. Add the vegetable oil and briefly stir-fry the chillies. Add the chicken and stir-fry briefly, then pour in the sauce.

6 Stir-fry for a further 2 minutes. Pour in enough water to cover the chicken and increase the heat to bring the sauce to the boil.

7 Once the mixture is boiling add the carrot and potatoes. Boil until the liquid has reduced by half. Add the cucumber, cabbage and onion.

8 Reduce the heat and part-cover the pan, then simmer until most of the liquid has evaporated and the chicken and vegetables are cooked but not overcooked. Stir occasionally during cooking to ensure that the ingredients do not burn.

9 Add the leek and glass noodles to the pan and mix the ingredients thoroughly. Serve the chicken with a side dish of *kimchi* or vegetable *namul*.

COOK'S TIP
Glass noodles are also known as transparent cellophane noodles, bean threads, Chinese vermicelli and *bai fun*. Made from the starch of mung beans they offer a good wheat-free ingredient.

Per portion Energy 538kcal/2254kJ; Protein 28.5g; Carbohydrate 51.5g, of which sugars 31.9g; Fat 25.5g, of which saturates 6.6g; Cholesterol 128mg; Calcium 64mg; Fibre 1.8g; Sodium 1961mg.

CHICKEN <u>WITH</u> SOY DRESSING

This dish, a favourite of the Korean royal court, smothers tender chicken in a rich mushroom sauce. Strips of poultry are coated with a sticky glaze that blends woodland flavours with soy sauce and ginger. Serve with rice, soup and Kimchi.

SERVES TWO

INGREDIENTS
1 leek, roughly sliced
10ml/2 tsp chopped fresh root
    ginger
300g/11oz chicken breast fillet
10ml/2 tsp sesame oil, plus extra
    for drizzling
salt and ground black pepper
For the sauce
6 dried shiitake mushrooms,
    soaked in warm water for about
    30 minutes
30ml/2 tbsp vegetable oil
1 garlic clove, finely chopped
10 oyster mushrooms, sliced
30ml/2 tbsp dark soy sauce
60ml/4 tbsp maple syrup
30ml/2 tbsp plain
    (all-purpose) flour
2 eggs, beaten
salt and ground black pepper

1 Place the leek, root ginger and chicken in a pan, cover with water and bring to the boil. After 5 minutes remove the chicken from the water with a slotted spoon. Strain the liquid into a measuring jug (cup).

2 When the soaked shiitake mushrooms have reconstituted and become soft, drain and slice them, discarding the tough stems.

3 Tear the cooked chicken into strips and add salt, pepper and sesame oil.

4 Stir-fry the garlic in the vegetable oil and add the mushrooms and soy sauce. Sauté for a few minutes.

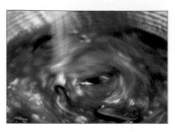

5 Pour in 300ml/½ pint/1¼ cups of stock. Add the maple syrup and stir. Bring the sauce to the boil, add the flour and simmer, stirring until the sauce thickens. Add the beaten egg, gently poaching it.

6 Place the strips of chicken on a serving platter, pour over the mushroom sauce and drizzle with sesame oil.

COOK'S TIP
Oyster mushrooms are available in colours that range from soft brown to grey. Their delicate, mild flavour and velvety texture are hard to match, but they can be substituted with cooked white mushrooms. Keep them refrigerated in paper bags and they will be fresh for up to 7 days.

Per portion Energy 567kcal/2381kJ; Protein 47.2g; Carbohydrate 39.7g, of which sugars 27.3g; Fat 25.6g, of which saturates 4.5g; Cholesterol 314mg; Calcium 95mg; Fibre 3.2g; Sodium 1321mg.

CHICKEN MARINATED <u>IN</u> CHILLI PASTE

HOT, SPICY, GARLICKY AND A LITTLE SWEET, THIS IS A TRULY TASTY DISH. GRIDDLED FOR A VERSION THAT IS QUICK TO PREPARE, IT HAS THE SAME DELICIOUS SCORCHED FLAVOUR AS THE SLOW-SMOKED VARIETY. STUFFED CUCUMBER KIMCHI MAKES A REFRESHING ACCOMPANIMENT.

SERVES FOUR

INGREDIENTS

   900g/2lb chicken breast fillet or
     boneless thighs
   2 round (butterhead) lettuces
   vegetable oil
   4 spring onions (scallions), shredded
For the marinade
   60ml/4 tbsp *gochujang* chilli paste
   45ml/3 tbsp mirin or rice wine
   15ml/1 tbsp dark soy sauce
   4 garlic cloves, crushed
   25ml/1½ tsp sesame oil
   15ml/1 tbsp grated fresh root
     ginger
   2 spring onions (scallions), finely
     chopped
   10ml/2 tsp ground black pepper
   15ml/1 tbsp lemonade

COOK'S TIP
In restaurants, lettuce wraps are usually offered as an appetizer, but they can also be a very successful main course. Children enjoy them as they can eat them with their hands.

1 Combine all the *gochujang* marinade ingredients thoroughly.

2 Cut the chicken into bitesize pieces, and coat it with the marinade.

3 Marinate the chicken in the refrigerator for about 3 hours.

4 Remove the outer leaves from the heads of lettuce, keeping them whole. Rinse well and place in a serving dish.

5 Lightly coat a heavy griddle pan or frying pan with vegetable oil and place it over a medium heat (the griddle can be used over charcoal).

6 Griddle the chicken for 15 minutes, or until the meat is cooked and has turned a deep brown. Increase the heat briefly to scorch the chicken and give it a smoky flavour.

7 Serve by wrapping the chicken pieces in lettuce leaves with a few shredded spring onions.

VARIATIONS
Butterhead lettuces are perfect to use as wraps because the leaves are so soft and tender, but you can choose to substitute them with red leaf lettuce, iceberg lettuce, romaine lettuce or the slightly bitter escarole.

Per portion Energy 279kcal/1178kJ; Protein 55g; Carbohydrate 2g, of which sugars 2g; Fat 5.7g, of which saturates 1.1g; Cholesterol 158mg; Calcium 39mg; Fibre 0.9g; Sodium 405mg.

PORK GOCHUJANG STEW

THIS DELICIOUS STEW OF TENDER PORK LOIN IS VIBRANTLY COLOURED WITH RED CHILLI AND HAS A FIERY TASTE TO MATCH. THE SUCCULENT PORK IS COOKED WITH AN ARRAY OF VEGETABLES IN AN AROMATIC, THICK SOUP WITH AN UPLIFTING KICK OF GINGER.

SERVES FOUR

INGREDIENTS
 250g/9oz pork loin
 30ml/2 tbsp vegetable oil
 1 garlic clove, crushed
 30ml/2 tbsp *gochujang* chilli paste
 5ml/1 tsp Korean chilli powder
 90g/3½oz potato, cubed
 20g/¾oz fresh root ginger, peeled
 1 green chilli, sliced
 ½ leek, sliced
 1 courgette (zucchini), sliced
 5ml/1 tsp sesame oil
 50g/2oz *minari*, watercress or rocket
  (arugula), roughly chopped
 5ml/1 tsp sesame seeds, to garnish

1 Trim any excess fat from the pork and roughly cut the meat into bitesize cubes. Place a heavy pan over a high heat and add the vegetable oil. Add the garlic and pork and stir until the meat is lightly browned on all sides. Then add the *gochujang* chilli paste and chilli powder, and briefly sauté the ingredients, evenly coating the meat with the spices.

2 Add the potato, fresh root ginger and chilli and then pour in enough water to cover all the ingredients. Bring the pan to the boil and add the leek, courgette and sesame oil. Stir the mixture well and cover the pan. Cook over a high heat for 3 minutes, then reduce the heat and simmer for a further 5 minutes. Skim off any excess fat from the surface as the dish stews.

3 Remove from the heat and stir in the *minari*, watercress or rocket. Discard the root ginger and ladle the stew into bowls. Garnish with the sesame seeds before serving.

COOK'S TIP
To make this dish spicier increase the quantity of *gochujang* chilli paste, but be careful as a little makes a big difference.

Per portion Energy 220kcal/918kJ; Protein 17.2g; Carbohydrate 15.2g, of which sugars 2.2g; Fat 10.6g, of which saturates 2g; Cholesterol 39mg; Calcium 45mg; Fibre 1.6g; Sodium 55mg.

GRIDDLED DOENJANG PORK

DOENJANG *SOYA BEAN PASTE GIVES A LOVELY ROAST-CHESTNUT FLAVOUR TO THE PORK IN THIS RECIPE, MARRYING WELL WITH THE GRIDDLED TASTE OF THE MEAT. THE MARINADE IS MILD AND GIVES THE PORK A SUCCULENT BARBECUE TEXTURE.*

SERVES THREE

INGREDIENTS
675g/1½lb pork loin
2 round (butterhead) lettuces
4 spring onions (scallions),
   shredded
For the marinade
30ml/2 tbsp *doenjang* soya bean
   paste
15ml/1 tbsp Thai fish sauce
22.5ml/4½ tsp sugar
1 spring onion (scallion), finely
   chopped
5ml/1 tsp grated fresh root ginger
1 onion, finely chopped
5ml/1 tsp cornflour (cornstarch)
1 garlic clove, crushed
15ml/1 tbsp *mirin* or rice wine
15ml/1 tbsp milk
salt and ground black pepper

COOK'S TIP
You can store fresh root ginger in an airtight container in the refrigerator for up to a month. It is also possible to freeze whole ginger pieces, or grated ginger, and it will thaw quickly. When buying ginger, look for sections that are plump, and avoid wrinkled skin.

1 Trim off any excess fat and roughly cut the pork into bitesize pieces.

2 To make the marinade, put the *doenjang* paste, Thai fish sauce, sugar, spring onion and ginger in a large bowl and then mix the ingredients together thoroughly.

3 Add the onion, cornflour and garlic, and pour in the *mirin* or rice wine and milk. Season with salt and pepper and mix well.

4 Add the pork to the bowl and coat it well with the marinade. Leave the mixture in the bowl for approximately 30 minutes.

5 Remove the outer leaves from the heads of lettuce, keeping them whole. Rinse them well and place them in a serving dish.

6 Place a heavy griddle pan or frying pan over a high heat and once hot reduce to a medium heat (the griddle can be used over charcoal). Add the marinated pork and cook well, turning as required. The meat should be well done, with the exterior seared and slightly blackened and no pinkness inside.

7 Serve by wrapping the meat in a lettuce leaf with pieces of shredded spring onions.

Per portion Energy 355kcal/1493kJ; Protein 50g; Carbohydrate 17.4g, of which sugars 12.4g; Fat 9.9g, of which saturates 3.4g; Cholesterol 142mg; Calcium 74mg; Fibre 1.7g; Sodium 168mg.

POACHED PORK WRAPPED ᴵᴺ CHINESE LEAVES

Meltingly tender pork, imbued with the flavours of doenjang *soya bean paste and garlic, is combined with a zesty radish stuffing and wrapped in parcels of Chinese leaves. This dish, called* bossam, *is perfect as an appetizer or as a nibble with drinks.*

SERVES THREE TO FOUR

INGREDIENTS

   1 head Chinese leaves (Chinese
     cabbage)
   5 garlic cloves, roughly chopped
   ½ onion, roughly chopped
   1 leek, roughly chopped
   15ml/1 tbsp *doenjang* soya bean
     paste
   120ml/4fl oz/½ cup sake or rice wine
   675g/1½lb pork neck
   salt
   sugar
For the stuffing
   500g/1¼lb Chinese white radish,
     peeled and thinly sliced
   3 chestnuts, sliced
   ½ Asian pear, sliced
   65g/2½oz *minari*, watercress,
     or rocket (arugula), chopped
   45ml/3 tbsp Korean chilli powder
   5ml/1 tsp Thai fish sauce
   2 garlic cloves, crushed
   2.5ml/½ tsp grated fresh root ginger
   5ml/1 tsp honey
   5ml/1 tsp sesame seeds

1 Soak the whole head of Chinese leaves in salty water (using 50g/2oz of salt) for about 1 hour, or until the leaves have softened.

2 To make the stuffing, put the white radish into a colander and sprinkle with salt. Leave to stand for 10 minutes, then rinse and transfer to a large bowl.

3 Add the chestnuts, pear and chopped *minari*, watercress or rocket to the bowl and mix together well.

4 Add the other stuffing ingredients, with salt to taste, and stir thoroughly.

5 Prepare the poaching liquid by putting the garlic, onion and leek in a large pan. Mix in the *doenjang* soya bean paste and sake or rice wine, and then add the pork. Add enough water to cover the pork and heat to bring the liquid to the boil.

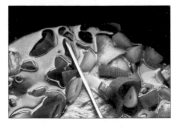

6 Cook the pork for 30–40 minutes, until tender. To test if the meat is ready, push a skewer into the meat – it should pass through cleanly.

7 Drain the Chinese leaves and tear off the leaves, keeping them whole, and place them on a serving plate.

8 Transfer the stuffing mixture to a serving dish. Once the pork is cooked, remove it from the liquid and slice it into thin bitesize pieces. Serve the pork with the stuffing and Chinese leaves.

9 To eat, take a slice of the pork and place it on a Chinese leaf. Then spoon a little of the stuffing on to the meat, and wrap it into a parcel before eating it.

Per portion Energy 332kcal/1391kJ; Protein 40.2g; Carbohydrate 18.7g, of which sugars 14.9g; Fat 7.9g, of which saturates 2.6g; Cholesterol 106mg; Calcium 136mg; Fibre 5.9g; Sodium 507mg.

SPICY PORK STIR-FRY

THIS SIMPLE DISH, CALLED CHEYUK BOKUM, *IS QUICK TO PREPARE AND MAKES THE THINLY SLICED PORK FABULOUSLY SPICY. THE POTENT FLAVOUR OF* GOCHUJANG *CHILLI PASTE THAT PREDOMINATES IN THE SEASONING FOR THE PORK WILL SET THE TASTEBUDS AFLAME. SERVE WITH A BOWL OF RICE.*

SERVES TWO

INGREDIENTS
    400g/14oz pork shoulder
    1 onion
    ½ carrot
    2 spring onions (scallions)
    15ml/1 tbsp vegetable oil
    ½ red chilli, finely sliced
    ½ green chilli, finely sliced
    steamed rice and miso soup, to serve
For the seasoning
    30ml/2 tbsp dark soy sauce
    30ml/2 tbsp *gochujang* chilli paste
    30ml/2 tbsp *mirin* or rice wine
    15ml/1 tbsp Korean chilli powder
    1 garlic clove, finely chopped
    1 spring onion (scallion), finely
      chopped
    15ml/1 tbsp grated fresh root ginger
    15ml/1 tbsp sesame oil
    30ml/2 tbsp sugar
    ground black pepper

COOK'S TIP
This dish also works well with chicken.
Replace the pork shoulder with
400g/14oz chicken thighs and omit the
ginger from the seasoning.

1 Freeze the pork shoulder for
30 minutes and then slice it thinly, to
about 5mm/¼in thick. Cut the onion
and carrot into thin strips and roughly
slice the spring onions lengthways.

3 Heat a wok or large frying pan, and
add the vegetable oil.

5 Once the pork has lightly browned
add the seasoning and thoroughly coat
the meat and vegetables. Stir-fry for 2
minutes more, or until the pork is
cooked through. Serve immediately with
rice and a bowl of miso soup to help
neutralize the spicy flavours of the dish.

2 To make the seasoning, combine the
seasoning ingredients in a large bowl,
mixing together thoroughly to form a
paste. Add a splash of water if needed.

4 Once the oil is smoking, add the pork,
onion, carrot, spring onions and chillies,
in that order. Stir-fry, keeping the
ingredients moving all the time.

Per portion Energy 430kcal/1799kJ; Protein 44.1g; Carbohydrate 21.3g, of which sugars 20.4g; Fat 19.2g, of which saturates 4.3g; Cholesterol 126mg; Calcium 44mg; Fibre 1.2g; Sodium 1216mg.

PORK BELLY <u>WITH</u> SESAME DIP

SAMGYUPSAL IS A HUGELY POPULAR DISH IN KOREA, AND IS OFTEN ENJOYED AS AN EVENING SNACK WITH A GLASS OF SOJU. THINLY SLICED PORK BELLY IS GRIDDLED UNTIL THE OUTSIDE IS CRISP, LEAVING A SMOOTH TEXTURED CENTRE. THE MEAT IS THEN IMMERSED IN A SALTY SESAME DIP, BEFORE BEING WRAPPED IN LETTUCE LEAVES WITH A SPOONFUL OF RED CHILLI SAUCE.

SERVES THREE

INGREDIENTS
  675g/1½lb pork belly
  2 round (butterhead) lettuces
For the dip
  45ml/3 tbsp sesame oil
  10ml/2 tsp salt
  ground black pepper
For the sauce
  45ml/3 tbsp *gochujang* chilli paste
  75ml/5 tbsp *doenjang* soya bean
    paste
  2 garlic cloves, crushed
  1 spring onion (scallion), finely
    chopped
  5ml/1 tsp sesame oil

1 Freeze the pork belly for 30 minutes and then slice it very thinly, to about 3mm/⅛in thick. (You could ask the butcher to do this, or buy the meat pre-sliced at an Asian store.)

2 To make the dip, combine the sesame oil, salt and pepper in a small serving bowl.

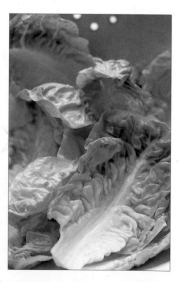

3 To make the sauce, blend the chilli paste, *doenjang* soya bean paste, garlic, spring onion and sesame oil in a bowl, mixing the oil thoroughly into the paste. Transfer to a serving bowl.

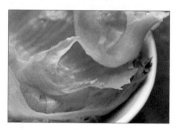

4 Remove the outer leaves from the heads of the lettuce, keeping them whole. Rinse well and place in a serving dish.

5 Heat a griddle pan or frying pan over a high heat (the griddle can be used over charcoal).Then add the sliced pork to the pan and cook until the surface of the pork is crisp and golden brown.

6 Serve the pork with the accompanying dishes of lettuce, sesame dip and chilli sauce. To eat, take a strip of pork and dip it into the sesame dip. Then place the meat in a lettuce leaf and add a small spoonful of the chilli sauce. Wrap the lettuce leaf into a parcel and enjoy.

COOK'S TIP
Any soft green leaf lettuce can be used; for example, Little Gem (Bibb) or any kind of crisphead lettuce such as iceberg. Rinse well before eating.

VARIATION
You can add other ingredients to the lettuce parcel, if you like. Some popular additions include shredded spring onion, sliced *kimchi* or sliced raw garlic.

Per portion Energy 991kcal/4093kJ; Protein 37g; Carbohydrate 1.1g, of which sugars 0.6g; Fat 93.1g, of which saturates 31.4g; Cholesterol 162mg; Calcium 37mg; Fibre 1.2g; Sodium 1475mg.

SWEET AND SOUR PORK

ALTHOUGH VERY SIMILAR TO THE CLASSIC CHINESE DISH, THIS KOREAN VERSION HAS A MORE SUBTLE TASTE AND A MORE DELICATE TEXTURE. CUBES OF TENDER GOLDEN PORK WITH A HINT OF GINGER COMBINE WITH CRUNCHY SWEET PEPPERS IN A DELIGHTFULLY STICKY SAUCE.

SERVES TWO

INGREDIENTS
  200g/7oz pork fillet (tenderloin), cubed
  90g/3½oz/¾ cup potato
    starch
  1 egg, beaten
  vegetable oil, for deep-frying
For the marinade
  5ml/1 tsp dark soy sauce
  7.5ml/1½ tsp *mirin* or rice wine
  15ml/1 tbsp finely grated fresh root
    ginger
For the sauce
  1 dried shiitake mushroom, soaked
    in warm water for about 30
    minutes until softened
  ½ onion
  ½ green (bell) pepper
  ¼ carrot
  25g/1oz pineapple
  15ml/1 tbsp vegetable oil
  10ml/2 tsp dark soy sauce
  60ml/4 tbsp sugar
  30ml/2 tbsp cider vinegar

1 Add the potato starch to 250ml/8fl oz/ 1 cup water and leave for 1 hour. The starch should sink to the bottom.

2 Marinate the pork with the soy sauce, *mirin* or rice wine, and grated ginger. Leave to marinate for 20 minutes.

3 When the soaked shiitake mushroom for the sauce has become soft, drain and finely slice it, discarding the stem.

4 Cut the onion, pepper and carrot into cubes. Finely chop the pineapple.

5 Drain the excess water from the top of the starch and water mixture. In a bowl combine the soaked starch with the beaten egg. Add the cubes of pork and evenly coat them in the batter.

6 Fill a wok or medium heavy pan one-third full of vegetable oil and heat over a high heat to 170°C/340°F, or when a small piece of bread dropped into the oil browns in 15 seconds. Add the battered pork and deep-fry for 1–2 minutes, or until golden brown. Remove the pork and drain on kitchen paper to remove any excess oil.

7 Coat a pan with the vegetable oil and place over a high heat. Add the onion, pepper and carrot and stir-fry.

8 Add 250ml/8fl oz/1 cup hot water, the soy sauce, sugar and vinegar, and simmer briefly before adding the mushroom and pineapple. Simmer for 1–2 minutes, add the egg mixture and stir until thickened.

9 Place the fried pork on a serving plate and pour the sauce liberally over the top. Serve the dish immediately.

Per portion Energy 727kcal/3035kJ; Protein 32.8g; Carbohydrate 76.5g, of which sugars 39.4g; Fat 32.8g, of which saturates 5.8g; Cholesterol 272mg; Calcium 85mg; Fibre 2.7g; Sodium 1048mg.

GRILLED GREEN TEA PORK <u>WITH</u> SOYA DIP

THE GREEN TEA IN THIS RECIPE ADDS A CRISP TEXTURE AND INVIGORATING FLAVOUR. THE COMBINATION OF DOENJANG AND GOCHUJANG PASTE IN THE DIP CREATES A FUSION OF NUTTY AND SPICY FLAVOURS, WHICH ACCENTUATE THE TASTE OF THE GRILLED MEAT PERFECTLY.

SERVES THREE TO FOUR

INGREDIENTS
- 675g/1½lb boneless pork belly, sliced
- 130g/4½oz Chinese chives
- ½ white onion, thinly sliced
- 1 small slice red cabbage, about 20g/¾oz, thinly sliced
- 15ml/1 tbsp Korean chilli powder
- 7.5ml/1½ tsp sesame oil
- 15ml/1 tbsp vinegar
- 7.5ml/1½ tsp soy sauce
- powdered green tea
- salt and ground black pepper
- sesame seeds, to garnish

For the dip
- 15ml/1 tbsp *doenjang* soya bean paste
- 7.5ml/1½ tsp *gochujang* chilli paste
- 1 spring onion (scallion)
- 5ml/1 tsp chopped garlic
- 30ml/2 tbsp grated white onion
- 7.5ml/1½ tsp sesame oil

1 Place the pork in a dish. Season with salt and pepper and leave to stand for 20 minutes.

2 Cut the chives into 4cm/1½in lengths and mix with the onion and red cabbage in a bowl of cold water as the vegetables are prepared.

3 Drain the chives and then add the chilli powder, sesame oil, vinegar and soy sauce. Combine the ingredients thoroughly and leave them to stand until the pork is cooked to allow the flavours to mingle.

4 Make the dip by combining the soya bean and chilli pastes with the spring onion, garlic, white onion and sesame oil in a bowl. Mix thoroughly.

5 Heat a pan over a medium heat. Dry the pork on kitchen paper and add to the pan. Sprinkle over half the green tea, then flip the pork over.

6 Coat the top of the pork with the remaining green tea and turn the pieces, then cook until the underneath is brown. Make sure both sides are browned evenly.

7 Arrange the pork and vegetables on plates and serve with small dishes of the dip, sprinkled with sesame seeds.

Per portion Energy 692kcal/2862kJ; Protein 28.5g; Carbohydrate 6g, of which sugars 1.6g; Fat 62g, of which saturates 22.4g; Cholesterol 122mg; Calcium 60mg; Fibre 0.8g; Sodium 264mg.

BARBECUED PORK RIB IN CHILLI SAUCE

POPULAR AS A SNACK TO ACCOMPANY A GLASS OF SOJU, THESE PORK RIBS ARE SERVED WITH GREEN LEAVES TO WRAP THE MEAT BEFORE EATING. THE PORK IS GLAZED WITH A SWEET AND SPICY SAUCE AND HAS A WONDERFULLY CHARRED, SMOKY TASTE WITH A LOVELY CHEWY TEXTURE.

SERVES FOUR

INGREDIENTS
- 1kg/2¼lb pork ribs
- 60ml/4 tbsp *gochujang* chilli paste
- 45ml/3 tbsp Korean chilli powder
- 30ml/2 tbsp sake or *mirin*
- 60ml/4 tbsp sugar
- 30ml/2 tbsp soy sauce
- ½ white onion, grated
- 4 garlic cloves, crushed
- 7.5ml/1½ tsp grated fresh root ginger
- 45ml/3 tbsp maple syrup
- 30ml/2 tbsp sesame oil
- salt and ground black pepper
- sesame seeds, to garnish

COOK'S TIP
The barbecued pork is best served with an accompaniment of green leaves, in which the meat can be wrapped before eating with fingers.

1 Place the pork ribs in a large bowl and pour in enough cold water to cover them, then leave them to soak for about 20 minutes. Drain the ribs and pat dry with kitchen paper.

2 Remove the bones from the ribs and trim off any excess fat. Slice the meat into 5cm/2in pieces.

3 Make the marinade. Mix the chilli paste and powder, sake or *mirin*, sugar, soy sauce, onion, garlic, ginger, maple syrup, sesame oil, salt and pepper in a bowl. Mix well. Add the meat and coat thoroughly with the mixture. Place in the refrigerator and leave it to marinate for at least 3 hours.

4 Heat a griddle or frying pan over a medium heat and add the pork with the marinade. Cook, turning the pieces once or twice, for 25–30 minutes, until the pork is properly cooked and the sauce has formed a glaze.

5 Arrange the pork on a serving plate. Sprinkle with sesame seeds to garnish and serve.

Per portion Energy 638kcal/2663kJ; Protein 49.9g; Carbohydrate 20g, of which sugars 13.8g; Fat 40.8g, of which saturates 14.1g; Cholesterol 165mg; Calcium 83mg; Fibre 1.1g; Sodium 994mg.

BEEF

Beef is a favourite meat among Koreans who like its rich flavours and textures. It is often barbecued, charcoal grilled or flame grilled. One popular dish is bulgogi, made from thin sirloin strips marinated in sesame oil and soy sauce and grilled, creating a delicious glaze. Beef is usually seasoned before cooking, to allow it to soak up the flavourings. A favourite summer meal is chilled ribbons of beef such as Ribbon Beef Tartare. Spicy beef soups, such as Simmered Short Ribs in Noodle Soup, are enjoyed in the winter for their hearty, nourishing quality.

SIMMERED SHORT RIBS <u>IN</u> NOODLE SOUP

THIS SLOW-COOKED DISH, CALLED GALBITANG, *CONTAINS SHORT RIBS AND CUBES OF ASIAN RADISH IN AN EXQUISITELY RICH SOUP, WITH FINE* DANGMYUN *NOODLES HIDING JUST BELOW THE SURFACE. A PIQUANT CHILLI SEASONING IS ADDED JUST BEFORE SERVING.*

2 Cut the radish into 2cm/½in cubes. Place the seasoning ingredients in a bowl and mix thoroughly.

3 Place the ribs in a large heavy pan and cover with 1 litre/1¾ pints/4 cups water. Cook over a high heat for 20 minutes and add the radish and salt. Reduce the heat and cook for 7 minutes, then add the noodles and cook for 3 minutes more.

4 Ladle the soup into bowls and add a generous spoonful of the seasoning just before serving.

COOK'S TIP
Made from sweet potatoes, *dangmyun* noodles are available at Asian stores.

SERVES FOUR

INGREDIENTS
   900g/2lb beef short ribs, cut into
     5cm/2in squares
   350g/12oz Chinese white radish,
     peeled
   5ml/1 tsp salt
   90g/3½oz *dangmyun*
     noodles
For the seasoning
   45ml/3 tbsp soy sauce
   15ml/1 tbsp chilli powder
   50g/2oz spring onions (scallions),
     roughly chopped
   5ml/1 tsp sesame oil
   1 chilli, finely sliced
   ground black pepper

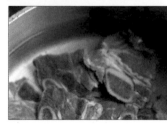

1 Soak the ribs in a bowl of cold water for 10 hours to drain the blood, changing the water halfway. Drain the ribs and place in a large pan, cover with water and place over a high heat. Once the water has boiled remove the ribs, rinse them in cold water and set aside.

Per portion Energy 437kcal/1830kJ; Protein 52.1g; Carbohydrate 19.8g, of which sugars 3.1g; Fat 17g, of which saturates 6.7g; Cholesterol 126mg; Calcium 40mg; Fibre 1.6g; Sodium 1174mg.

BARBECUED BEEF SHORT RIBS

THE SECRET TO THIS DISH, CALLED GALBI, IS TO MARINATE THE BEEF OVERNIGHT TO ALLOW THE FLAVOURS TO INFUSE. THE NATURAL FRUIT ACIDITY IN THE PEAR HELPS TO TENDERIZE THE MEAT, AND THE SAKE ADDS A SLIGHTLY SWEET EDGE. STUFFED CUCUMBER KIMCHI MAKES A PERFECT SIDE DISH.

SERVES FOUR

INGREDIENTS
900g/2lb beef short ribs, cut
  into 5cm/2in squares
shredded spring onions (scallions),
  seasoned with Korean chilli powder
  and rice vinegar, to serve
For the marinade
4 spring onions (scallions), finely sliced
½ onion, finely chopped
1 Asian pear
60ml/4 tbsp dark soy sauce
60ml/4 tbsp sugar
30ml/2 tbsp sesame oil
15ml/1 tbsp sake or rice wine
10ml/2 tsp ground
  black pepper
5ml/1 tsp sesame seeds
2 garlic cloves, crushed
5ml/1 tsp grated fresh
  root ginger

1 To make the marinade, place the spring onions and onion in a large bowl. Core and chop the Asian pear, being careful to save the juices, and add to the bowl. Add the remaining marinade ingredients and mix together thoroughly.

COOK'S TIP
Butchers should be happy to prepare short ribs for you; ask for pieces approximately 5cm/2in square.

2 Add the short ribs to the marinade, stirring to coat them. Leave to stand for at least 2 hours to allow the flavours to permeate and the meat to soften.

3 Heat a heavy griddle pan or frying pan and add the ribs. Keep turning them to cook the meat evenly. When they become crisp and dark brown, serve immediately with a bowl of seasoned shredded spring onions.

Per portion Energy 373kcal/1563kJ; Protein 49.5g; Carbohydrate 9.4g, of which sugars 9.3g; Fat 15.5g, of which saturates 6.7g; Cholesterol 126mg; Calcium 35mg; Fibre 0.5g; Sodium 852mg.

BRAISED BEEF STRIPS WITH SOY AND GINGER

FINE STRIPS OF BRAISED BEEF ARE ENHANCED BY A RICH, DARK SOY AND GARLIC SAUCE, WITH A PIQUANT KICK OF ROOT GINGER AND JALAPEÑO CHILLIES. MUSCOVADO SUGAR ADDS AN IMPERCEPTIBLE SWEETNESS. THIS IS AN EXCELLENT SIDE SERVING TO ACCOMPANY A LARGER STEW OR NOODLE DISH.

SERVES TWO TO THREE

INGREDIENTS
  450g/1lb beef flank
  25g/1oz piece fresh root ginger,
    peeled
  100ml/3½fl oz/scant ½ cup dark soy
    sauce
  75g/3oz light muscovado (brown)
    sugar
  12 garlic cloves, peeled
  6 jalapeño chillies

COOK'S TIP
With a beef cut other than the flank, the meat should be cut into thin strips to ensure it is tender when cooked.

1 Bring a large pan of water to the boil and add the beef. Cook for around 40 minutes until tender. Drain the meat and rinse it in warm water. Leave the beef to cool, then roughly slice it into strips about 5cm/2in long.

2 Place the peeled root ginger in a large pan with the beef and add 300ml/½ pint/1¼ cups water. Bring to the boil, cover and then reduce the heat and simmer for 30 minutes. Skim the fat from the surface of the liquid as the meat cooks. The liquid should have reduced to half its initial volume.

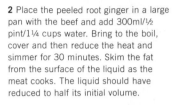

3 Add the soy sauce, muscovado sugar and garlic, and simmer for a further 20 minutes. Then add the jalapeño chillies, and cook for a further 5 minutes.

4 Discard the root ginger, and serve in bowls with generous quantities of the garlic and chillies.

Per portion Energy 408kcal/1713kJ; Protein 37.8g; Carbohydrate 34.3g, of which sugars 29.1g; Fat 14.2g, of which saturates 5.7g; Cholesterol 87mg; Calcium 33mg; Fibre 1.4g; Sodium 2472mg.

BRAISED SHORT RIBS STEW

THIS SLOW COOKED, RICHLY COLOURED STEW IS A POPULAR FEAST DISH, WHICH IS TRADITIONALLY EATEN ON NEW YEAR'S DAY. NAMUL VEGETABLES MAKE AN IDEAL ACCOMPANIMENT, SERVED ALONGSIDE RADISH KIMCHI AND A BOWL OF STEAMED RICE.

SERVES FOUR

INGREDIENTS
　900g/2lb short ribs, cut into 5cm/
　　2in squares
　3 dried shiitake mushrooms, soaked
　　in warm water for about 30 minutes
　　until softened
　½ onion, roughly cubed
　½ carrot, roughly cubed
　½ potato, roughly cubed
　75g/3oz Chinese white radish, peeled
　　and roughly diced
　2 spring onions (scallions), finely
　　sliced
　4 chestnuts
　2 red dates
　30ml/2 tbsp *mirin* or rice wine
　4 ginkgo nuts, to garnish
For the seasoning
　½ Asian pear or kiwi fruit
　60ml/4 tbsp light soy sauce
　20ml/4 tsp sugar
　2 garlic cloves, crushed
　5ml/1 tsp finely grated fresh root
　　ginger
　15ml/1 tbsp sesame seeds
　20ml/4 tsp sesame oil
　ground black pepper

1 Soak the short ribs in a large bowl of cold water for approximately 3 hours to help drain the blood from the meat. Change the water halfway through, once it has discoloured.Then drain the ribs thoroughly.

2 Place the ribs in a large pan, cover with water and put over a high heat. Bring to the boil and then remove the ribs and rinse them in cold water. Strain the cooking liquid into a jug (pitcher), and set aside.

3 When the soaked shiitake mushrooms have reconstituted and become soft, drain and slice them, discarding the stems.

4 To make the seasoning, peel and core the Asian pear or kiwi fruit, and grate into a large bowl to catch the juice.

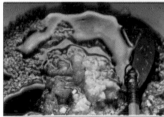

5 Add the other seasoning ingredients to the bowl and mix them together.

6 Use a knife to make deep cuts in the ribs and place them in the bowl of seasoning. Coat the meat, working the mixture well into the slits, and leave it to absorb the flavours for 20 minutes.

7 Transfer the ribs and seasoning mixture to a large pan. Add the sliced mushrooms and the chunks of onion, carrot, potato, radish and spring onions.

8 Then add the whole chestnuts and red dates. Pour 200ml/7fl oz/scant 1 cup water over the ingredients and set the pan over high heat.

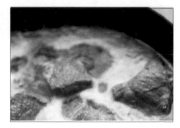

9 Once the liquid begins to boil add the *mirin* or rice wine and cover the pan. Reduce the heat and simmer for 1 hour, or until the meat has become very tender. If necessary, top up the level of liquid from the jug so that there is enough to cover all of the ingredients. Serve with a garnish of ginkgo nuts.

Per portion Energy 533kcal/2223kJ; Protein 49.6g; Carbohydrate 16.7g, of which sugars 10.3g; Fat 30.1g, of which saturates 9g; Cholesterol 126mg; Calcium 35mg; Fibre 1.5g; Sodium 147mg.

GRIDDLED BEEF <u>WITH</u> SESAME <u>AND</u> SOY

Bulgogi is one of Korea's most popular dishes. Thin strips of sirloin are marinated in sesame oil and soy sauce, then grilled over a charcoal brazier. The meat with its delicious glaze is often enjoyed with a piquant dipping sauce or with fresh green leaves.

2 Shred one of the spring onions and set aside for a garnish. Finely slice the remaining spring onions, the onion and pear. Combine all the marinade ingredients in a large bowl to form a paste, adding a little water if necessary.

3 Mix the beef in with the marinade, making sure that it is well coated. Leave in the refrigerator for at least 30 minutes or up to 2 hours (if left longer the meat will become too salty).

SERVES FOUR

INGREDIENTS
    800g/1¾lb sirloin steak
For the marinade
    4 spring onions (scallions)
    ½ onion
    1 Asian pear
    60ml/4 tbsp dark soy sauce
    60ml/4 tbsp sugar
    30ml/2 tbsp sesame oil
    10ml/2 tsp ground black pepper
    5ml/1 tsp sesame seeds
    2 garlic cloves, crushed
    15ml/1 tbsp lemonade

1 Finely slice the steak, and tenderize by bashing with a meat mallet or rolling pin for a few minutes. Then cut into bitesize strips.

4 Heat a griddle pan gently. Add the meat and cook over a medium heat. Once the meat is cooked through, transfer it to a large serving dish, garnish with the spring onion and serve.

Per portion Energy 330kcal/1382kJ; Protein 47.3g; Carbohydrate 8.2g, of which sugars 8.1g; Fat 12.1g, of which saturates 4.5g; Cholesterol 102mg; Calcium 22mg; Fibre 0.2g; Sodium 141mg.

GRILLED BEEF IN SWEET SOY MARINADE

Dark soy sauce has a characteristic taste complemented by the refined sweetness of the honey. Marinating the beef makes the meat tender, and also creates a crispy coating when it is pan-fried. This dish can be accompanied by rice, fresh vegetables or a crisp salad.

SERVES TWO TO THREE

INGREDIENTS
   200g/7oz sirloin or fillet steak
For the marinade
   75ml/5 tbsp dark soy sauce
   30ml/2 tbsp sesame oil
   2 garlic cloves, crushed
   15ml/1 tbsp honey
   15ml/1 tbsp sesame seeds
   vegetable oil, for cooking
   1 spring onion (scallion), finely
     shredded, to garnish

5 Transfer the steak to a serving dish, garnish with the spring onions and serve immediately.

4 Heat a griddle pan or frying pan over a high heat, then add a little vegetable oil. Remove the beef from the marinade, allowing the excess to drip off, and lay it in the pan. Cook for 2–3 minutes on each side, until it is browned and only just cooked.

1 Beat the steak gently on a board with a steak mallet or the bottom of a heavy pan until it is about 1cm/½in thick.

2 Combine the soy sauce, sesame oil, garlic and honey in a shallow bowl and stir in the sesame seeds until all the ingredients are thoroughly mixed.

3 Add the steak to the bowl with the soy and sesame mixture and turn it several times to ensure that it is well coated with the marinade and the sesame seeds. Cover and leave to marinate for an hour.

Per portion Energy 264kcal/1095kJ; Protein 15.4g; Carbohydrate 2.1g, of which sugars 2g; Fat 21.6g, of which saturates 4.2g; Cholesterol 41mg; Calcium 39mg; Fibre 0.4g; Sodium 743mg.

BEEF <u>AND</u> MUSHROOM CASSEROLE

IN THIS PERFECT EXAMPLE OF A KOREAN CASSEROLE DISH, CALLED BEOSEOT CHUNGOL, A MEDLEY OF MUSHROOMS ARE SLOW COOKED WITH BEEF IN A SAUCE SEASONED WITH GARLIC AND SESAME. IDEAL AS A WINTER DISH, ITS EARTHY MUSHROOM FLAVOUR IS ENLIVENED WITH SPRING ONIONS AND CHILLIES.

SERVES TWO

INGREDIENTS
150g/5oz beef
2 dried shiitake mushrooms, soaked
in warm water for about 30 minutes
until softened
25g/1oz enoki mushrooms
1 onion, sliced
400ml/14fl oz/1⅔ cups water
or beef stock
25g/1oz oyster mushrooms, thinly
sliced
6 pine mushrooms, cut into
thin strips
10 spring onions (scallions),
sliced
2 chrysanthemum leaves or spinach,
and ½ red and ½ green chilli,
seeded and shredded, to garnish
steamed rice, to serve
For the seasoning
30ml/2 tbsp dark soy sauce
3 spring onions (scallions),
sliced
2 garlic cloves, crushed
10ml/2 tsp sesame seeds
10ml/2 tsp sesame oil

VARIATION
You can choose to omit the beef
and add a selection of vegetables to
suit your taste to create a good
vegetarian alternative.

1 Slice the beef into thin strips and
place in a bowl. Add the seasoning
ingredients to the beef and mix well,
coating the beef evenly. Leave to absorb
the flavours for 20 minutes.

2 When the soaked shiitake
mushrooms have fully reconstituted
and become soft, drain and thinly slice
them, discarding the stems in the
process. Discard the caps from the
enoki mushrooms.

3 Place the seasoned beef and the
onion in a heavy pan or flameproof
casserole and then add the water or
beef stock.

4 Add all the mushrooms and the
spring onions to the beef mixture in
the pan, and then bring the mixture
to the boil.

5 Once the pan is bubbling reduce
the heat and simmer the mixture for a
further 20 minutes.

6 Transfer the contents of the pan to a
serving dish, or alternatively you can
serve the dish directly from the
casserole. Garnish the dish with the
chrysanthemum leaves or spinach, and
the shredded chilli, and then serve the
dish at the table accompanied by
steamed rice.

COOK'S TIPS
• Pine mushrooms can be difficult
to find; in this case other wild
mushrooms will also work well.
• Chrysanthemum leaves have a
distinctive flavour and a bright green
colour. The cooked greens have a dark
colour, a thick texture and a fragrant and
addictive texture.
• When preparing steamed rice, always
rinse the rice before cooking to get rid
of any impurities. You should also soak
the rice immediately after rinsing. If any
rice floats on the water, then discard
these grains.

VARIATIONS
• Although this recipe is designed to be
simmered to achieve a more delicate
taste, for a more traditional *chungol*
dish, serve the casserole as soon as it
has boiled to maintain the freshness of
the ingredients.
• If you can't find chrysanthemum
leaves, spinach leaves can be used as a
good substitute. The leaves are usually
blanched briefly to soften them, but
young leaves can be served raw.

Per portion Energy 227kcal/945kJ; Protein 21.1g; Carbohydrate 5.5g, of which sugars 4.4g; Fat 13.6g, of which saturates 3.9g; Cholesterol 44mg; Calcium 72mg; Fibre 2.4g; Sodium 1125mg.

BEEF VEGETABLE RICE WITH QUAIL'S EGGS

IN THIS DISH, CALLED BIBIMBAP, *VEGETABLES GARNISH A BED OF PEARLY STEAMED RICE, WHICH IS THEN SEASONED WITH SESAME AND SOY SAUCE. LIGHTLY BROWNED BEEF IS ADDED AND THE DISH IS TOPPED WITH A FRIED QUAIL'S EGG AND A SCOOP OF* GOCHUJANG *CHILLI PASTE.*

SERVES FOUR

INGREDIENTS
    400g/14oz/2 cups short grain
      rice or pudding rice, rinsed
    a drop of sunflower oil
    1 sheet dried seaweed
    4 quail's eggs
    vegetable oil, for shallow-frying
    sesame seeds, to garnish
For the marinade
    30ml/2 tbsp dark soy sauce
    15ml/1 tbsp garlic, crushed
    15ml/1 tbsp sliced spring onions
      (scallions)
    5ml/1 tsp sesame oil
    5ml/1 tsp rice wine
    200g/7oz beef, shredded
    10ml/2 tsp vegetable oil
    salt and ground black pepper
For the *namul* vegetables
    150g/5oz white radish, peeled
    1 courgette (zucchini)
    2 carrots
    150g/5oz/generous ½ cup soya
      beansprouts, trimmed
    150g/5oz fern fronds (optional)
    6 dried shiitake mushrooms, soaked
      in warm water for about 30 minutes
      until softened
    ½ cucumber
For the *namul* seasoning
    10ml/2 tsp sugar
    17.5ml/3½ tsp salt
    35ml/2½ tbsp sesame oil
    7.5ml/1½ tsp crushed garlic
    a splash of dark soy sauce
    1.5ml/¼ tsp chilli powder
    5ml/1 tsp sesame seeds
    vegetable oil, for stir-frying
For the *gochujang* sauce
    45ml/3 tbsp *gochujang* chilli paste
    7.5ml/1½ tsp sugar or honey
    10ml/2 tsp sesame oil

1 Place the rice in a pan and add water to 5mm/¼in above the rice. Add the sunflower oil, cover and bring to the boil. Lower the heat and simmer. Do not remove the lid. After 12–15 minutes turn off the heat and steam for 5 minutes.

2 For the marinade, blend the soy sauce, garlic, spring onions, sesame oil, rice wine, and salt and pepper. Add the beef, mix and marinate for 1 hour. Roll up the seaweed and slice into thin strips.

3 Mix the ingredients for the *gochujang* sauce and place them in a serving bowl. Cut the white radish, courgette and carrots into thin strips.

4 Blend 5ml/1 tsp sugar, 5ml/1 tsp salt and 5ml/1 tsp sesame oil, with 2.5ml/½ tsp crushed garlic, and coat the radish strips. Flash fry. Repeat with the carrots.

5 Blend 5ml/1 tsp salt and 5ml/1 tsp sesame oil with 2.5ml/½ tsp crushed garlic and a little water. Coat the courgette.

6 Heat 5ml/1 tsp vegetable oil in a wok and flash fry the courgette until soft.

7 Briefly cook the soya beansprouts in boiling water. Mix 15ml/1 tbsp sesame oil with 2.5ml/½ tsp salt, 1.5ml/¼ tsp chilli powder and 2.5ml/½ tsp sesame seeds. Sweeten with a pinch of sugar and use to coat the soya beansprouts.

8 Drain and slice the shiitake mushrooms, discarding the stems. Quickly stir-fry in 5ml/1 tsp vegetable oil and season with a pinch of salt. Transfer to the plate.

9 Seed the cucumber, cut into thin strips and transfer to the plate.

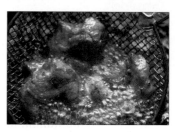

10 Heat 10ml/2 tsp vegetable oil in the wok and stir-fry the beef until tender and golden brown.

11 Divide the rice among four bowls and arrange the *namul* vegetables and beef on top. Fry the quail's eggs, and place one in the centre of each bowl. Garnish with a sprinkling of sesame seeds and ribbons of dried seaweed. Serve with the *gochujang* sauce.

Per portion Energy 645kcal/2688kJ; Protein 23.7g; Carbohydrate 88.5g, of which sugars 7.7g; Fat 21.4g, of which saturates 4.4g; Cholesterol 86mg; Calcium 73mg; Fibre 2.3g; Sodium 1781mg.

BEEF RISSOLES

By combining the beef with a selection of distinctively Korean ingredients this recipe is full of rich and complex flavours. While the meat in the middle of the rissole remains succulent, pan-frying gives this hearty dish a lovely crisp coating.

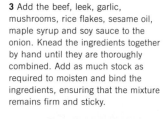

3 Add the beef, leek, garlic, mushrooms, rice flakes, sesame oil, maple syrup and soy sauce to the onion. Knead the ingredients together by hand until they are thoroughly combined. Add as much stock as required to moisten and bind the ingredients, ensuring that the mixture remains firm and sticky.

4 Once the ingredients are combined, shape small handfuls of the mixture into small round patties.

5 Heat a frying pan over a medium heat and add a little vegetable oil. Add the patties and fry them, turning once, until they are golden brown on both sides and cooked through.

6 Drain the patties on kitchen paper and serve hot, garnished with the ground pine nuts.

COOK'S TIP
Glutinous rice flakes are available at Asian supermarkets but can be hard to track down. Roughly ground sticky rice makes a suitable alternative.

SERVES TWO TO THREE

INGREDIENTS
    a little vegetable oil
    ½ small white onion, finely chopped
    300g/11oz beef sirloin or rib, minced (ground)
    1 thick slice leek, finely chopped
    2 garlic cloves, crushed
    40g/1½oz button (white) mushrooms, finely chopped
    90ml/6 tbsp glutinous rice flakes
    15ml/1 tbsp sesame oil
    15ml/1 tbsp maple syrup
    90ml/6 tbsp soy sauce
    about 105ml/7 tbsp beef stock
    15ml/1 tbsp pine nuts, to garnish

1 Grind the pine nuts with a mortar and pestle in preparation for the garnish.

2 Heat the vegetable oil in a pan or wok and cook the chopped onion gently until it browns. Transfer to a bowl.

Per portion Energy 419kcal/1743kJ; Protein 23.7g; Carbohydrate 32g, of which sugars 7.7g; Fat 22g, of which saturates 7.7g; Cholesterol 60mg; Calcium 41mg; Fibre 1.9g; Sodium 1164mg.

KNEADED SIRLOIN STEAK

THIS RECIPE RELIES ON THE FLAVOUR OF HIGH-QUALITY SIRLOIN STEAK. KNEADING THE MEAT WITH SALT MAKES IT DELICIOUSLY TENDER. ACCOMPANIED BY A BOWL OF SOUP, THE SMOKY AROMA AND GRILLED TASTE OF THIS DISH ARE WITHOUT EQUAL.

SERVES FOUR

INGREDIENTS
  450g/1lb beef sirloin
  2 round (butterhead) lettuces
For the marinade
  8 garlic cloves, chopped
  75g/3oz oyster mushrooms, sliced
  3 spring onions (scallions), finely
    chopped
  20ml/4 tsp *mirin* or rice wine
  10ml/2 tsp salt
  salt and ground black pepper
For the spring onion mixture
  8 shredded spring onions
    (scallions)
  20ml/4 tsp rice vinegar
  20ml/4 tsp Korean chilli powder
  2 tsp sugar
  10ml/2 tsp sesame oil

1 Slice the beef into bitesize strips and place in a bowl. Add the garlic, mushrooms and spring onions. Pour in the mirin or rice wine and add the salt and several twists of black pepper.

2 Mix the marinade together, evenly coating the beef. Knead the meat well to tenderize. Chill, and leave for 2 hours.

3 Mix the spring onion mixture ingredients together. Remove the outer leaves from the lettuce and rinse well.

4 Place a griddle pan over a medium heat and add the beef. Cook until the meat has darkened. Wrap the meat in a lettuce leaf with a pinch of the spring onion mixture and serve.

Per portion Energy 188kcal/786kJ; Protein 27.6g; Carbohydrate 4g, of which sugars 3.9g; Fat 6.9g, of which saturates 2.6g; Cholesterol 57mg; Calcium 26mg; Fibre 0.9g; Sodium 83mg.

RIBBON BEEF TARTARE

Succulent raw beef is cut into fine ribbons and tossed in a sesame oil seasoning. Its delicate, silky texture is contrasted with toasted pine nuts and lettuce. Use the freshest cuts of meat for this recipe to ensure the best flavour.

SERVES FOUR

INGREDIENTS
    400g/14oz beef, skirt (flank) or
      topside loin
    1 Asian pear
    1 lettuce
    30ml/2 tbsp pine nuts
    1 egg yolk
    3 garlic cloves, thinly sliced
For the seasoning
    60ml/4 tbsp soy sauce
    30ml/2 tbsp sugar
    1 spring onion (scallion), finely
      chopped
    1 garlic clove, crushed
    15ml/1 tbsp sesame seeds
    20ml/4 tsp sesame oil
    ground black pepper

1 Freeze the beef for 30 minutes before preparation for cooking.

2 Cut the Asian pear into thin strips. Line a serving platter with fresh lettuce leaves and arrange the strips of pear around the outside, leaving a space in the centre.

3 Toast the pine nuts in a dry pan until lightly browned. Set aside.

4 Remove the beef from the freezer and slice into ribbon-thin strips, discarding any fatty sections. Put the beef into a bowl, and add all the seasoning ingredients. Mix thoroughly by hand, kneading the meat gently.

5 Place the seasoned beef into the middle of the lettuce-lined platter, and gently lay the unbroken egg yolk on the top. Sprinkle with the pine nuts and sliced garlic, and serve.

6 To eat, break the egg yolk and mix it with the beef. Transfer to individual bowls or plates. Diners should eat the beef with a little pear and garlic for the best possible combination of flavours.

Per portion Energy 263kcal/1106kJ; Protein 25.8g; Carbohydrate 14.9g, of which sugars 14.2g; Fat 11.6g, of which saturates 2.6g; Cholesterol 100mg; Calcium 70mg; Fibre 2.2g; Sodium 797mg.

BEEF <u>WITH</u> DANGMYUN NOODLES

ONE OF KOREA'S MOST POPULAR NOODLE DISHES, CHAPCHAE IS TRADITIONALLY SERVED AT CELEBRATIONS. QUICK AND EASY TO PREPARE, THE DELICATE TEXTURE OF THE GLASS NOODLES COMBINES WELL WITH THE CRUNCHY VEGETABLES AND THE RICH, SESAME-INFUSED STRIPS OF BEEF.

SERVES FOUR

INGREDIENTS
   250g/9oz *dangmyun* or glass noodles
   5 dried shiitake mushrooms, soaked
      in warm water for about 30 minutes
      until softened
   275g/10oz beef
   1 carrot
   90g/3½oz spinach
   15ml/1 tbsp sesame oil, plus extra
      for drizzling
   2 eggs, beaten
   25ml/1½ tbsp vegetable oil
   1 spring onion (scallion), roughly
      sliced
   salt
   sesame seeds, to garnish
For the marinade
   2 garlic cloves, crushed
   30ml/2 tbsp soy sauce
   15ml/1 tbsp sesame oil
   5ml/1 tsp sugar
   10ml/2 tsp *mirin* or rice wine
For the seasoning
   30ml/2 tbsp soy sauce
   15ml/1 tbsp sugar
   1 garlic clove, crushed

1 Soak the *dangmyun* noodles in warm water for 30 minutes.

2 When the soaked shiitake mushrooms have become soft, drain and slice them, discarding the stems.

3 Combine the marinade ingredients. Slice the beef into thin strips and add with the mushrooms to the marinade. Coat and marinate for 20 minutes.

4 Cut the carrot into thin strips. Blanch the spinach for 1 minute then rinse. Squeeze out any liquid and season with salt and 15ml/1 tbsp sesame oil.

5 Add a pinch of salt to the beaten eggs. Coat a frying pan with 10ml/2 tsp vegetable oil and heat over a medium heat. Add the beaten egg and make a thin omelette. Remove from the pan and cut into thin strips, then set aside.

6 Coat a large frying pan or wok with the remaining vegetable oil and heat over a medium heat. Add the marinated beef and mushrooms, then stir-fry until the meat is golden brown. Remove the beef and mushrooms, and set aside.

7 Use the same pan (preserving any cooking juices from the meat) to stir-fry the carrot, spinach and spring onion. Add the seasoning ingredients to the vegetables in the pan and coat well. Reduce the heat under the pan. Stir in the beef and mushrooms, mixing all the ingredients well.

8 Drizzle with a little sesame oil and transfer to a shallow serving dish. Garnish the mixture with the strips of omelette and a sprinkling of sesame seeds before serving.

Per portion Energy 458kcal/1911kJ; Protein 22.8g; Carbohydrate 54.5g, of which sugars 3.4g; Fat 15.8g, of which saturates 4.2g; Cholesterol 135mg; Calcium 71mg; Fibre 1g; Sodium 390mg.

VEGETABLES, SALADS & TOFU

Korea's high mountain slopes provide an array of wild vegetables, which

are the inspiration for many classic dishes, such as the Vegetable

Buckwheat Crêpe with Mustard Dip. Salads, both with and

without meat, are made of ingredients that include green leaves, white

cabbage, bamboo and spinach. Tofu is a versatile soya beancurd used

mainly for pan-fried, stewed or blanched dishes. Each method creates a

different flavour, from the creamy texture of Stuffed Pan-fried Tofu, to

the smoky richness of Blanched Tofu with Soy Dressing.

PAN-FRIED CHILLI PARSNIP AND SHIITAKE MUSHROOMS

THIS DISH HAS ITS ROOTS IN THE TEMPLES OF KOREA, ALTHOUGH THIS CONTEMPORARY VERSION ADDS MORE SPICES AND SEASONING THAN THE ORIGINALS. THE NATURAL SWEETNESS OF THE PARSNIPS IS BALANCED BY THE SPICINESS OF THE DRESSING.

SERVES FOUR

INGREDIENTS
  150g/5oz parsnips, finely sliced
  a little vegetable oil
  115g/4oz fresh shiitake
    mushrooms
  salt
  15ml/1 tbsp pine nuts, ground, to
    garnish
  sesame oil, to season
For the sauce
  45ml/3 tbsp *gochujang* chilli paste
  5ml/1 tsp Korean chilli powder
  15ml/1 tbsp maple syrup
  5ml/1 tsp sugar
  5ml/1 tsp soy sauce
  5ml/1 tsp sesame oil

1 Place the parsnips in a bowl and add a little sesame oil and salt. Coat the slices evenly. Set aside for 10 minutes.

2 For the sauce, mix the chilli paste and powder, maple syrup, sugar, soy sauce and sesame oil with a little water.

3 Heat a frying pan and add a little vegetable oil. Sauté the finely sliced parsnips until they are softened and lightly browned. Then transfer the parsnips to a bowl and add enough of the chilli sauce to coat them well.

4 Discard the stalks from the shiitake mushrooms and spoon the remaining chilli sauce into the caps.

5 Return the sautéed parsnips to the pan, with their sauce, and then add the mushrooms.

6 Cook the parsnip and mushroom mixture over low heat, allowing the chilli mixture to fully infuse the vegetables and form a sticky glaze. Then add more of the *gochujang* chilli sauce if necessary.

7 When the vegetables are cooked and the liquid has reduced, transfer them to a serving dish, season with sesame oil and sprinkle with ground pine nuts.

Per portion Energy 86kcal/362kJ; Protein 2.3g; Carbohydrate 10.4g, of which sugars 6.4g; Fat 4.4g, of which saturates 0.5g; Cholesterol 0mg; Calcium 26mg; Fibre 2.1g; Sodium 106mg.

STUFFED AUBERGINE WITH RICE WINE AND GINGER SAUCE

THE SUCCULENT BEEF FILLING COMPLEMENTS THE CREAMY TEXTURE OF THE BRAISED AUBERGINE BEAUTIFULLY, AND THE WHOLE DISH IS INFUSED WITH THE FLAVOURS OF RICE WINE AND GINGER; AN ADDITIONAL FIERY KICK IS SUPPLIED BY CHILLIES.

SERVES TWO

INGREDIENTS
   2 aubergines (eggplants)
   1 egg
   25ml/1½ tbsp vegetable oil
   1 sheet dried seaweed
   90g/3½oz/scant ½ cup minced
      (ground) beef
   15ml/1 tbsp *mirin* or rice wine
   15ml/1 tbsp dark soy sauce
   1 garlic clove, crushed
   5ml/1 tsp sesame oil
   1 red chilli, seeded and
      shredded
   1 green chilli, seeded and
      shredded
   salt and ground black pepper
   steamed rice, to serve
For the sauce
   30ml/2 tbsp mirin or rice wine
   30ml/2 tbsp dark soy sauce
   5ml/1 tsp fresh root ginger, peeled
      and grated

COOK'S TIP
If you would like to reduce the heat of the dish, then avoid using the red chilli and just use the green chilli.

1 Clean the aubergines, and cut into slices about 2.5cm/1in thick.

2 Make two cross slits down the length of each aubergine slice, making sure that you don't cut all the way through. Then sprinkle each one with a little salt and set aside.

3 Beat the egg and season with a pinch of salt. Coat a frying pan with 10ml/2 tsp vegetable oil and heat over medium heat.

4 Add the beaten egg and make a thin omelette, browning gently on each side. Remove the omelette from the pan and cut it into thin strips. Wait until it is cool and then chill in the refrigerator.

5 Heat the remaining vegetable oil over high heat. Cut the seaweed into strips and stir fry with the beef, *mirin* or rice wine, soy sauce and garlic. Once cooked, drizzle the beef with the sesame oil.

6 Place the chillies in a bowl. Add the egg strips and the beef, and mix together. Rinse the aubergines and stuff each slice with a little of the beef mixture.

7 Place all the ingredients for the sauce into a frying pan, add 200ml/7fl oz/ scant 1 cup of water and salt to taste, and heat over medium heat. Once the sauce is blended and bubbling add the stuffed aubergine slices. Spoon the sauce over the aubergines and simmer for 15 minutes, or until the aubergines are soft and the skin has become shiny. Transfer to a shallow dish and serve with steamed rice.

Per portion Energy 273kcal/1134kJ; Protein 14.3g; Carbohydrate 5.9g, of which sugars 5.3g; Fat 19.9g, of which saturates 5.2g; Cholesterol 122mg; Calcium 42mg; Fibre 4g; Sodium 1145mg.

VEGETABLE BUCKWHEAT CRÊPE <u>WITH</u> MUSTARD DIP

THIS HISTORIC DISH CELEBRATES THE RANGE OF VEGETABLES NATIVE TO KOREA. THE INGREDIENTS FORM A MEDLEY OF TASTES AND COLOURS, ALL WRAPPED IN A BUCKWHEAT CRÊPE. SLICING THE CRÊPE BEFORE SERVING CREATES BITESIZE PIECES REMINISCENT OF JAPANESE MAKI ROLL.

SERVES FOUR

INGREDIENTS
 50g/2oz *minari* or watercress
 50g/2oz/½ cup beansprouts
 400g/14oz Chinese white radish,
  finely sliced
 25g/1oz dried shiitake mushrooms
 1 garlic clove, crushed
 5ml/1 tsp spring onion (scallion),
  finely chopped
 5ml/1 tsp soy sauce
 5 red dates, finely chopped
 vegetable oil, for cooking
 1 small carrot
For seasoning
 sesame oil
 sesame seeds
 salt
 sugar
For the buckwheat crêpe
 115g/4oz/1 cup buckwheat flour
 50g/2oz/1 cup wholemeal
  (whole-wheat) flour
 1 egg white, lightly whisked
 5ml/1 tsp salt
For the dip
 15ml/1 tbsp Korean mustard powder
  or German mustard
 15ml/1 tbsp vinegar
 7.5ml/1½ tbsp sugar
 2.5ml/½ tsp soy sauce

1 Bring a pan of water to the boil and add a pinch of salt. Add the watercress and beansprouts, bring back to the boil, then immediately drain them and rinse under cold water. Drain thoroughly, place in a bowl and season with a little sesame oil. Sprinkle lightly with sesame seeds, then set aside.

COOK'S TIPS
• When turning crêpes, slide a knife under the edge to loosen. Then move a spatula as close to the centre as possible and flip to the other side.
• To keep crêpes warm, cover with plastic wrap (clear film) and a thick towel.

2 Prepare another pan of salted boiling water. Add the Chinese radish and boil for about 10 minutes, until cooked and tender. Drain, place the radish in a bowl and season with salt, sesame oil and sesame seeds, then set aside.

3 Soak the shiitake mushrooms in warm water to cover for about 15 minutes, until they have softened.

4 Drain and thinly slice the mushrooms, discarding their stalks. Mix them with the garlic, spring onions and soy sauce. Season with a pinch each of salt and sugar, a little sesame oil and a sprinkling of sesame seeds.

5 Heat a frying pan or wok. Add a little vegetable oil and stir-fry the mushrooms until they are cooked and tender, then remove from the pan and set aside.

6 To make the crêpes, sift the buckwheat and wholemeal flours into a bowl. Add the egg white and a little water, stirring gently.

7 Continue to stir and add more water to make a smooth batter. Leave to rest for 30 minutes before cooking.

8 Heat a pan and pour in a little vegetable oil. Tilt the pan to coat in oil, then pour in a ladleful of batter. Tilt the pan to spread the batter thinly and cook for 30 seconds, until set and browned.

9 Turn the crêpe and cook on the second side. Then remove from the pan and place on a plate. Cover loosely with foil and keep hot in a warm oven. Cook the remaining batter to make additional crêpes.

10 Place a little of each vegetable and some chopped dates in each crêpe and roll up. Slice into bitesize pieces and arrange on a serving platter.

11 To make the mustard dip, mix the mustard powder, vinegar and sugar with the soy sauce and 15ml/1 tbsp water. Transfer to individual dishes and serve with the crêpes.

Per portion Energy 167kcal/699kJ; Protein 6.3g; Carbohydrate 34.9g, of which sugars 2.8g; Fat 1.2g, of which saturates 0.2g; Cholesterol 0mg; Calcium 71mg; Fibre 3g; Sodium 410mg.

GREEN LEAF SALAD <u>IN</u> CHILLI DRESSING

SERVED AS AN ACCOMPANIMENT TO GRILLED SEAFOOD, THE SANGCHI IN THIS RECIPE ADDS A HINT OF BITTERNESS WHILE THE SHARP SPICINESS OF THE DRESSING GIVES A REFRESHING EDGE. A VARIETY OF GREEN SALAD LEAVES CAN BE USED IN THIS RECIPE, HOWEVER, DEPENDING ON WHAT IS IN SEASON.

SERVES TWO TO THREE

INGREDIENTS

- 250g/9oz green salad leaves or Korean *sangchi*
- 115g/4oz leeks, finely sliced
- 1 white onion, finely sliced
- 2 green chillies, seeded and finely sliced
- 1 red chilli, seeded and finely sliced
- 15ml/1 tbsp sesame seeds, to garnish

For the dressing

- 5ml/1 tsp pine nuts, ground
- 15ml/1 tbsp Korean chilli powder
- 5ml/1 tsp sesame oil
- 1 garlic clove, crushed
- 30ml/2 tbsp light soy sauce
- 30ml/2 tbsp fish stock or water

1 Tear the leaves or *sangchi* into bitesize pieces. Mix the leeks, onion and green and red chillies.

2 For the salad dressing, mix the pine nuts with the chilli powder, sesame oil, garlic, soy sauce and stock or water in a bowl.

3 Stir the dressing gently, allowing the flavours to mingle, and then add the chillies, onion and leeks.

4 Place the green leaves or *sangchi* in a salad bowl and pour over the dressing. Toss the salad, garnish with sesame seeds and serve.

Per portion Energy 54kcal/224kJ; Protein 2.5g; Carbohydrate 4.1g, of which sugars 4g; Fat 3.2g, of which saturates 0.4g; Cholesterol 0mg; Calcium 58mg; Fibre 1.7g; Sodium 719mg.

CHINESE CHIVE AND ONION SALAD

THIS LIVELY SALAD IS A COMBINATION OF CRUNCHY SALAD LEAVES AND CABBAGE WITH A CHILLI POWDER AND SOY DRESSING. IT IS DELICIOUS SERVED ON ITS OWN AS A VEGETABLE DISH OR AS A REFRESHING ACCOMPANIMENT TO GRILLED MEAT OR SEAFOOD.

SERVES TWO TO THREE

INGREDIENTS
50g/2oz Chinese chives
1 thin wedge Chinese leaves (Chinese cabbage), finely sliced
1 thin slice red cabbage, finely sliced
¼ white onion, finely sliced
For the dressing
15ml/1 tbsp soy sauce
7.5ml/1½ tbsp Korean chilli powder
7.5ml/1½ tbsp sesame seeds
7.5ml/1½ tbsp sesame oil
5ml/1 tsp cider vinegar
5ml/1 tsp lemon juice
5ml/1 tsp sugar
1 garlic clove, crushed

1 Trim both ends off the Chinese chives and cut them into 5cm/2in long pieces.

2 Soak the onion, and the red cabbage and Chinese leaves, separately in two bowls of iced water for about 5 minutes, to soften the flavour of the cabbage.

3 Drain the onion and cabbage, then combine them with the chives in a serving dish and mix thoroughly.

4 For the dressing, combine the soy sauce, chilli powder, sesame seeds and oil, vinegar, lemon juice, sugar and garlic in a bowl. Mix the ingredients.

5 Drizzle the dressing over the chive mixture and serve.

Per portion Energy 47kcal/197kJ; Protein 1.7g; Carbohydrate 6.2g, of which sugars 5.7g; Fat 1.9g, of which saturates 0.3g; Cholesterol 0mg; Calcium 53mg; Fibre 1.8g; Sodium 362mg.

SPINACH KIMCHI SALAD

THIS APPETISING SUMMER SALAD IS SIMPLE TO MAKE AND IS A PERFECT ACCOMPANIMENT FOR ANY NOODLE DISH. WHILE THE INGREDIENTS FOR THE DRESSING ARE THE SAME AS FOR TRADITIONAL KIMCHI, THIS IS NOT PRESERVED AND SO THE TASTE IS LIGHTER.

2 Place the rice in a medium pan. Add 50ml/2fl oz/¼ cup water and bring to the boil over a high heat. Reduce the heat, part cover the pan and simmer for about 20 minutes, until the liquid turns milky. Add the chilli powder, spring onions, anchovy sauce and green and red chillies. Mix thoroughly and remove from the heat. Then add the garlic and the ginger.

3 Toss the leek and onions with the spinach in a large serving dish. Pour over the dressing and toss the salad. Serve immediately.

SERVES TWO TO THREE

INGREDIENTS
　500g/1¼lb spinach
　1 leek, finely sliced
　2 mild onions, finely sliced
For the dressing
　15ml/1 tbsp glutinous rice
　90ml/6 tbsp Korean chilli powder
　　(40g/1½oz in weight)
　8 spring onions, finely sliced
　30ml/2 tbsp anchovy sauce
　1 green chilli, seeded and finely
　　chopped
　1 red chilli, seeded and finely chopped
　3 garlic cloves, crushed
　5ml/1 tsp grated fresh root ginger

1 Trim off any tough stems from the spinach with a sharp knife and then slice the leaves into large pieces. Rinse the spinach leaves under cold running water. Drain them well and then set aside.

Per portion Energy 112kcal/468kJ; Protein 10.8g; Carbohydrate 9.7g, of which sugars 5g; Fat 3.4g, of which saturates 0.5g; Cholesterol 8mg; Calcium 405mg; Fibre 5.9g; Sodium 807mg.

WHITE CABBAGE SALAD <u>IN</u> KIMCHI DRESSING

THE WHITE CABBAGE USED HERE HAS A NATURAL SWEETNESS AND DELICIOUS CRISP TEXTURE WHICH IS COMPLEMENTED BY THE SPICINESS OF A TRADITIONAL KIMCHI DRESSING. THIS SALAD IS A QUICK, REVITALIZING DISH TO ENJOY YEAR ROUND AS A SIDE SERVING OR LIGHT LUNCH.

SERVES FOUR

INGREDIENTS
1 Chinese leaves (Chinese
   cabbage)
25g/1oz/2 tbsp salt
10g/¼oz/2½ tsp short grain rice or
   pudding rice
2 leeks, finely sliced
1 white onion, finely sliced
115g/4oz spring onions (scallions),
   roughly chopped
15ml/1 tbsp sesame seeds
For the dressing
50g/2oz Korean chilli powder
½ white onion, finely grated
15ml/1 tbsp fermented shrimps,
   finely chopped
30ml/2 tbsp anchovy sauce
2 garlic cloves, crushed
7.5ml/1½ tsp grated fresh root
   ginger

COOK'S TIP
The *kimchi* dressing adds a spicy heat to
a cool salad, making this a perfect
summer dish.

VARIATION
Adapt the *kimchi* dressing by serving it
with chunky noodles that have been
cooked lightly in butter, spiked with
salty fish and blanketed with the
fiery dressing.

1 Cut the Chinese leaves lengthways
into quarters. Place in a bowl and
sprinkle with the salt. Leave to stand for
30 minutes and then drain off any
liquid that has collected in the bowl.

2 Place the rice in a small pan with
50ml/2fl oz/¼ cup water and simmer
over a low heat, stirring gently, until the
grains break down to give a smooth,
milky mixture.

3 For the dressing, mix the chilli
powder, onion, shrimps, anchovy sauce,
garlic and ginger in a bowl, then add
the milky cooked rice. Stir gently to
combine the flavours.

4 Slice off the core from the Chinese
leaves and separate the leaves. Place
the leaves in a large bowl.

5 Add the leeks, white onion and
spring onions to the bowl, and pour
over the dressing. Mix thoroughly so
that the leaves are well coated with
the dressing. Garnish with sesame
seeds and serve.

Per portion Energy 90kcal/377kJ; Protein 5.8g; Carbohydrate 9.2g, of which sugars 5.2g; Fat 3.5g, of which saturates 0.6g; Cholesterol 19mg; Calcium 134mg; Fibre 3.8g; Sodium 169mg.

BAMBOO SHOOT SALAD WITH PERSIMMON

CRUNCHY BAMBOO COMBINES PERFECTLY WITH SEASONED BEEF AND PERSIMMON AND ADDS AN APPETIZING SWEETNESS. PEPPERY WATERCRESS AND CRISP BEANSPROUTS MAKE THIS INTO AN UNMISSABLE SALAD.

SERVES ONE TO TWO

INGREDIENTS
- 200g/7oz bamboo shoots
- 2 dried shiitake mushrooms, soaked in warm water for about 30 minutes until softened
- 50g/2oz beef flank, thinly sliced
- 25ml/1½ tbsp vegetable oil
- 90g/3½oz/scant ½ cup beansprouts
- 1 egg
- 90g/3½oz watercress or rocket (arugula)
- salt
- ½ red chilli, seeded and thinly sliced, to garnish

For the seasoning
- 7.5ml/1½ tsp dark soy sauce
- 10g/¼oz red persimmon, finely chopped
- ½ spring onion (scallion), finely chopped
- 1 garlic clove, crushed
- 5ml/1 tsp sesame seeds
- 2.5ml/½ tsp sesame oil
- ground white pepper

For the dressing
- 60ml/4 tbsp dark soy sauce
- 60ml/4 tbsp water
- 30ml/2 tbsp rice vinegar
- 40g/1½oz red persimmon, finely chopped
- 5ml/1 tsp sesame seeds

2 Put the beef slices in a bowl. Add the seasoning ingredients and the shiitake mushrooms, and mix together well, so that the meat is thoroughly coated.

3 Heat 15ml/1 tbsp of the vegetable oil in a frying pan over a medium heat. Stir-fry the beef and mushrooms until cooked, then remove from the pan and chill.

6 Beat the egg and coat a frying pan with the remaining vegetable oil over a medium heat. Add the beaten egg and make a thin omelette, browning each side. Remove and cut into thin strips.

7 Serve the beef with the bamboo shoots, watercress and beansprouts, garnished with chilli and egg strips.

1 Thinly slice the bamboo shoots and cut into bitesize pieces. When the soaked shiitake mushrooms have become soft, drain and thinly slice them, discarding the tough stems.

4 Trim the beansprouts and blanch gently in boiling water for 3 minutes. Drain. Blanch the bamboo shoots for about 3 minutes. Drain.

5 In a bowl combine all the dressing ingredients and mix well. Set aside.

Per portion Energy 268kcal/1115kJ; Protein 17g; Carbohydrate 9.1g, of which sugars 6.1g; Fat 18.6g, of which saturates 3.6g; Cholesterol 119mg; Calcium 164mg; Fibre 3.5g; Sodium 2489mg.

BEEF <u>AND</u> ASIAN PEAR SALAD

PAN-FRIED BEEF AND ASIAN PEAR COMBINE WITH PINE NUTS AND CHESTNUTS IN THIS DISH, TO CREATE A SALAD THAT PROVIDES THE QUINTESSENTIAL LIGHT SUMMER SUPPER IN KOREA.

SERVES FOUR

INGREDIENTS
    300g/11oz fillet steak, thinly sliced
    15ml/1 tbsp dark soy sauce
    1 garlic clove, crushed
    10ml/2 tsp sesame oil
    1 Asian pear
    15ml/1 tbsp sugar
    15ml/1 tbsp rice vinegar
    30ml/2 tbsp pine nuts
    5 cooked chestnuts, finely
      chopped
    salt and ground black pepper
    vegetable oil, for cooking

1 Mix the steak with the soy sauce, garlic, sesame oil and a little salt and pepper and marinate for 20 minutes.

2 Meanwhile, peel, core and slice the pear, then cut the slices into fine strips. Place in a small bowl and pour in cold water to cover.

3 Stir the sugar and rice vinegar into the bowl. Leave to stand for 5 minutes. Then drain and set aside.

4 Heat a frying pan over a high heat and add a little vegetable oil. Add the beef with its marinade and sauté briefly, then reduce the heat and fry gently until the meat is well cooked.

5 Transfer the beef to a serving dish. Add the pear, pine nuts and chestnuts, toss the ingredients together and serve immediately.

Per portion Energy 234kcal/976kJ; Protein 18.6g; Carbohydrate 8.9g, of which sugars 5.2g; Fat 14g, of which saturates 3.5g; Cholesterol 44mg; Calcium 15mg; Fibre 1.5g; Sodium 300mg.

BRAISED TOFU

TOFU IS A VERY POPULAR DISH IN KOREA. THE INGREDIENTS IN THE SAUCE PROVIDE A RANGE OF TASTES: SWEET, SALTY, NUTTY AND SPICY, AND REDUCING THE SAUCE DURING COOKING FORMS A STICKY GLAZE FOR THE CUBED TOFU THAT IS QUITE IRRESISTIBLE.

SERVES TWO TO THREE

INGREDIENTS
    1 block firm tofu, diced
    250ml/8fl oz/1 cup anchovy or
      seafood stock
    45ml/3 tbsp soy sauce
    1 sheet dried kelp, chopped
    15ml/1 tbsp honey
    1 garlic clove, crushed
    ½ white onion, finely chopped
    1 green chilli, seeded and sliced
    1 red chilli, seeded and sliced
    15ml/1 tbsp Korean chilli
      powder
    5ml/1 tsp sesame seeds, to
      garnish

1 Cut the tofu into 1cm/½in cubes and place in a pan. Add 250ml/8fl oz/1 cup cold water, the anchovy or seafood stock, soy sauce and kelp.

2 Stir in the honey and garlic, then bring to the boil. Cover and boil for 5 minutes.

3 Add the onion, chillies and chilli powder. Reduce the heat and simmer, uncovered, for a further 10 minutes, until the liquid has reduced to a small amount of sauce.

4 Transfer to a serving dish and garnish with sesame seeds.

Per portion Energy 118kcal/490kJ; Protein 8.2g; Carbohydrate 14g, of which sugars 8.8g; Fat 3.7g, of which saturates 0.4g; Cholesterol 0mg; Calcium 385mg; Fibre 1.9g; Sodium 1076mg.

SPICY SOFT TOFU STEW

The underlying fiery spiciness of this dish, called SUNDUBU CHIGE, *really helps to emphasize its seafood flavours. Clams and prawns are served in a piquant soup with a medley of vegetables, with creamy tofu melting into the rich sauce.*

SERVES TWO TO THREE

INGREDIENTS
1 block soft tofu
15ml/1 tbsp light soy sauce
6 prawns (shrimp)
6 clams
25g/1oz enoki mushrooms
15ml/1 tbsp vegetable oil
50g/2oz beef, finely chopped
7.5ml/1½ tsp Korean chilli powder
5ml/1 tsp crushed garlic
500ml/17fl oz/generous 2 cups water
  or beef stock
⅓ leek, sliced
½ red chilli, sliced
½ green chilli, sliced
2.5ml/½ tsp dark soy sauce
1.5ml/¼ tsp Thai fish sauce
salt

1 Break the block of tofu into small pieces with your hands, place them in a bowl and marinate with the light soy sauce and a pinch of salt for about 1 hour.

2 Scrub the clams in cold running water. Discard the caps from the enoki mushrooms.

3 To shell the prawns, gently pull off the tail shell. Twist off the head. Peel away the soft body shell and the small claws beneath. Rinse well.

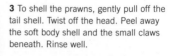

4 In a flameproof casserole dish or heavy pan, heat the vegetable oil over a high heat. Add the chopped beef and stir-fry until the meat has browned.

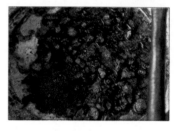

5 Add the chilli powder, garlic and a splash of water to the pan. Stir-fry, coating the meat with the spices. Add the water or stock and bring to the boil.

6 Add the clams, prawns and tofu, and boil for a further 4 minutes.

7 Reduce the heat slightly and add the leek, chillies and mushrooms. Continue to cook until the leek has softened. Then stir in the dark soy sauce and Thai fish sauce. Season with salt if necessary, and serve.

VARIATION
To give the dish a spicy tang, add 50g/2oz chopped *kimchi* while you are stir-frying the beef.

Per portion Energy 170kcal/709kJ; Protein 21.4g; Carbohydrate 2.1g, of which sugars 1.5g; Fat 8.4g, of which saturates 1.5g; Cholesterol 140mg; Calcium 378mg; Fibre 0.8g; Sodium 734mg.

SOYA BEAN PASTE STEW

THIS RICH STEW, DOENJANG CHIGE, *IS A REALLY THICK AND HEARTY CASSEROLE. THE SLOW COOKING IMPARTS A DEEP, COMPLEX FLAVOUR FULL OF SPICINESS. IT IS A SATISFYINGLY WARM DISH, IDEAL FOR COLD EVENINGS, AND GOES PARTICULARLY WELL WITH THE FLAVOUR OF FLAME-GRILLED MEAT.*

SERVES TWO

INGREDIENTS
    ½ courgette (zucchini)
    25g/1oz enoki mushrooms
    15ml/1 tbsp sesame oil, plus extra
      for drizzling
    50g/2oz beef, finely chopped
    30ml/2 tbsp *doenjang* soya bean
      paste
    ½ onion, finely chopped
    10ml/2 tsp finely chopped garlic
    550ml/18fl oz/2½ cups fish stock
    1 red chilli, seeded and sliced
      diagonally
    ½ block firm tofu, diced
    1 spring onion (scallion), sliced,
      to garnish

1 Thickly slice the courgette, and then cut the slices into quarters. Discard the caps from the enoki mushrooms.

2 In a casserole dish or heavy pan, heat the sesame oil over a high heat. Add the beef and soya bean paste to the pan, and cook until golden brown. Then add the onion and garlic to the pan and sauté gently. Add the fish stock and bring to the boil.

3 Next add the chilli and courgette slices and boil for 5 minutes. Add the tofu and mushrooms and boil for a further 2 minutes. Reduce the heat and simmer the stew gently for 15 minutes.

4 Garnish with sliced spring onion and a drizzle of sesame oil, and serve.

COOK'S TIPS
• When making fish stock, you can use stock (bouillon) cubes for convenience, but to make an authentic fish stock from scratch, simply simmer a handful of dried anchovies in 1 litre/1¾ pints/ 4 cups water for 30 minutes, and then strain the stock into a jug (pitcher).
• This dish is traditionally cooked in a heavy stone pot known as a *tukbaege*, although a heavy pan or casserole will work as well. Serve the dish in the heavy cooking pot so it remains warm and continues to cook once it is on the table.
• Enoki mushrooms are sometimes found in supermarkets under the name of snow puff mushrooms.

Per portion Energy 166kcal/690kJ; Protein 13g; Carbohydrate 4.8g, of which sugars 3.2g; Fat 10.7g, of which saturates 2.2g; Cholesterol 15mg; Calcium 169mg; Fibre 3.1g; Sodium 25mg.

VEGETABLE ᴬᴺᴰ TOFU CAKE ᵂᴵᵀᴴ MUSTARD DIP

THIS DISH IS FILLED WITH A MOUTHWATERING BLEND OF TASTES AND TEXTURES, YET IS REMARKABLY SIMPLE TO PREPARE. THE CONTRAST BETWEEN THE DELICATE TEXTURE OF THE TOFU AND THE CRUNCHINESS OF THE MANGETOUTS IS DELIGHTFUL, AND THE SESAME SEEDS ADD A HINT OF NUTTINESS. EATEN WITH THE MUSTARD DIP, IT IS PERFECT AS A SNACK OR AS A SIDE DISH.

SERVES TWO

INGREDIENTS
1 block firm tofu
1 carrot, finely chopped
115g/4oz mangetouts (snow peas),
  sliced
3 eggs
5ml/1 tsp sake or *mirin*
10ml/2 tsp salt
5ml/1 tsp grated fresh root
  ginger
5ml/1 tsp sesame oil
5ml/1 tsp sesame seeds
ground black pepper
vegetable oil, for greasing
  mould
For the mustard dip
  45ml/3 tbsp Dijon mustard
  15ml/1 tbsp sugar syrup
    (see below)
  7.5ml/1½ tsp soy sauce
  30ml/2 tbsp rice vinegar
  salt
To make sugar syrup
  1 part white sugar to 2 parts water
  (see cook's tip)

1 Bring a large pan of salted water to the boil. Add the block of tofu and then bring it back to the boil.

2 Use a large fish slice, metal spatula, or sieve (strainer) to remove and drain the tofu from the pan.

3 Crumble the block of tofu on to a piece of muslin (cheesecloth), and then squeeze it to drain off any excess water.

4 Bring a fresh batch of water to the boil and blanch the carrot for 1 minute.

5 Add the mangetouts, bring back to the boil and then drain the vegetables. The vegetables should be slightly cooked but retain their crunchy texture.

6 Beat the eggs and sake or *mirin* together briefly, then add them to the crumbled tofu.

7 Mix in the mangetouts and carrots, ginger, sesame oil and sesame seeds. Season with a little black pepper and mix well.

8 Grease a 18cm/7in mould with a little oil. Pour the mixture into the mould and place in a steamer. Lay a piece of foil over the top of the mould, to keep steam out and steam over boiling water for 20 minutes, until the mixture is set and firm.

9 Meanwhile, for the dip, mix the mustard, syrup, soy sauce and vinegar. Season with a little salt. Mix thoroughly and pour into two small serving bowls.

10 Slide a metal spatula or palette knife between the tofu and the mould. Cover with a serving plate and then invert mould and plate. Remove the mould and serve the tofu sliced, with the dipping sauce.

COOK'S TIP
To make sugar syrup, dissolve 1 part white sugar in 2 parts water over a low heat.

Stir until the sugar has dissolved, then bring to the boil for 1 minute. Remove from the heat and leave to cool. Store the syrup in a screw-top jar in the refrigerator for up to 2 weeks. You can also freeze it in ice cube trays.

Per portion Energy 320kcal/1334kJ; Protein 23g; Carbohydrate 16.4g, of which sugars 14.9g; Fat 18.7g, of which saturates 3.7g; Cholesterol 285mg; Calcium 662mg; Fibre 3.8g; Sodium 657mg.

BLANCHED TOFU WITH SOY DRESSING

THE SILKY CONSISTENCY OF THE TOFU ABSORBS THE DARK SMOKY TASTE OF THE SOY DRESSING IN THIS RICH AND FLAVOURFUL DISH. TOFU HAS A NUTTY QUALITY THAT BLENDS AGREEABLY WITH THE SALTY SWEETNESS OF THE SOY SAUCE AND THE HINTS OF GARLIC AND SPRING ONION.

SERVES TWO

INGREDIENTS
  2 blocks firm tofu
  salt
For the dressing
  10ml/2 tsp finely sliced spring
    onion (scallion)
  5ml/1 tsp finely chopped
    garlic
  60ml/4 tbsp dark soy sauce
  10ml/2 tsp chilli powder
  5ml/1 tsp sugar
  10ml/2 tsp sesame seeds

1 Mix the spring onion and garlic with the soy sauce, chilli powder, sugar and sesame seeds. Leave to stand for a few minutes.

2 Meanwhile, bring a large pan of water to the boil, and add a pinch of salt. Place the whole blocks of tofu in the water, being careful not to let them break apart.

3 Blanch the tofu for 3 minutes. Remove and place on kitchen paper to remove any excess water.

4 Transfer the tofu to a plate, and cover with the dressing. Serve, slicing the tofu as desired.

COOK'S TIP
Koreans traditionally eat this dish without slicing the tofu, preferring instead to either eat it directly with a spoon or pick it apart with chopsticks. It may be easier, however, to slice it in advance if you are serving it as an accompanying dish.

Per portion Energy 160kcal/669kJ; Protein 16.1g; Carbohydrate 6.7g, of which sugars 5.6g; Fat 7.8g, of which saturates 0.9g; Cholesterol 0mg; Calcium 954mg; Fibre 0.1g; Sodium 2144mg.

STUFFED PAN-FRIED TOFU

AN EASY ACCOMPANIMENT FOR A MAIN COURSE, OR A GREAT APPETIZER. SQUARES OF FRIED TOFU STUFFED WITH A BLEND OF CHILLI AND CHESTNUT GIVE A PIQUANT JOLT TO THE DELICATE FLAVOUR. THE TOFU HAS A CRISPY COATING, SURROUNDING A CREAMY TEXTURE, WITH A CRUNCHY FILLING.

SERVES TWO

INGREDIENTS
  2 blocks firm tofu
  30ml/2 tbsp Thai fish sauce
  5ml/1 tsp sesame oil
  2 eggs
  7.5ml/1½ tsp cornflour
    (cornstarch)
  vegetable oil, for shallow-frying
For the filling
  2 green chillies, finely chopped
  2 chestnuts, finely chopped
  6 garlic cloves, crushed
  10ml/2 tsp sesame seeds

1 Cut the two blocks of tofu into 2cm/¾in slices and then cut each slice in half. Place the tofu slices on pieces of kitchen paper to blot and absorb any excess water.

2 Mix together the Thai fish sauce and sesame oil. Transfer the tofu slices to a plate and coat them with the fish sauce mixture. Leave to marinate for 20 minutes. Meanwhile, put all the filling ingredients into a bowl and combine them thoroughly. Set aside.

3 Beat the eggs in a shallow dish. Add the cornflour and whisk until well combined. Take the slices of tofu and dip them into the beaten egg mixture, ensuring an even coating on all sides.

VARIATION
Alternatively, you can serve the tofu with a light soy dip instead of the spicy filling.

4 Place a frying pan or wok over a medium heat and add the vegetable oil. Add the tofu slices to the pan and sauté, turning over once, until they are golden brown.

5 Once cooked, make a slit down the middle of each slice with a sharp knife, without cutting all the way through. Gently stuff a large pinch of the filling into each slice, and serve.

Per portion Energy 291kcal/1213kJ; Protein 23g; Carbohydrate 7.8g, of which sugars 1.3g; Fat 19.1g, of which saturates 3.4g; Cholesterol 209mg; Calcium 1014mg; Fibre 0.8g; Sodium 88mg.

VEGETABLE ACCOMPANIMENTS

The Korean table features a host of smaller dishes to accompany the main courses. Vegetable accompaniments alter with the seasons, giving meals changing interest all year round. Sangchae are tangy, crunchy salads made with vegetables coated in a spicy dressing, whereas namul *dishes use seasoned vegetables and have a more delicate quality. Both* namul *and* sangchae *contain only one vegetable, making the most of the individual flavours. This section also features delicious condiments for grilled dishes, such as Sweet Lotus Root and Black Beans with Sweet Soy.*

WHITE RADISH SANGCHAE

The red chilli and sesame oil dressing adds an understated spiciness and nutty aftertaste to this healthy dish. The white radish, also known as daikon, is a commonly used ingredient in Asian cooking and is valued for its medicinal properties.

SERVES TWO

INGREDIENTS
225g/8oz Chinese white radish, peeled
½ red chilli, shredded, and 1.5ml/
¼ tsp sesame seeds, to garnish
For the marinade
5ml/1 tsp cider vinegar
2.5ml/½ tsp sugar
1.5ml/¼ tsp salt
7.5ml/1½ tsp lemon juice
2.5ml/½ tsp Korean chilli powder

VARIATIONS
• The radish takes on the red colour of the chilli powder, but for an interesting alternative replace the chilli powder with 2.5ml/½ tsp wasabi. This will give the radish a green tint and a sharper taste.
• Make an alternative sesame oil marinade with 2.5ml/½ tsp sesame oil 2.5ml/½ tsp vegetable oil, 120ml/ 4fl oz/½ cup white wine vinegar, 50g/2oz/¼ cup sugar, 1.5ml/¼ tsp salt and a pinch of pepper.

1 Cut the radish into thin strips approximately 5cm/2in long.

2 To make the marinade, mix the vinegar, sugar, salt, lemon juice and chilli powder together in a small bowl, and ensure that the ingredients are thoroughly blended.

3 Place the radish in a bowl, and add the marinade. Leave to marinate for 20 minutes, then place in the refrigerator until the dish has chilled thoroughly.

4 Mix well again, then garnish with the shredded red chilli pepper and the sesame seeds before serving.

Per portion Energy 22kcal/91kJ; Protein 1g; Carbohydrate 3.2g, of which sugars 3.2g; Fat 0.7g, of which saturates 0.2g; Cholesterol 0mg; Calcium 27mg; Fibre 1.1g; Sodium 209mg.

CUCUMBER SANGCHAE

THE REFRESHING, SUCCULENT TASTE OF THIS SIMPLE SALAD MAKES A PERFECT ACCOMPANIMENT FOR A MAIN MEAL ON A HOT SUMMER'S NIGHT. SMALL PICKLING CUCUMBERS ARE THE BEST FOR THIS DISH; THEY ARE NOT AS WATERY AS THE LARGER SPECIMENS AND THEY DO NOT REQUIRE PEELING.

SERVES FOUR

INGREDIENTS
    400g/14oz pickling or salad
        cucumber
    30ml/2 tbsp salt
For the dressing
    2 spring onions (scallions), finely
        chopped
    2 garlic cloves, crushed
    5ml/1 tsp cider vinegar
    5ml/1 tsp salt
    2.5ml/½ tsp Korean chilli powder
    10ml/2 tsp toasted sesame seeds
    10ml/2 tsp sesame oil
    5ml/1 tsp *gochujang* chilli paste
    10ml/2 tsp sugar

1 Cut the cucumber lengthways into thin slices and put into a colander. Sprinkle with the salt, mix well and leave for 30 minutes.

2 Place the cucumber slices in a damp dish towel and gently squeeze out as much of the water as possible.

3 Place the spring onions in a large bowl. Add the crushed garlic, vinegar, salt and chilli powder, and combine. Sprinkle in the sesame seeds and mix in the sesame oil, chilli paste and sugar.

4 Blend the cucumber with the dressing. Chill before serving.

Per portion Energy 105kcal/432kJ; Protein 3.3g; Carbohydrate 9.2g, of which sugars 7.4g; Fat 6.2g, of which saturates 0.9g; Cholesterol 0mg; Calcium 78mg; Fibre 2.2g; Sodium 1973mg.

KOREAN CHIVE SANGCHAE

THE KOREAN CHIVE HAS A GARLIC NUANCE IN BOTH TASTE AND AROMA, AND THE LEAVES HAVE A SOFT, GRASSLIKE TEXTURE. THIS DISH IS THE PERFECT ACCOMPANIMENT TO ANY GRILLED MEAT, AND IS A TASTY ALTERNATIVE TO THE CLASSIC SHREDDED SPRING ONION SALAD.

SERVES TWO

INGREDIENTS
    200g/7oz fresh Korean or Chinese
        chives
    1 green chilli, seeded and finely
        sliced
    10ml/2 tsp sesame seeds, to
        garnish
For the seasoning
    30ml/2 tbsp dark soy sauce
    2 garlic cloves, crushed
    10ml/2 tsp Korean chilli powder
    10ml/2 tsp sesame oil
    10ml/2 tsp sugar

COOK'S TIP
Korean chives are available in most Asian markets in 225g/½lb or 450g/1lb bundles. When shopping for these chives, try to select those that are bright green with a crisp texture.

1 Clean the chives, then trim off the bulbs and discard. Slice roughly into 4cm/1½in lengths. Combine with the chilli in a bowl.

2 To make the seasoning, mix the soy sauce, garlic, chilli powder, sesame oil and sugar together, and then add it to the bowl with the chives and chilli. Mix until well coated, then chill.

3 Garnish with sesame seeds and serve. The chives can be attractively arranged in alternating layers laid at right angles.

VARIATION
For a traditional alternative use 150g/ 5oz shredded spring onion (scallion) in place of the chives, and add 15ml/ 1 tbsp cider vinegar and 15ml/1 tbsp soy sauce to the seasoning.

Per portion Energy 105Kcal/434kJ; Protein 4.3g; Carbohydrate 7g, of which sugars 6.7g; Fat 6.7g, of which saturates 0.9g; Cholesterol 0mg; Calcium 196mg; Fibre 2.3g; Sodium 1196mg.

COURGETTE NAMUL

*THE FRESH TASTE OF THE COURGETTE IN THIS NAMUL DISH MINGLES WITH THE FLAVOURS OF SESAME
OIL AND A HINT OF SEAFOOD. THE DRIED SHRIMP GIVES A PLEASING CRUNCHINESS, WHICH CONTRASTS
NICELY WITH THE SOFTER TEXTURE OF THE COURGETTE.*

SERVES TWO

INGREDIENTS
  2 courgettes (zucchini), finely sliced
  10ml/2 tsp sesame oil
  30ml/2 tbsp vegetable oil
  2 garlic cloves, crushed
  40g/1½oz dried shrimp
  finely chopped spring onion (scallion)
    and sesame seeds, to garnish
  salt

1 Place the courgettes in a colander, lightly sprinkle them with salt and leave to stand for 20 minutes. Drain off any excess liquid and transfer to a bowl.

2 Add the sesame oil to the courgette slices and mix together to coat.

3 Coat a frying pan or wok with the vegetable oil and heat over a high heat. Add the seasoned courgettes and crushed garlic, and stir-fry briefly. Add the dried shrimp and stir-fry quickly until they become crispy, but the courgettes should retain their bright green colour.

4 Remove from the heat, and transfer to a shallow dish. Garnish with the spring onion, and sprinkle over the sesame seeds before serving.

COOK'S TIP
You will find dried shrimp at most specialist Asian stores.

VARIATION
Chopped fresh prawns (shrimp) can be substituted as an alternative to dried shrimp; they will provide a similar flavour, although won't have the same crunchy texture.

Per portion Energy 213kcal/883kJ; Protein 15g; Carbohydrate 3.9g, of which sugars 3.7g; Fat 15.3g, of which saturates 2g; Cholesterol 101mg; Calcium 294mg; Fibre 2g; Sodium 869mg.

SHIITAKE MUSHROOM NAMUL

IN THIS TEMPTING NAMUL DISH THE DISTINCTIVE TASTE OF SESAME OIL EMPHASIZES THE RICH AND MEATY FLAVOUR OF THE SHIITAKE MUSHROOMS. THE LATTER ARE QUICKLY SAUTÉED TO SOFTEN THEM AND TO ACCENTUATE THEIR CHARACTERISTIC EARTHY TASTE.

SERVES TWO

INGREDIENTS
    12 dried shiitake mushrooms, soaked
        in warm water for about 30 minutes
        until softened
    10ml/2 tsp sesame seeds
    2 garlic cloves, crushed
    30ml/2 tbsp vegetable oil
    ½ spring onion (scallion), finely
        chopped
    10ml/2 tsp sesame oil
    salt

1 When the soaked shiitake mushrooms have reconstituted and become soft, drain and slice them, discarding the stems, and then place them in a bowl. Add the sesame seeds, crushed garlic and a pinch of salt, and blend the ingredients together.

2 Coat a frying pan or wok with the vegetable oil and place over high heat. Add the seasoned mushroom slices and quickly stir-fry them, so that they soften slightly but do not lose their firmness.

3 Remove from the heat and stir in the spring onion and sesame oil. Transfer to a shallow dish and serve.

COOK'S TIP
It is important that the shiitake mushrooms are drained thoroughly to ensure that their dark colour does not overwhelm the dish. Having drained them, then squeeze the mushrooms gently to remove all the excess liquid, and finally pat them dry with kitchen paper.

Per portion Energy 167kcal/689kJ; Protein 2.2g; Carbohydrate 1.1g, of which sugars 0.2g; Fat 17.2g, of which saturates 2.2g; Cholesterol 0mg; Calcium 38mg; Fibre 1.2g; Sodium 4mg.

WHITE RADISH NAMUL

THIS SUBTLE DISH BLENDS THE SWEETNESS OF WHITE RADISH WITH A DELICIOUS NUTTY AFTERTASTE.
BLANCHING THE WHITE RADISH SOFTENS IT, LEAVING IT WITH A SILKY TEXTURE.

SERVES TWO

INGREDIENTS
400g/14oz Chinese white radish,
  peeled
50g/2oz leek, finely sliced
20ml/4 tsp sesame oil, plus extra for
  drizzling
5ml/1 tsp salt
60ml/4 tbsp vegetable oil
½ red chilli, seeded and finely
  shredded, to garnish

1 Slice the radish into 5cm/2in
matchstick lengths. Blanch in a pan of
boiling water for 30 seconds. Drain, and
gently squeeze to remove any excess
water. Pat dry with kitchen paper.

2 Mix the leek with the sesame oil and
salt in a large bowl.

3 Sauté the radish in the vegetable oil
for 1 minute. Add the leeks and sauté
for a further 2 minutes. Garnish with the
chilli and a drizzle of sesame oil.

Per portion Energy 137kcal/565kJ; Protein 1.8g; Carbohydrate 4.5g, of which sugars 4.3g; Fat 12.5g, of which saturates 1.8g; Cholesterol 0mg; Calcium 45mg; Fibre 2.4g; Sodium 1005mg.

SPINACH NAMUL

USING THE STEMS AS WELL AS THE LEAVES OF THE SPINACH GIVES A SUBTLE CRUNCH TO THIS DISH.
THE HINT OF BITTERNESS IN THE SPINACH IS BALANCED BY THE SALTY SOY SAUCE.

SERVES TWO

INGREDIENTS
500g/1¼lb spinach
60ml/4 tbsp dark soy sauce
2 small garlic cloves, crushed
20ml/4 tsp sesame oil
2.5ml/½ tsp rice wine
20ml/4 tsp sesame seeds
30ml/2 tbsp vegetable oil
salt

1 Trim the ends of the spinach stalks.
Cut the leaves and stalks into
10cm/4in lengths. Blanch the spinach
in a pan of lightly salted water for
approximately 30 seconds. Drain the
spinach, and rinse well under cold
running water.

2 Mix the soy sauce, garlic, sesame
oil and rice wine together in a
large bowl. Add the spinach and
thoroughly coat the leaves and stems
with the seasoning mixture. In a dry
pan lightly toast the sesame seeds
until they are golden brown, then
set aside.

3 Heat the vegetable oil in a frying
pan or wok, and sauté the spinach
over a high heat for 20 seconds.
Transfer to a serving dish and
garnish with the toasted sesame
seeds before serving.

Per portion Energy 293kcal/1208kJ; Protein 10.1g; Carbohydrate 7.4g, of which sugars 6.1g; Fat 24.8g, of which saturates 3.2g; Cholesterol 0mg; Calcium 499mg; Fibre 6.2g; Sodium 2488mg.

CUCUMBER NAMUL

THIS SAUTÉED DISH RETAINS THE NATURAL SUCCULENCE OF THE CUCUMBER, WHILE ALSO INFUSING THE RECIPE WITH A PLEASANTLY REFRESHING HINT OF GARLIC AND CHILLI.

SERVES TWO

INGREDIENTS
200g/7oz cucumber
15ml/1 tbsp vegetable oil
5ml/1 tsp spring onion (scallion),
  finely chopped
1 garlic clove, crushed
5ml/1 tsp sesame oil
sesame seeds, and seeded and
  shredded red chilli, to garnish
salt

COOK'S TIP
You can adapt this dish and tone
down the hot chilli garnish by
substituting the red chilli for a milder
green chilli.

1 Thinly slice the cucumber and place the slices in a colander. Sprinkle with salt, then leave to stand for about 10 minutes. Then drain off any excess liquid and transfer the cucumber to a clean bowl.

2 Coat a frying pan or wok with the vegetable oil, and heat it over a medium heat. Add the spring onion, garlic and cucumber, and quickly stir-fry together.

3 Remove from the heat, add the sesame oil and toss lightly to blend the ingredients. Place in a shallow serving dish and garnish with the sesame seeds and shredded chilli before serving.

Per portion Energy 74kcal/304kJ; Protein 0.8g; Carbohydrate 1.7g, of which sugars 1.6g; Fat 7.1g, of which saturates 0.9g; Cholesterol 0mg; Calcium 20mg; Fibre 0.7g; Sodium 4mg.

SOYA BEANSPROUT NAMUL

THE DELICATE SPICINESS OF THE RED CHILLI AND NUTTY FLAVOUR OF THE SESAME OIL CREATE A TANTALIZING DISH. CRISPY SOYA BEANSPROUTS CAN BE REPLACED WITH MUNG BEANSPROUTS.

SERVES TWO

INGREDIENTS
300g/11oz/generous 1 cup soya
  beansprouts
60ml/4 tbsp vegetable oil
⅔ red chilli, seeded and
  sliced
1 baby leek, finely sliced
10ml/2 tsp sesame oil
salt

VARIATION
Try this with different beansprouts.

1 Wash the soya beansprouts, and trim the tail ends. Cover them with a light sprinkling of salt, and leave them to stand for 10 minutes.

2 Bring a pan of water to the boil, and add the beansprouts. Cover and boil for 3 minutes, then drain.

3 Place a frying pan or wok over medium heat and add the vegetable oil.

4 Add the soya beansprouts, and sauté gently for 30 seconds. Add the chilli and leek, and stir-fry together so that the ingredients are thoroughly blended.

5 Transfer to a shallow dish and then drizzle with a little sesame oil before serving the *namul*.

Per portion Energy 282kcal/1167kJ; Protein 5.2g; Carbohydrate 7.5g, of which sugars 4.4g; Fat 26g, of which saturates 3.2g; Cholesterol 0mg; Calcium 42mg; Fibre 3.4g; Sodium 9mg.

BRAISED SHIITAKE MUSHROOM AND ONION

IN THIS DISH, THE EARTHY FLAVOURS OF THE MUSHROOMS ARE BALANCED BY THE NATURAL SWEETNESS OF THE ONION AND GARLIC. A KOREAN STAPLE AND AN IDEAL ACCOMPANIMENT FOR FISH AND SEAFOOD.

SERVES TWO TO THREE

INGREDIENTS
    10 fresh shiitake mushrooms
    ½ white onion, finely diced
    5 garlic cloves, crushed
    1 spring onion (scallion),
        shredded
    5ml/1 tsp sesame seeds
For the sauce
    60ml/4 tbsp dark soy sauce
    15ml/1 tbsp sesame oil
    10ml/2 tsp maple syrup

1 Discard the stalks from the shiitake mushrooms and cut each cap in half.

2 Boil 350ml/12fl oz/1½ cups water. Add the soy sauce, sesame oil, maple syrup, mushrooms, onion and garlic.

3 Reduce the heat under the pan and simmer until the mushrooms are tender and the cooking liquid has reduced to form a rich sauce.

4 Transfer to a dish and serve sprinkled with spring onion and sesame seeds.

COOK'S TIP
Substitute the shiitake mushrooms with field (portobello), cremini or button (white) mushrooms.

Per portion Energy 117kcal/489kJ; Protein 3.5g; Carbohydrate 14.9g, of which sugars 13g; Fat 5.3g, of which saturates 0.8g; Cholesterol 0mg; Calcium 40mg; Fibre 2.2g; Sodium 1103mg.

SHREDDED LEEK WITH SESAME

THIS SIMPLE VEGETABLE DISH IS A CLASSIC AND SOMETIMES INDISPENSABLE ACCOMPANIMENT TO BARBECUED OR GRILLED MEAT DISHES, ESPECIALLY PORK-BASED ONES.

SERVES THREE TO FOUR

INGREDIENTS

    250g/9oz leeks or spring onions
      (scallions)
    15ml/1 tbsp Korean chilli powder
    10ml/2 tsp sesame oil
    1 garlic clove, crushed
    5ml/1 tsp cider vinegar
    5ml/1 tsp sugar
    10ml/2 tsp sesame seeds
    salt

1 Finely shred the leeks or spring onions diagonally with a sharp knife and place in a large bowl. Pour in cold water and add a quantity of ice, then leave the leeks to soak for about 5 minutes.

2 Meanwhile, to make a dressing, put the chilli powder, sesame oil, garlic and vinegar in a bowl and mix together well.

3 Add the sugar and stir until it dissolves into the mixture.

4 Add the sesame seeds and season to taste with a little salt.

5 Drain the leeks and place them in a serving bowl.

6 Pour the dressing over the leeks and toss well before serving.

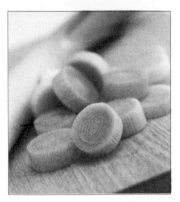

Per portion Energy 58kcal/242kJ; Protein 2g; Carbohydrate 4.5g, of which sugars 2.7g; Fat 3.8g, of which saturates 0.6g; Cholesterol 0mg; Calcium 39mg; Fibre 1.6g; Sodium 3mg.

ACORN JELLY AND SEAWEED IN SOY DRESSING

ACORN JELLY IS A DELICACY RARELY FOUND OUTSIDE OF KOREA. THE JELLY HAS A SUBTLE BITTERNESS, BUT THE SEAWEED BRINGS OUT ITS DISTINCTIVE NUTTY FLAVOUR, WHILE THE SOY DRESSING ADDS OVERTONES OF SWEETNESS AND SALTINESS. BEST SERVED WITH NOODLES AS A LIGHT SUMMER DISH.

SERVES FOUR

INGREDIENTS
50g/2oz/½ cup acorn powder
5ml/1 tsp salt
15ml/1 tsp sesame oil
5ml/1 tsp sesame seeds
30ml/2 tbsp dark soy sauce
dried seaweed paper or Japanese nori

COOK'S TIP
Acorn powder is available at most Asian supermarkets.

2 Pour the acorn mixture into a pan and stir until the liquid boils, then simmer for 2–3 minutes. Add the salt and 1 teaspoon of the sesame oil, and simmer for 5 minutes, until the liquid reduces and becomes sticky.

3 Pour the liquid into a mould and leave it to cool and set.

4 Mix the sesame seeds with the soy sauce and add the remaining sesame oil.

5 Cut the seaweed paper into a manageable size. Turn out the jelly, cut into slices and arrange on a plate. Crumble the seaweed over, then drizzle with the dressing before serving.

1 Stir 750ml/1¼ pints/3 cups water into the acorn powder. Stir until the powder and water are well mixed together.

Per portion Energy 57kcal/236kJ; Protein 0.7g; Carbohydrate 5.2g, of which sugars 1.4g; Fat 3.8g, of which saturates 0.6g; Cholesterol 0mg; Calcium 16mg; Fibre 0.6g; Sodium 1027mg.

SWEET LOTUS ROOT

THE ROOT OF THE LOTUS FLOWER HAS A UNIQUE FLAVOUR AND CLEAN, CRISP TASTE AND IS A GREATLY OVERLOOKED INGREDIENT IN THE WESTERN KITCHEN. HISTORICALLY, THIS KOREAN SPECIALITY WAS EATEN BY THE KING AS A DESSERT, BRAISED WITH SUGAR RATHER THAN SOY, AS HERE.

SERVES TWO TO THREE

INGREDIENTS
  15ml/1 tbsp cider vinegar
  300g/11oz lotus root, peeled
  60ml/4 tbsp soy sauce
  30ml/2 tbsp sugar
  45ml/3 tbsp maple syrup
  10ml/2 tsp sesame oil
  sesame seeds, to garnish

1 Pour 750ml/1¼ pints/3 cups water into a bowl and add the vinegar. Cut the lotus root into slices about 1cm/½in thick and place them in the vinegar water. Leave to soak for about 30 minutes, then drain. Be careful not to leave the lotus root in the water for too long or it will begin to turn black.

2 Bring 750ml/1¼ pints/3 cups water to the boil in a pan and add the lotus root. Boil for 2 minutes and then drain the lotus root and rinse the slices thoroughly under cold water.

3 Return the slices to the rinsed-out pan and add just enough water to cover them. Add the soy sauce. Bring to the boil and cook for 20 minutes, by which time the lotus root should have taken on the colour of the soy sauce.

4 Add the sugar and maple syrup, then reduce the heat and simmer for about 30 minutes. Mix in the sesame oil, coating the lotus root slices carefully. Transfer to a serving dish and garnish with a sprinkle of sesame seeds.

COOK'S TIPS
• Once peeled fresh lotus root will discolour very quickly. Treat it in the same way you would an apple, ensuring that it is soaked in the acidulated water as soon as it is peeled will slow down this process.
• If possible use a mature lotus root for this recipe, as the starchy quality of the larger roots will be ideal for absorbing the flavours during the cooking process. Smaller lotus roots are often eaten raw and are delicious in salads.

Per portion Energy 131kcal/555kJ; Protein 1.2g; Carbohydrate 28.3g, of which sugars 28.1g; Fat 2.2g, of which saturates 0.3g; Cholesterol 0mg; Calcium 54mg; Fibre 1.1g; Sodium 1525mg.

BLACK BEANS WITH SWEET SOY

SIMPLE TO MAKE, AND POPULAR AS AN ACCOMPANIMENT, THIS IS AMONG THE OLDEST OF TRADITIONAL DISHES AND IS A STAPLE OF THE CUSTOMARY KOREAN TABLE. THE BLACK BEANS HAVE A SWEET, NUTTY TASTE THAT IS WELL MATCHED BY THE SALTY TANG OF SOY SAUCE.

SERVES TWO TO THREE

INGREDIENTS

300g/11oz/2 cups canned black
   beans, drained
120ml/4fl oz/½ cup maple
   syrup
30ml/2 tbsp sugar
100ml/3½fl oz/scant ½ cup light
   soy sauce
5ml/1 tsp sesame seeds, to
   garnish

1 Rinse the beans, then drain them.

2 Bring 750ml/1½pints/3 cups water to the boil in a pan and add the beans. Boil the beans for 5 minutes, by which time any odour from them should have disappeared. Drain the beans and rinse out the pan.

3 Bring 450ml/¾ pint/scant 2 cups water to the boil in the pan. Add the beans and maple syrup.

4 Boil for 3 minutes, then add the sugar and soy sauce.

5 Reduce the heat under the pan and simmer over low heat, until the liquid has reduced to form a thick, rich sauce.

6 Remove from the heat and leave to cool. Transfer the cooled beans to a dish and garnish with sesame seeds before serving.

VARIATION
If you liquidize this tasty recipe, it makes a delicious accompaniment to fish, such as grilled sea bass or red snapper fillets.

Per portion Energy 275kcal/1166kJ; Protein 7.8g; Carbohydrate 61.1g, of which sugars 47.8g; Fat 1.5g, of which saturates 0.2g; Cholesterol 0mg; Calcium 94mg; Fibre 5.8g; Sodium 2840mg.

PICKLED GARLIC

Although the preparation involved in this dish takes some work, once the garlic is preserved it will last for months. Served with grilled dishes or as part of a table setting with rice, soup and kimchi, this is a ubiquitous part of the Korean dining experience.

SERVES EIGHT

INGREDIENTS
    25 garlic bulbs
    350ml/12fl oz/1½ cups cider
        vinegar
    450ml/¾ pint/scant 2 cups soy
        sauce
    200g/7oz/1 cup sugar

1 Peel off the outer layers of the garlic, taking care to keep the bulbs intact. Rinse the garlic bulbs, then drain them well.

2 Take a large heatproof jar with an airtight lid. It must be big enough to hold the garlic and 1.2 litres/2 pints/ 5 cups liquid. Pour in 750ml/1¼ pints/ 3 cups water and the vinegar. Then add the bulbs of garlic and cover the jar. Leave at room temperature for 3 days.

3 Drain off the vinegar solution from the jar, leaving the garlic in place. Heat 350ml/12fl oz/1½ cups water in a pan and add the soy sauce and sugar. Simmer for 5 minutes, then pour the liquid over the garlic in the jar.

4 Cover the jar immediately, closing it tightly, and store in a cool dark place for 1 month before eating.

Per portion Energy 171kcal/723kJ; Protein 5.8g; Carbohydrate 38.4g, of which sugars 29g; Fat 0.4g, of which saturates 0.1g; Cholesterol 0mg; Calcium 29mg; Fibre 2.6g; Sodium 1784mg.

SWEETS, CAKES
& DRINKS

*Sweet flavours are uncommon in Korea, and when they do
feature they tend to be served with tea rather than as a dessert at the end
of a meal. Popular sweet dishes are the fluffy Sweet Rice Balls and
Three-colour Ribbon Cookies, which contain crushed pumpkin, apricot and
seaweed. Sweet drinks appear in many varieties, such as Citron and
Pomegranate Punch, and they are a great way to finish a meal. Green teas
and grain teas are available everywhere, with common favourites being the
soothing Green Tea Latte and refreshing Barley Tea.*

POACHED PEAR WITH PEPPERCORNS

FOR THIS DISH, CALLED BAESUK, ASIAN PEARS ARE GENTLY POACHED UNTIL TENDER IN LIQUID SWIMMING WITH BLACK PEPPERCORNS AND SLICED GINGER. IT IS SWEET, BUT HAS A DELICATE SPICINESS WHICH MAKES FOR A CLEANSING AND REFRESHING END TO A MEAL.

SERVES FOUR

INGREDIENTS
2 Asian pears
20 black peppercorns
10g/¼oz fresh root ginger, peeled
   and sliced
25g/1oz/2 tbsp sugar
pine nuts, to decorate

1 Peel and core the Asian pears with a sharp knife. Then cut each one into six pieces.

COOK'S TIP
When choosing Asian pears at the market, pick those that are most even in shape, firm and free of any soft spots.

2 Press two or three peppercorns into the smooth outer surface of each piece.

3 Place 750ml/1¼ pints/3 cups water in a large pan and add the ginger. Bring to the boil and cook for 10 minutes, or until the flavour of the ginger has suffused the water. Add the sugar and then the pears. Reduce the heat, and simmer for 5 minutes, or until the pears have softened.

4 Transfer the fruit and liquid to a bowl. Cool, remove the sliced ginger and place the bowl in the refrigerator to chill for a while.

5 Place three pieces of pear in a bowl for each person. Pour over the poaching liquid and decorate with pine nuts.

VARIATION
Asian pears are crisp and mild, whereas European pears tend have a more aromatic and buttery flavour. If Asian pears are not available, then Conference pears can be used in their place. They should be cored and used whole – one per person – rather than sliced.

Per portion Energy 60kcal/253kJ; Protein 0.3g; Carbohydrate 15.4g, of which sugars 15.4g; Fat 0.1g, of which saturates 0g; Cholesterol 0mg; Calcium 12mg; Fibre 1.7g; Sodium 3mg.

SWEET BEANS <u>ON</u> ICE FLAKES

FOR THIS REFRESHING, CHILLED DESSERT, UNIQUE TO KOREA, CRUNCHY ICE FLAKES ARE COATED WITH A PURÉE OF RED BEANS AND MAPLE SYRUP AND THEN TOPPED WITH FRESH FRUIT. THIS IS UNQUESTIONABLY THE MOST POPULAR CHOICE FOR A HOT SUMMER'S DAY IN KOREA.

SERVES TWO

INGREDIENTS
    75g/3oz/½ cup red kidney beans,
        soaked overnight
    115g/4oz/generous ½ cup sugar
    5ml/1 tsp salt
    30ml/2 tbsp maple syrup
    ice cubes
    30ml/2 tbsp condensed milk
    90ml/6 tbsp milk
    1 kiwi fruit, sliced
    2 strawberries

1 Place the red kidney beans in a pan, cover with water and bring to the boil. Boil fast for 10 minutes, then simmer until the beans have softened. Drain and leave to cool, then roll them between the palms of your hands to remove the skins.

2 Put the peeled beans, sugar, salt and maple syrup into a food processor or blender and purée together to a fine paste. Put the puréed beans into a pan and simmer them until the paste has reduced to the consistency of a custard. Cool, then chill.

3 Use an ice crusher, food processor or blender to crush the ice into flakes (you will need 2 litres/3½ pints/8 cups of ice flakes) and transfer to a serving bowl.

4 Mix the condensed milk and milk in a jug (pitcher) and pour over the ice flakes in the bowl. Pour the bean paste over the top and decorate with the kiwi fruit and strawberries before serving.

VARIATIONS
A variety of fruits can be used depending on what is available or in season. Blueberries and raspberries both make delicious alternatives.

Per portion Energy 462kcal/1968kJ; Protein 11.4g; Carbohydrate 105.1g, of which sugars 88.4g; Fat 2.5g, of which saturates 1.2g; Cholesterol 6mg; Calcium 145mg; Fibre 7g; Sodium 1063mg.

SWEET RICE BALLS

FLUFFY RICE BALLS ARE FILLED WITH A DELICIOUS SWEET BEAN PASTE TO CREATE A LIGHT, SUCCULENT DESSERT. THE SWEETS ARE COATED WITH RED DATES, CHESTNUTS AND SESAME SEEDS, WHICH GIVE THEM AN UNUSUAL TEXTURE. THE FRUIT AND NUTS CONTRAST WITH THE MELTINGLY TENDER RICE.

3 Sift the flour and salt into a bowl and add 300ml/½ pint/1¼ cups warm water. Mix well and knead for 10 minutes. Take a small piece of dough, make an indent with your finger and add a little bean paste. Wrap the dough over and form into a ball.

4 Bring a large pan of water to the boil and add the rice balls. Cook for 7 minutes, then drain and rinse well in cold water.

5 Separate the rice balls into three groups. Roll one third in the chopped dates, another third in the chestnuts and the last in the toasted sesame seeds. Arrange on a serving platter.

SERVES FOUR

INGREDIENTS
    375g/13oz/2 cups red kidney beans, soaked overnight
    200g/7oz/1 cup sugar
    30ml/2 tbsp black sesame seeds
    20 red dates, stoned (pitted) and finely chopped
    20 chestnuts, finely chopped
    400g/13oz/3½ cups sweet rice flour
    5ml/1 tsp salt

1 Place the beans in a pan, cover with water and bring to the boil. Boil fast for 20 minutes, then drain and leave to cool. Roll them between the palms of your hands to remove the skins. Purée the peeled beans and sugar to a fine paste. Simmer the purée in a pan until the paste resembles a custard consistency.

2 Toast the sesame seeds in a dry pan. Place the dates, chestnuts and sesame seeds in three separate shallow dishes.

Per portion Energy 973kcal/4111kJ; Protein 30.1g; Carbohydrate 199.9g, of which sugars 66g; Fat 7.9g, of which saturates 1.1g; Cholesterol 0mg; Calcium 224mg; Fibre 19.8g; Sodium 34mg.

SWEET RICE WITH RED DATES

TRADITIONALLY USED FOR ANCESTRAL MEMORIAL SERVICES, BIRTHDAYS AND WEDDINGS, THIS SWEET CAKE IS NOW ENJOYED TO CELEBRATE ANY OCCASION. THE RED DATES HAVE A RICH FRUITY FLAVOUR THAT PERMEATES THE RICE, CREATING A SWEET, APPETIZING DESSERT.

SERVES FOUR

INGREDIENTS
  400g/14oz/2 cups glutinous rice
  115g/4oz/½ cup brown sugar
  8 cooked chestnuts, finely
    chopped
  8 dried red dates, seeded and
    chopped
  15ml/1 tbsp sesame oil
  30ml/2 tbsp raisins
  5ml/1 tsp ground cinnamon
  pine nuts
  salt

1 Soak the rice in plenty of cold water for 20 minutes. Drain the rice and place it in a heavy pan or a rice cooker.

2 Add the brown sugar and 200ml/ 7fl oz/scant 1 cup water to the pan. Stir all the ingredients well.

COOK'S TIPS
• If you are cooking on the type of electric cooker that retains heat, when the water boils, transfer it to another ring on the lowest setting to prevent the rice from cooking too quickly and sticking to the bottom of the pan.
• Rice cookers are relatively inexpensive to buy, and are particularly useful for cooking Korean recipes which always include rice. The cookers are thermostatically controlled and very useful for preventing burning. To use a rice cooker for this recipe, follow the manufacturer's instructions and cook until the rice is fully cooked and the liquid has been fully absorbed.

3 Add the chestnuts, dates, sesame oil and raisins to the rice. Add a little of the cinnamon and a pinch of salt. Add water until it covers the rice by about 2cm/¾in.

4 Bring to the boil, reduce the heat to the lowest setting and stir the rice once. Cover the pan tightly and cook as gently as possible for 20 minutes.

5 Remove the pan from the heat and leave to stand, without uncovering the pan, for 15 minutes.

6 Arrange a portion of rice on each plate. Mould it neatly in a small ring or ramekin dish, if liked. Decorate the dish with the pine nuts and a dusting of cinnamon.

Per portion Energy 582kcal/2450kJ; Protein 9.5g; Carbohydrate 125.3g, of which sugars 44.5g; Fat 4.9g, of which saturates 0.5g; Cholesterol 0mg; Calcium 50mg; Fibre 1.4g; Sodium 13mg.

PERSIMMON SORBET IN GINGER PUNCH

*THE SWEET, AUTUMNAL FLAVOUR OF RIPE PERSIMMON GIVES THIS DESSERT A WONDERFULLY MELLOW
TASTE. THE RICH, CREAMY SORBET SITS IN A BOWL OF PUNCH WHERE THE AROMATIC QUALITY OF THE
FRUIT IS OFFSET BY THE INVIGORATING PEPPERY TASTE OF THE GINGER.*

SERVES FOUR

INGREDIENTS
   300g/11oz persimmon purée
   75g/3oz dextrose or glucose
   10ml/2 tsp caster (superfine) sugar
   30ml/2 tbsp lemon juice
   Persimmon and walnut punch, to
      serve (see page 247)

COOK'S TIPS
• Dextrose is another name for glucose.
This is available in powder form from
health food shops or among speciality
sweeteners and sugars.
• The sorbet can also be made in
an ice cream maker, following the
manufacturer's instructions.

1 Heat the persimmon purée in a pan
over a low heat. Add the dextrose and
use a whisk to stir it into the purée.

2 Add the sugar and bring to the boil.
Once the mixture begins to bubble pour
into a bowl, and leave to cool.

3 Stir in the lemon juice and chill the
mixture thoroughly in the refrigerator,
for about 10 hours.

4 Turn the freezer to the fast freeze
setting, following the manufacturer's
instructions. Transfer the mixture to a
shallow freezer container.

5 Freeze the mixture, removing the
container and stirring every 30
minutes or so to break up ice crystals
as they form. The sorbet should be
smooth and creamy.

6 To serve, place a scoop of sorbet in
each bowl and pour over the ginger and
persimmon punch.

Per portion Energy 109kcal/461kJ; Protein 0.3g; Carbohydrate 28.3g, of which sugars 28.3g; Fat 0.1g, of which saturates 0g; Cholesterol 0mg; Calcium 14mg; Fibre 1.1g; Sodium 4mg.

GREEN TEA ICE CREAM

IN KOREA IT IS UNUSUAL TO EAT A DESSERT, BUT FRESH FRUIT AND PUNCH ARE POPULAR CHOICES TO CONCLUDE A MEAL. THIS EASTERN TAKE ON A TRADITIONAL WESTERN DESSERT CREATES A LOVELY MIX OF FLAVOURS, WITH THE ENERGIZING PROPERTIES OF GREEN TEA.

SERVES FOUR

INGREDIENTS
    2 egg yolks
    200ml/7fl oz/scant 1 cup whole
      milk
    30ml/2 tbsp caster (superfine) sugar
    30ml/2 tbsp green tea powder or
      maca
    120ml/4fl oz/½ cup hot water
    200ml/7fl oz/scant 1 cup double
      (heavy) cream

1 Turn the freezer to the fast freeze setting, or in step 6 if time allows for chilling the mixture before freezing.

2 Whisk the egg yolks in a large heatproof bowl. Add the milk and sugar and stir until the sugar has dissolved.

3 Place the bowl over a pan of barely simmering water over a low heat. Stir until this custard mixture thickens slightly, to coat the back of a mixing spoon thinly. Remove from the heat.

4 Add the green tea powder or maca to the hot water and stir until dissolved.

5 Cool the green tea mixture a bit before adding to the custard.

6 Stand the bowl containing the custard and green tea inside a larger one. Add ice and water to the outer bowl to cool the custard quickly. Stir during cooling.

7 Whip the double cream until thick and light, but not stiff, then fold it into the custard. Transfer it to a shallow freezer container. If possible. Chill the mixture for 6–12 hours before freezing, as this helps to prevent ice crystals from forming and makes the mixture smoother. Place in the freezer. For best results, stir the mixture every 30 minutes or so, until it is thick and smooth and creamy.

COOK'S TIP
If using an ice-cream making machine, follow the manufacturer's instructions. The double cream will not have to be whisked before it is added to the custard and frozen.

Per portion Energy 308kcal/1273kJ; Protein 2.3g; Carbohydrate 8.7g, of which sugars 8.7g; Fat 29.6g, of which saturates 17.5g; Cholesterol 169mg; Calcium 40mg; Fibre 0g; Sodium 16mg.

THREE-COLOUR RIBBON COOKIES

THESE DELIGHTFUL RIBBON COOKIES, CALLED MAEJAKGWA, *TASTE AS GOOD AS THEY LOOK. THE CRISP TWISTS OF WAFER-THIN DOUGH ARE TINTED IN PASTEL SHADES OF GREEN, YELLOW AND PINK, AND HAVE A HINT OF GINGER. THEY ARE PERFECT SERVED WITH A SWEET DRINK OR A CUP OF GREEN TEA.*

SERVES FOUR

INGREDIENTS
    30ml/2 tbsp pine nuts, finely ground
    vegetable oil, for deep-frying
For the green cookies
    115g/4oz/1 cup plain
    (all-purpose) flour
    2.5ml/½ tsp salt
    10g/¼oz grated fresh root ginger
    30ml/2 tbsp seaweed, finely ground
For the yellow cookies
    115g/4oz/1 cup plain
    (all-purpose) flour
    2.5ml/½ tsp salt
    10g/¼oz grated fresh root ginger
    50g/2oz sweet pumpkin, finely
    minced (ground)
For the pink cookies
    115g/4oz/1 cup plain
    (all-purpose) flour
    2.5ml/½ tsp salt
    10g/¼oz grated fresh root ginger
    50g/2oz apricot flesh, finely minced
    (ground)
For the syrup
    250ml/8fl oz/1 cup water
    200g/7oz/1 cup sugar
    30ml/2 tbsp honey
    2.5ml/½ tsp cinnamon
    salt

1 To make the green cookies, sift the flour and salt into a large bowl and mix in the grated ginger, ground seaweed and a splash of water. Knead gently into a smooth, elastic dough.

2 Place on a lightly floured surface and roll out the dough to about 3mm/⅛in thick. Cut the dough into strips 2cm/¾in wide and 5cm/2in long.

3 To make the yellow cookies, sift the flour and salt into a large bowl and mix in the grated ginger, minced pumpkin and a splash of water. Continue as for the green cookies, kneading the dough, rolling out and cutting into strips 2cm/¾in wide and 5cm/2in long.

4 To make the pink cookies, sift the flour and salt into a large bowl and mix in the grated ginger, minced apricot and a splash of water. Continue as for the green cookies.

5 Score three cuts lengthways into each cookie, and bring one end of the strip back through the centre slit to form a loose knot.

6 To make the cinnamon syrup, put the water, sugar and honey in a pan, and add a pinch of salt. Bring to the boil without stirring, then add the cinnamon and continue to boil, stirring until the syrup becomes sticky. Pour into a bowl.

7 Pour a generous amount of vegetable oil into a heavy pan, and heat over a medium heat to 150°C/300°F, or when a small piece of bread browns in about 20 seconds. Add the cookies and deep-fry until golden brown.

8 Drain the cookies on kitchen paper, then dip into the cinnamon syrup. Arrange on a serving plate and dust the cookies with the ground pine nuts before serving.

COOK'S TIPS
• Although getting the cookies to form the right shape can seem difficult at first, it will become much easier with practice. Don't lose heart.
• As an alternative to ingredients that colour the dough, you can use edible food colourings to introduce other colours and make them more appealing for children.

Per portion Energy 669kcal/2827kJ; Protein 9.7g; Carbohydrate 126.5g, of which sugars 60.7g; Fat 17.3g, of which saturates 1.8g; Cholesterol 0mg; Calcium 154mg; Fibre 3.2g; Sodium 498mg.

SAKE <u>AND</u> GINGER COOKIES

YAKWA ARE AMONG THE BEST KNOWN AND MOST TRADITIONAL SWEETS IN KOREA. LIGHT AND CRISP, THESE COOKIES HAVE A UNIQUE TASTE CREATED BY A COMBINATION OF MAPLE SYRUP AND SAKE, COMPLEMENTED BY A DELICIOUS HINT OF GINGER. PERFECT SERVED WITH A CUP OF GREEN TEA.

SERVES TWO

INGREDIENTS

   350g/12oz/3 cups plain
     (all-purpose) flour
   45ml/3 tbsp sesame oil
   25g/1oz fresh root ginger, peeled and
     grated
   90ml/6 tbsp sake or rice wine
   90ml/6 tbsp golden (light corn) syrup
     or maple syrup
   2.5ml/½ tsp white pepper
   30ml/2 tbsp pine nuts
   vegetable oil, for deep-frying
For the syrup
   250ml/8fl oz/1 cup water
   200g/7oz/1 cup sugar
   30ml/2 tbsp honey
   5ml/1 tsp cinnamon
   salt

1 Sift the flour and add the sesame oil. Mix in the grated ginger, sake or rice wine, syrup, pepper and a splash of water. Knead into an elastic dough.

2 Roll the dough out on a floured surface to about 1cm/½in thick. Use a biscuit (cookie) cutter to cut the cookie shapes out of the dough.

3 Place the water, sugar and honey in a pan, and add a pinch of salt. Bring to the boil without stirring, then add the cinnamon and cook, stirring, until the syrup thickens and becomes sticky. Pour into a bowl and set aside.

4 Grind the pine nuts to a fine powder in a mortar and pestle.

5 Place a generous amount of vegetable oil in a pan, and heat over a medium heat until a small piece of bread browns in about 20 seconds. Add the cookies and deep-fry until golden brown.

6 Remove any excess oil by blotting the cookies on kitchen paper and then dip them into the syrup. Arrange on a serving plate and dust the cookies with ground pine nuts.

Per portion Energy 719kcal/3027kJ; Protein 6.7g; Carbohydrate 119.8g, of which sugars 76.9g; Fat 25.1g, of which saturates 3g; Cholesterol 0mg; Calcium 111mg; Fibre 1.9g; Sodium 67mg.

FLOWER PETAL RICE CAKES IN HONEY

THIS GORGEOUS SPRING DISH, CALLED HWACHUN, *USES EDIBLE FLOWER PETALS TO FLAVOUR RICE CAKES, WHICH ARE THEN DRIZZLED WITH HONEY. ITS SOPHISTICATED APPEARANCE IS MATCHED BY ITS REFINED, EXQUISITE TASTE. SERVE WITH A CUP OF GREEN TEA.*

SERVES FOUR

INGREDIENTS
    20 edible flower petals
    225g/8oz/2 cups sweet
      rice flour
    2.5ml/½ tsp salt
    vegetable oil, for shallow-frying
    honey, for drizzling

1 Rinse the flower petals, and gently pat them dry with kitchen paper.

2 Sift the flour and salt into a bowl and add 300ml/½ pint/1¼ cups of warm water. Mix well and knead for 10 minutes. Place on a lightly floured surface and roll out the dough to 1cm/½in thick. Use a floured 5cm/2in biscuit (cookie) cutter to cut the dough into rounds.

3 Heat the oil in a frying pan over a low flame. Add the rice cakes and fry for 2 minutes, or until lightly browned. Flip over and cook on the other side, and then remove from the pan. Place on kitchen paper to blot the excess oil, then arrange on a serving platter.

4 Sprinkle the petals over the rice cakes, and then drizzle with honey.

COOK'S TIPS
• A number of different flowers have edible petals, including roses, azaleas, apple blossom, carnations and chrysanthemums, and they can sometimes be found at supermarkets or grocery stores.
• If you have food or pollen allergies, check with your doctor before consuming flower petals to avoid any adverse reaction.
• Do not eat petals from flowers that have been sprayed with pesticides, so either grow your own, or check the growing conditions with the supplier.

Per portion Energy 255kcal/1065kJ; Protein 3.6g; Carbohydrate 45.1g, of which sugars 0g; Fat 6g, of which saturates 0.7g; Cholesterol 0mg; Calcium 14mg; Fibre 1.1g; Sodium 249mg.

SWEET POTATO JELLY

WHILE DESSERTS ARE UNCOMMON IN KOREA, THIS DELICATELY SWEET JELLY IS SOMETIMES SERVED AFTER A MEAL. IT IS ALSO POPULAR AS A SNACK OR AS A LIGHT ACCOMPANIMENT TO AFTERNOON TEA. THE MAPLE SYRUP GIVES IT A DISTINCTIVE UNDERTONE.

2 Drain and mash the potatoes until completely smooth, then mix in the maple syrup and sesame seeds. Bring 200ml/7fl oz/scant 1 cup water to simmering point over a medium heat. Add the gelatine and stir until dissolved.

3 Add the sweet potato to the pan and stir well. Simmer for 5 minutes, stirring frequently, and remove from the heat.

4 Grease a mould with a little oil. Pour in the potato mixture and cool. Then chill until the jelly has set.

5 Cover the mould with a board and invert. Lift the mould off the jelly. Slice and arrange on a shallow dish to serve.

SERVES TWO

INGREDIENTS
  2 small sweet potatoes
  60ml/4 tbsp maple syrup
  30ml/2 tbsp black sesame seeds
  15ml/1 tbsp powdered gelatine
  vegetable oil, for greasing mould

1 Peel the sweet potatoes and cut them into chunks, then place them in a pan. Add enough water to cover and then bring to the boil over a high heat. Reduce the heat slightly and simmer the potatoes for approximately 15 minutes, until they are tender.

Per portion Energy 310kcal/1309kJ; Protein 4.6g; Carbohydrate 55.8g, of which sugars 32.3g; Fat 9.2g, of which saturates 1.4g; Cholesterol 0mg; Calcium 142mg; Fibre 4.8g; Sodium 144mg.

CITRON AND POMEGRANATE PUNCH

DUE TO THE SCARCITY OF POMEGRANATES IN KOREA THIS PUNCH WAS HISTORICALLY ONLY ENJOYED BY THE ARISTOCRACY. WITH A BLEND OF SHARPNESS AND SWEETNESS, THIS PUNCH IS WONDERFULLY THIRST QUENCHING AND A GREAT WAY TO FINISH A MEAL IN THE SUMMERTIME.

SERVES THREE

INGREDIENTS
    200g/7oz sugar
    1 citron
    ½ Asian pear
    45ml/3 tbsp pomegranate seeds
    15ml/1 tbsp pine nuts

1 Place 1.2 litres/2 pints/5 cups water in a bowl and add the sugar. Stir until the sugar has dissolved completely, then chill well.

2 Pare off the outer surface of the rind from the citron in fine shreds with a zester. Alternatively, use a fairly coarse grater, and set aside, then halve the fruit and squeeze out the juice. Add a pinch of sugar to the citron juice and set it aside.

5 Finely slice the Asian pear and divide the slices among three glasses.

6 Add a little of the sliced white citron rind to each glass and divide the citron juice among them.

7 Top up with the sugar water and sprinkle with citron zest. Cover and chill for 20 minutes to allow the citron flavour to infuse the punch.

8 Add a tablespoon of pomegranate seeds to each glass and decorate with the pine nuts before serving.

COOK'S TIPS
• Citron fruit will be available in many Asian grocery stores. If it is not available, instead use the juice and zest of one large lemon, without using the rind.
• Use lime and orange slices, or pomegranate seeds and pineapple chunks, for a colourful garnish.
• To remove the seed sacs from a pomegranate, score the pomegranate and put in a bowl of water. Break the fruit open underwater so that the seeds sink to the bottom and the white membrane floats to the top. Then strain the membrane out and remove the seed sacs. You can refrigerate or freeze them for later use.

3 Scrape the remainder of the squeezed flesh from the rind along with soft pith. Cut the pieces of rind in half.

4 Use a sharp knife to cut the inner white layer from the yellow outer layer of rind. Finely slice the white rind.

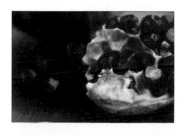

Per portion Energy 311kcal/1323kJ; Protein 1.2g; Carbohydrate 73.4g, of which sugars 73.4g; Fat 3.5g, of which saturates 0.2g; Cholesterol 0mg; Calcium 48mg; Fibre 1.2g; Sodium 5mg.

SWEET RICE PUNCH

A THIRST-QUENCHING RICE AND MALT PUNCH, SHIKHAE HAS A LOVELY SWEET TASTE WITH A HINT OF SPICE. IT IS THE MOST WIDELY ENJOYED OF KOREAN DRINKS, PARTICULARLY ON A HOT DAY WHEN NOTHING BEATS A BOWL OF THE FRAGRANT CHILLED LIQUID WITH ICE CUBES FLOATING ON TOP.

SERVES FOUR

INGREDIENTS
  450g/1lb/4 cups malt
  30ml/2 tbsp caster (superfine)
    sugar
  350g/12oz/3 cups cooked rice
  10g/¼oz fresh root ginger, peeled
    and sliced
  1 cinnamon stick
  1 red date, thinly sliced, pine nuts,
    and ice cubes, to serve

COOK'S TIP
The sorbet can be made in an ice cream maker, following the manufacturer's instructions.

1 Roughly blend the malt in a food processor, then place in a large bowl. Add 1.5 litres/2½ pints/6¼ cups water and leave for 1 hour. Drain the liquid through muslin (cheesecloth) into a bowl, reserving the malt in the cloth. Repeat this process again, pouring the liquid repeatedly through the malt-lined cloth. After three or four times the liquid should thicken and become opaque. Discard the malt.

2 Add the sugar and increase the heat. Bring the mixture to the boil, removing the pan from the heat as soon as the mixture begins to bubble Pour the mixture into a bowl, then leave to cool.

3 Put the cooked rice into a large pan and add the malt liquid. Heat gently to 40°C/104°F or hand hot and keep at that temperature for about 5 hours. Once the rice grains begin to float on the surface, remove the rice from the liquid, cool it down and place in a bowl in the refrigerator to chill.

4 Turn the heat under the malt liquid to high. Once it is boiling, add the sliced ginger and the cinnamon stick, then simmer for a few minutes. Discard the ginger and cinnamon, and transfer the liquid to a jug (pitcher). Cool and chill in the refrigerator.

5 In a small bowl combine the chilled rice and malt liquid. Add a sprinkling of sliced red date, a handful of pine nuts and some ice cubes before serving.

Per portion Energy 186kcal/791kJ; Protein 3.5g; Carbohydrate 42.5g, of which sugars 8.4g; Fat 1.4g, of which saturates 0.3g; Cholesterol 0mg; Calcium 26mg; Fibre 1.8g; Sodium 2mg.

PERSIMMON AND WALNUT PUNCH

THIS NON-ALCOHOLIC PUNCH IS A POPULAR DESSERT IN KOREA. THE SWEETNESS OF THE DRIED PERSIMMONS IS MATCHED BY THE SHARPNESS OF THE CINNAMON, AND THE DISH HAS A REFRESHING FRUITY KICK THAT EFFECTIVELY BALANCES OUT A SPICY MAIN MEAL.

SERVES FOUR

INGREDIENTS
    12 dried persimmons
    12 walnuts
    150g/5oz fresh root ginger, peeled
      and thinly sliced
    1 cinnamon stick/½ tsp ground
      cinnamon
    450g/1lb/2 cups light muscovado
      (brown) sugar
    30ml/2 tbsp maple syrup or golden
      (light corn) syrup
    30 pine nuts

1 Seed the dried persimmons and soak them in cold water until they have softened. Then make an incision into the centre of each, and stuff each one with a walnut. Set aside.

2 Pour 1 litre/1¾ pints/4 cups water into a pan and add the ginger and cinnamon stick or powder. Place over a low heat and simmer gently for 15 minutes, or until the water has taken on the flavour of the ginger and cinnamon.

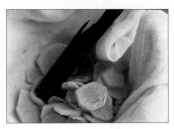

3 When the liquid has reduced by about a fifth to a quarter, strain it through muslin (cheesecloth) into a large jug (pitcher).

4 Pour the liquid back into the pan, add the sugar and maple or golden syrup and then bring the contents to the boil again.

5 Remove the pan from the heat and pour the punch into a jug. Cool, then chill in the refrigerator.

6 Place three persimmons in a small serving bowl for each person, and then pour over the chilled liquid. Decorate each bowl with a sprinkling of pine nuts, and serve.

Per portion Energy 379kcal/1589kJ; Protein 4.9g; Carbohydrate 48.4g, of which sugars 48.3g; Fat 19.8g, of which saturates 1.6g; Cholesterol 0mg; Calcium 47mg; Fibre 1.6g; Sodium 31mg.

GREEN TEA LATTE

This Asian twist on an Italian classic is a delightful, sweet beverage. The green tea has a refreshing quality and imbues the hot milk with its distinctive flavour, a little like that of green tea ice cream. Use water instead of milk to enhance the green tea flavour.

SERVES FOUR

INGREDIENTS
  1 litre/1¾ pints/4 cups milk
  60ml/4 tbsp green tea powder or
    maacha
  30ml/2 tbsp sugar
  120ml/4fl oz/½ cup whipping
    cream
  10ml/2 tsp caster (superfine) sugar

VARIATION
You can replace the caster suger with
the same amount of honey.

1 Heat the milk in a pan over a low heat until it simmers gently. Add the green tea powder and sugar and stir well.

2 Remove from the heat and pour the tea into a bowl or jug (pitcher). Leave to cool before chilling.

3 When ready to serve the tea, whisk the cream until it begins to thicken. Then add the caster sugar and continue to whisk until the cream is light and fluffy.

4 Pour the chilled green tea into tall glasses and top with whipped cream. Dust each glass with a little green tea powder and serve.

Per portion Energy 269kcal/1126kJ; Protein 9.2g; Carbohydrate 23g, of which sugars 23g; Fat 16.4g, of which saturates 10.3g; Cholesterol 46mg; Calcium 323mg; Fibre 0g; Sodium 116mg.

GRAIN TEAS

THESE SIMPLE TEAS ARE A HEALTHY CHOICE AND PERFECT FOR THOSE WHO PREFER TO AVOID CAFFEINE. UBIQUITOUS IN KOREAN HOUSEHOLDS, THEY USE BARLEY, CORN AND BROWN RICE, ALL NATIVE TO THE COUNTRY, AND THE ROASTED GRAINS CREATE A SUBTLE SMOKY TASTE.

VERSION 1: BARLEY TEA
75ml/5 tbsp barley

VERSION 2: CORN TEA
75ml/5 tbsp dried corn

VERSION 3: BROWN RICE TEA
75ml/5 tbsp husked brown rice

BARLEY TEA
1 Heat a heavy pan over a medium heat and add the barley.

2 Toast the barley in the dry pan, shaking it all the time, until lightly browned. Take care not to burn the grains. Remove from the heat and transfer to a dish.

3 Bring 500ml/17fl oz/generous 2 cups water to the boil and add the barley.

4 Remove the pan from the heat and leave to infuse for about 5 minutes, until the water has taken on the colour of the barley.

5 Strain and serve the tea in cups or heatproof glasses.

CORN TEA
1 To make the corn tea, bring 500ml/17fl oz/generous 2 cups water to the boil in a pan and then add the dried corn to the pan.

2 Bring the pan back to the boil, reduce the heat and cover the pan. Simmer for 20 minutes.

3 Strain the tea through a fine sieve (strainer) in order to remove the grain. To serve the tea, pour the liquid into cups or heatproof glasses.

BROWN RICE TEA
1 Rinse the rice under running water in a sieve. Drain and then dry thoroughly on a dish towel.

2 Toast the rice as for the barley (see above), until it is golden brown. Bring 500ml/17fl oz/generous 2 cups water to the boil and add the toasted rice.

3 Reduce the heat, cover the pan and simmer for 30–40 minutes. Strain to remove the rice and serve the tea in cups or in heatproof glasses.

Per portion Energy 8kcal/32kJ; Protein 0.8g; Carbohydrate 1.2g, of which sugars 0g; Fat 0g, of which saturates 0g; Cholesterol 0mg; Calcium 12mg; Fibre 0g; Sodium 0mg.

GLOSSARY

anju bar snacks
baechu Chinese cabbage
ban cooked rice
banchan side dishes
bansang table setting
bap cooked rice
bapsang table setting
bibimbap mixed rice and meat
  dish
boricha roasted barley tea
buchimgae kimchi fritters
buchu Korean chives
bulgalbi beef stew
bulgogi grilled beef
bungeoppang fish-shaped
  sweet pastry
Busan city in South Korea
chechi baby clams
Cheju island of South Korea
chige casserole
cho gochujan chilli paste and
  vinegar sauce
Chobok one of the three
  hottest summer days
Cholla province in South
  Korea
Chonchon river in North Korea
Chosun dynasty 1392–1910
Chungchong province in
  South Korea
chungju Korean wine
chungol tofu casserole
chup side dish
Chuseok autumn harvest
  festival
Daegu city in South Korea
daepa large spring onion
  (scallion)
dahima dried kelp
daikon Japanese radish
dangmyun sweet potato
  noodles, glass noodles

dashikonbu dried kelp
doenjang soya bean paste
Dol 1st birthday
dol hareubang stone
  grandfather statue
Donji winter solstice festival
enokitake enoki mushrooms
galbi tang beef stew
gochugaru chilli powder
gochujang chilli paste
gool pajeon oyster pancakes
gujeolpan elaborate dish for
  wedding feasts
gukwappang flower-shaped
  sweet pastry
Gyeonggi province in South
  Korea
gyeranppang shell-shaped
  sweet pastry
hae san mool jungol mixed
  meat and fish dish
Halla-san mountain on Cheju
  island
Hamgyong province in North
  Korea
Hamhung city in North Korea
Hangul Korean phonetic script
hotteok sweet pancakes
Hwanghae province in North
  Korea
Hwangop 60th birthday
jakju rice liquor
Jeongwol Daeboreum First
  Full Moon Day
jeotgal fermented preserved
  seafood
jeotgarak chopsticks
jujube red dates
Jungbok one of the three
  hottest summer days
kalguksu handmade flat
  noodles

Kangwon South Korean
  province
kenip wild sesame leaf
kim flat dark seaweed
kimbap rice and meat snack
  roll
kimchi pickled and fermented
  vegetables
kimchi pajeon kimchi pancake
kimjang season for preparing
  kimchi
Koguro one of the Three
  Kingdoms
Koh-cui 70th birthday
Koryo Buddhist dynasty
Kyongsang province in South
  Korea
makgoli alcoholic rice drink
maki sushi dish from Japan
Malbok one of the three
  hottest summer days
mandu savoury dumplings
memil buckwheat noodles
minari salad leaf
mirin Japanese rice wine
miyuk seaweed
momil wheat noodles
mooli Japanese radish
mugeun namul medley of
  vegetable dishes
myongtae dried fish
myulchi dried anchovies
myun cooked noodles
myunsang table setting
namul vegetable side dishes
nori flat dark seaweed
ogokbap mixed grain rice
Paekje one of the Three
  Kingdoms
pajeon pancake
patjuk red bean porridge
perilla wild sesame leaf
pyogo shiitake mushrooms
Pyongan North Korean province
Pyongyang capital city of
  North Korea
Racktong river in South Korea
Sambok summer festival
samgyetang hot chicken soup
samgyupsal three-layer pork
  dish
sang table
sashimi sushi dish from Japan
Seoul South Korea capital city
seuck bak ji cod kimchi

Silla one of the Three
  Kingdoms
soju grain or sweet potato spirit
somyun wedding noodles
songpyeon rice cakes
ssal short-grain rice
sujunggwa spiced persimmon
  punch
sukgot chrysanthemum leaves
surasang twelve-chup meal
sutgarak spoon
takju rice liquor
tong baechu Chinese cabbage
torantang tora soup
tteok rice cakes
tteokguk soup with rice
tukbaege earthenware
  casserole dish
udon noodles from Japan
Ullung-do island famed for
  squid
wakame seaweed
yangnyum seasoning
yangnyum gochujang stir-fried
  chilli paste
Yi Syeong-Gye, Founder of the
  Chosun dynasty
yukgejang soup with fern
  fronds

SHOPPING INFORMATION

AUSTRALIA

Ettason
www.ettason.com
Importer of Asian food

Welcome Fresh Food
Shop 91, Sunnybank Plaza
Cnr. Mains Rd and
McCullough Street
Sunnybank
Brisbane Qld 4109
Tel: 07 3345 7688
www.welcomefreshfood.com.au
Asian supermarket

CANADA

T & T Supermarkets
www.tnt-supermarket.com
Chain of Asian supermarkets
(refer to website for further
stores)

T & T Supermarket
#800–999 36th Street N.E.
Calgary
Alberta T2A 7X6
Tel: 403 569 6888

T & T Supermarket
Middlefield & Steeles
5661 Steeles Avenue East,
Scarborough
Ontario M1V 5P6
Tel: 416 321 8113

T & T Supermarket
Keefer & Abbott
179 Keefer Place
Vancouver
B.C. V6B 6C1
Tel: 604 899 8836

UK

Centre Point Food Store
20–21 St. Giles High Street
London WC2H 8LN
Tel: 020 7836 9860
www.cpfs.co.uk
Korean supermarket

H-Mart
Unit 1, Leigh Close
New Malden
Surrey KT3 3NW
Korean grocer

Japan Centre
Tel: 020 3405 1246
www.japancentre.com
Japanese and Korean food

Jinmi Super
127 Kingston Road
New Malden KT3 3NX
Tel: 020 8336 1882
Korean grocer

Korea Foods
Unit 5
Wyvern Industrial Estate
Beverley Way
New Malden
Surrey KT3 4PH
www.koreafoods.co.uk
Importer of Korean food

Kingston Korean Festival
The Fairfield
Kingston Town Centre
Kingston Upon Thames
www.kingston.gov.uk
Summer festival

Lotte Shopping
126 Malden Road
New Malden KT3 6DD
Tel: 020 8942 9552
Korean grocer

Nak Won
89 Kingston Road
New Malden KT3 3PA
Tel: 020 8949 6474
Korean rice cake shop

Oriental Mart
6-8 Heathcoat Street
Nottingham NG1 3AA
Tel: 0115 9506615
www.orientalmart.co.uk
Eastern ingredients

Ran
58–59 Great Marlborough
Street, London W1F 7JY
Tel: 020 7434 1650
www.ranrestaurant.com
*Korean restaurant in the heart
of Soho*

SeeWoo
18–20 Lisle Street
London WC2H 7BE
Tel: 020 7439 8325
Oriental food specialists

SeeWoo
The Point
29 Saracen Street
Hamilton Hill
Glasgow G22 5HT
Tel: 0845 078 8818
www.seewoo.com

Seoul Mate
29 Museum Street
London WC1A 1LH
Tel: 020 7636 4787

Tazaki Foods
www.tazakifoods.com
Specialist Korean ingredients

XO
29 Belsize Ln
London NW3 5AS
Tel: 020 7433 0888
Pan-Asian restaurant

USA

99 Ranch Market
Tel: 1-800-600-8292
www.99ranch.com
Chain of Asian markets

Asian Food Market
1011 Route 22 West
North Plainfield, NJ 07060
Tel: 001 (908) 668-8382
Specialist Asian food market

Asian Food Market
1797 South Avenue
Staten Island, NY 10314
Tel: 001 (718) 698-8898
www.asianfoodmarkets.com
Specialist Asian food market

Franchia
12 Park Avenue
New York, NY 10016
Tel: 001 (212) 213-1001
www.franchia.com
Korean teahouse and shop

H-Mart
300 Chubb Avenue
Lyndhurst, NJ 07071
www.hmart.com
Online superstore

Koamart
3692 Grayburn Road
Pasadena, CA 91107
www.koamart.com
Online superstore

Posharp Inc.
219 Quincy Ave
Quincy, MA 02169
www.posharpstore.com

Sunrise Asian Food Market
70 West 29th Avenue
Eugene, Oregon 97405
Tel: 001 (541) 343-3295
www.see.org/sunrise
Fresh Asian food and spices

SOUTH AFRICA

Korean Market
451 Premier Centre
Main Road, Observatory
Cape Town
Western Cape 7925
Tel: 021 448 3420
Korean grocer

Yat Sang Chinese
Supermarket
Penge St
Pretoria 0081
Tel: 012 991 3020
www.yatsang.co.za
*Supermarket with
Korean food*

INDEX

PUBLISHER'S ACKNOWLEDGEMENTS

The publishers would like to thank the following for permission to reproduce their images: t = top; b = bottom; r = right; l = left p6t Chad Ehlers/Alamy; p6b YONHAP/epa/Corbis; p7tr ImageState/Alamy; p8t LOOK Die Bildagentur der Fotografen GmbH/Alamy; p8b Carl and Ann Purcell/Corbis; p9tl Bohemian Nomad Picturemakers/Corbis; p9ml LOOK Die Bildagentur der Fotografen GmbH/Alamy; p9bl Alain Nogues/Corbis; p9r Atlantide Phototravel/Corbis; p10t KCNA/epa/Corbis; p10b Alain Nogues/ Corbis; p11t Eye Ubiquitous/Alamy; p11b Alain Nogues/Corbis; p12t Catherine Karnow/Corbis; p12b Neil Beer/Corbis; p13t STF/ epa/Corbis; p13b Catherine Karnow/Corbis; p14t Christophe Boisvieux/Corbis; p14b Kim Kyung-Hoon/Reuters /Corbis; p15t istock; p15b Michel Setboun/Corbis; p16t Kim Kyung-Hoon/ Reuters/Corbis; p16b Nathan Benn/Corbis; p17t Atlantide Phototravel/Corbis; 17b Cha Young-Jin/epa/Corbis; 18t Earl and Nazima Kowall/Corbis; p18bl Michel Setboun/Corbis; p18br LOOK Die Bildagentur der Fotografen GmbH/Alamy; p19 KCNA/epa/ Corbis/p20t Michael Freeman/Corbis; p20br Bob Krist/Corbis;

p21 Tropix Photo Library; p22t Gerald Bourke/Reuters/Corbis; p24 Michael Setboun/Corbis; p24b and p25t Tropix Photo Library; p25b Horizon International Images Limited/Alamy; p26tl and 26tr Tropix Photo Library; p27t Studio Eye/Corbis; p28 Nathan Benn/Corbis; p29t and p29b Tropix Photo Library; p30t Michel Setboun/Corbis; p30b and p31b Tropix Photo Library; p32 Michael Freeman/Corbis; p36bl istock; p60bl Tropix Photo Library; p61tl Peter Jordan/Alamy. All other photographs © Anness Publishing.

With grateful thanks to Ran Restaurant at 58–59 Great Marlborough Street, London for their help with photographing equipment. Also to Veronica Birley of Tropix Photo Library for her trip to Korea with our project in mind.